THE GROOM'S GUIDE

Acknowledgment

I would like to thank Richard Grohowski for his fine editorial research and many hours spent discussing marriage from a man's viewpoint. Special thanks as well to all the grooms who shared their personal experiences. This book is all the richer because of your contributions.

— M. S.

Projects like this are the result of many peoples' efforts and influences. I would especially like to thank Bridgett Wingert, Nancy Wey, and Monica Dietrich for their support of my work when it really counted.

— C. R.

Published by Ronnie Sellers Productions, Inc.
Portland, Maine

Copyright 2005 © PM Design Group, Inc.
Text © Ronnie Sellers Productions, Inc.
Photography 2005 © Carol Ross
All rights reserved.
www.carolrossphotography.com

Text by Marguerite Smolen

Series Editor: Robin Haywood
Production Editor: Mary Baldwin
Associate Editor: Jessica Curran
Design: Nina Barnett

P.O. Box 818, Portland, Maine 04104
For ordering information:
Toll free: 800-625-3386 Fax: (207) 772-6814
Visit our Web site: www.rsvp.com
E-mail: rsp@rsvp.com

ISBN: 1-56906-577-2
Library of Congress Control Number: 2004097469

Printed in China

THE GROOM'S GUIDE

A Gentleman's Indispensable Wedding Planner

by Marguerite Smolen
photography by Carol Ross

CONTENTS

CHAPTER 1: FIRST THINGS FIRST   **17**

The Marriage Proposal;
The most important question of your life

- Asking permission, or not
- The perfect proposal
- Buying the engagement ring
- Spreading the news

CHAPTER 2: GETTING STARTED   **33**

When, Where, How Much, and Who

- Getting organized
- The groom's role
- The groom's countdown
- Budgets and finances

Introduction

—◁ww▷—

You have found the woman of your dreams and after asking her to marry you, she has said yes. Take that in for a second. Give it time to linger in your thoughts. Let it inspire you as you begin to plan with your bride what will certainly be one of the most extraordinary experiences of your life — your wedding.

As an editor in the bridal business for nearly two decades, I had always been struck by how many books there are in the marketplace devoted to the bride, but how few, if any, were devoted to the groom. This book fills that gap. It provides an insider's guidebook of the information you need to know, from buying the perfect ring to planning a memorable honeymoon. I will help you through the nuptial gauntlet of working with your bride to create a registry, choose a photographer, and commandeer a caterer. Plus, I've included a wealth of advice just for you, from choosing your formal wear, to surviving the bachelor party, to speech giving, all the while keeping your sense of humor and your budget intact. It's all in here, as well as some noble lessons and strategies learned (often from mistakes or mishaps!) from other grooms who have successfully navigated the intricacies of wedding planning.

This is more than a how-to book; it's an indispensable guide to what to do and how to do it best. Civilized, humorous, and forthright, this book is what every man needs who wants his wedding, and the months of planning leading up to it, to be a class act.

How to Use This Book

TO MAKE PLANNING YOUR BIG DAY EASIER, WE'VE organized this handy book so that you can pick it up and turn to any section quickly . . . or flip to the Weddings A to Z dictionary if you want clarification on a word or phrase. We've included easy-to-use timelines, so that you'll know where to start — often the biggest challenge! If you want advice on how to propose, Chapter 1 will help with some creative, romantic ideas, in addition to being your complete guide to buying the engagement ring. Chapter 2 outlines the traditional responsibilities of the groom and provides a countdown; it also includes tips for getting organized, brainstorming your wedding style, and setting up a budget. To help you begin the wedding planning process, Chapter 3 offers a wedding Who's Who — and includes every role and its responsibilities, from best man to ringbearer. It also covers wardrobe essentials, from formal wear to finishing touches, and provides guidance in buying the wedding bands. Chapter 4 prepares you for handling social occasions as smoothly as 007, by putting you through Mister Manners 101 and giving you ideas on how to give a toast. It is also your essential planning guide for all the pre-wedding events. Chapter 5 covers the Main Event! It prepares you by explaining what to expect on the big day, from the time you wake up to when you bid your friends and family farewell. Finally, Chapter 6 helps you plan the perfect honeymoon and gives you some realistic, sensible advice for setting up house, managing your money as a couple, and keeping your marriage strong. We've filled this book with at-a-glance checklists, worksheets, and planning tips to help make planning your wedding easy and fun. Before you know it, your wedding day will be here, so why shouldn't the planning process be just as special as the big day?

At-A-Glance One-Year Timeline

	MONTH 1	MONTH 2	MONTH 3	MONTH 4	MONTH 5
Announce engagement	✔				
Prepare budget	✔				
Set the date	✔				
Select venues	✔				
Meet with officiant		✔			
Determine guest list		✔			
Select wedding party		✔			
Book videographer		✔			
Register for gifts			✔		
Book photographer			✔		
Book musicians/DJ			✔		
Book florist				✔	
Select invitations				✔	
Plan rehearsal dinner					✔
Send save the date card					✔
Plan/book honeymoon					
Book hotels for guests					
Arrange transportation					
Select formal wear					
Select wedding bands					
Finalize guest list					
Select menu, bar & cake					
Mail invitations					
Finish premarital req.					
Prepare ceremony program					
Buy gifts for groomsmen					
Get marriage license & BT					
Attend bachelor party					
Prepare seating plan					
Gift & card for bride					
Pack for honeymoon					

If you have a year to plan, use this chart as a quick overview of the tasks involved in planning a wedding and when they should be completed.

MONTH 6	MONTH 7	MONTH 8	MONTH 9	MONTH 10	MONTH 11	MONTH 12
✔						
	✔					
	✔					
		✔				
		✔				
			✔			
			✔			
				✔		
				✔		
					✔	
					✔	
					✔	
						✔
						✔
						✔
						✔

At-A-Glance Six-Month Timeline

If you have six months to plan, use this chart as a quick overview of the tasks involved in planning a wedding and when they should be completed.

	MONTH 1	MONTH 2	MONTH 3	MONTH 4	MONTH 5	MONTH 6
Set the date	✔					
Prepare budget	✔					
Select venues		✔				
Meet with officiant		✔				
Determine guest list		✔				
Select wedding party		✔				
Book photographer			✔			
Book videographer			✔			
Book musicians/DJ			✔			
Book florist			✔			
Select invitations			✔			
Select menu, bar, cake				✔		
Select formal wear				✔		
Mail invitations				✔		
Select wedding bands					✔	
Plan/book honeymoon					✔	
Get marriage license/BT						✔
Prepare ceremony program						✔

Weddings A to Z

—~m~—

WEDDINGS HAVE A VOCABULARY ALL THEIR OWN, and you've almost certainly managed to avoid weddingspeak thus far in your lifetime. Below are some wedding planning terms you'll come to know well. We've made it easy for you to look them up as you need to, by listing them alphabetically.

Announcement — 1) A notice sent to the newspaper designed to inform the public that you and your fiancée have become engaged, customarily printed in the newspaper the day after the engagement party; 2) A card sent in the mail informing friends and family that the two of you have married; typically used when a large, formal wedding cannot take place, due to a death in the family, or if the marriage takes place abroad.

Attendants — Men, women, and children who accompany the bride or stand with the groom throughout the wedding ceremony.

Blood test — (or BT) is a screen test for venereal disease, rubella (measles), and genetic disorders such as sickle-cell anemia or Tay-Sachs disease. Some states require blood tests before issuing a marriage license and may refuse to issue one based on the results.

Boutonniere — A flower or small floral bouquet that is traditionally worn by a man in the buttonhole of the left lapel. If there is no buttonhole, the flower is pinned to the lapel.

Bouquet — Floral ornament carried by the bride down the aisle. The bouquet toss occurs at the end of the wedding, prior to the couple's departure for the honeymoon.

Bride's gift — Brides and grooms customarily exchange gifts with one another to commemorate the wedding. The bride's gift should be something that your wife will treasure through the years and has a sentimental value for her. It does not have to be costly.

Bride's table — At formal weddings, the table at which the bride and groom and their attendants are seated.

Champagne toast — A traditional highlight of the wedding reception, when a glass of bubbly is raised and a few celebratory words are delivered, first to the bride by the best man and then to the groom, with others joining in — the bride to her parents, the groom to his, and so on.

Cocktail music — Music played during the cocktail hour, at a volume that easily facilitates conversation while setting a mood.

Couple's first dance — The first dance with your bride as a married couple, in front of all the wedding guests.

Enclosure card — Additional cards enclosed with the invitation to the wedding ceremony, such as a card inviting the recipient of the invitation to a reception after the ceremony and an RSVP card that the recipient fills out and sends back confirming attendance at the wedding. The invitation and enclosure cards are placed inside in an unsealed envelope.

Favors — A wedding memento imprinted with the couple's name and the wedding date, traditionally given to guests at the reception.

Garter toss — A modern wedding reception tradition in which the bride sits or stands in the center of the dance floor while the groom reaches under her gown to remove a garter. The groom throws the bride's garter into a crowd of single men. The man who catches the garter is said to be the next man to marry.

Gift registry — A service offered by many types of stores and mail-order catalogs, to help ensure the couple does not receive duplicate gifts or gifts they do not want or need.

Groom's cake — A second cake, typically of a smaller size and a different flavor from the wedding cake, served alongside the wedding cake. Fruitcake and chocolate are types of cake traditionally associated with the groom's cake, which appears to have originated as a custom at weddings in the American South. Sometimes it is the groom's cake, instead of the bride's cake, that is cut up and placed in boxes for guests to take home. At contemporary weddings, the groom's cake is often designed to reflect one of the groom's hobbies or interests.

Guest book — A book with a decorative binding (usually to match the color or theme of the wedding) and lined, blank pages on the inside, where guests who attend the wedding sign their names prior to entering the reception hall. May also include a small note from each guest and is often kept as a memento by the couple.

Hospitality room — A room that is set aside for the wedding party to freshen up in during the reception.

Incidental music — Light music of an informal nature played as guests arrive and before the formal function begins.

Maître d' — The headwaiter, in charge of seating guests and ensuring the service runs smoothly.

Marriage certificate — A certified document that serves as official proof of your marriage. Immediately after the ceremony, the couple, the officiant, and witnesses are required to sign an official form or "certificate." The officiant files the signed certificate with the appropriate county official. A certified copy of the certificate is sent to the newly married couple about two weeks later. (Some brides ask people to sign a fancy or reproduction Victorian wedding certificate. A highlight of a Jewish wedding is the signing of the *ketubah*, the heavily decorated ancient Jewish marriage contract specifying the groom's obligations to the bride.)

Noncontinuous contract — A contract that provides that the musicians can take a break every hour.

Officiant/clergy — Priest, minister, rabbi, justice of the peace, judge, or other official who conducts the wedding ceremony. Other cultures have officiants specific to their culture; for example, tribal chiefs officiate at Native American weddings.

Open bar — When drinks are served for "free" to guests (that is, paid for by the reception's hosts).

Pew (row) card — A card from the bride's mother or the groom's mother that is enclosed with the wedding invitation indicating that the guest is invited to sit within the rows reserved for family members (bride's to the left, groom's to the right).

Photo release — A clause in a wedding photography contract granting all rights to your image and likeness to the photographer. If you wish to buy "all rights" to your wedding-day photographs, you should expect to pay a higher fee.

Prix fixe — A set, or "fixed," per person price for a meal on a limited menu.

Processional — The entrance of the wedding party into the ceremony site, usually accompanied by a specific musical piece chosen by the couple. The processional ends with the entrance of the bride.

Program book — A pamphlet that lists the highlights of the wedding ceremony in the order they occur during the wedding. It often includes copies of the poems and readings recited during the ceremony, remembrances to deceased loved ones, the names of the officiant and bridal party members, and songs played. The book serves as a memento for you and your guests.

Rehearsal — A walk-through of the ceremony typically held the night before the wedding at the place of worship or other ceremony location.

Recessional — The departure of the wedding party after the ceremony, beginning with the bride and the groom. The recessional is accompanied by a selected musical piece.

Receiving line — The hostess (usually the mother of the bride), host, and wedding party members who stand in a line to welcome guests to the wedding reception and receive their congratulations.

"Save the date" card — A modern trend. Most wedding invitations are sent out six to eight weeks in advance, but in cases where couples are concerned that might not be enough notice for family and friends, or if the wedding will be held during peak/popular vacation times, they send out a card at an even earlier date asking people to reserve the date. The formal invitation then follows at a later date. Sometimes the "save the date" is designed as a creative, visual reminder such as a sticker, magnet, or card.

Service — 1) A religious wedding ceremony; 2) How meals at a reception hall are served to guests: French, plated tableside; American, plated in the kitchen and brought to the table; ultra-class French, prepared and plated within view; buffet, dishes arranged on a table; stations, wait staff stands behind a table featuring a single type of food (e.g., omelet, beef, salad, taco) and serves the item to guests one at a time, upon request.

Unity candle — A large candle, often decorated, that is lighted during some Christian wedding ceremonies to symbolize the union of two people and two families as they become one in marriage. Variations of this tradition are often incorporated into nondenominational ceremonies.

Viennese pastry table — A table of sweets, pastries, liqueurs, and coffees served at the conclusion of some weddings.

Wait staff — A generic term referring to waiters, waitresses, and other banquet servers. The higher the ratio of wait staff to guests, the better (and more expensive) the service should be.

Wedding planner — 1) A person who specializes in planning weddings; 2) A wedding organizer (see below).

Wedding organizer — A book akin to a beefed-up Day Planner, with timelines, checklists, and record sheets designed to help brides and grooms plan a wedding.

FIRST THINGS FIRST

FIRST THINGS FIRST

The marriage proposal;
the most important question of your life

❖ **Asking Permission, or Not**
❖ **The Perfect Proposal**
❖ **Buying the Engagement Ring**
❖ **Spreading the News**

The importance of the marriage proposal cannot be underestimated. Because the proposal will be an important memory for both you and your future wife, this chapter helps you to design a proposal that captures the spirit of the special and unique relationship you share and provides tips on buying that all-important ring.

Few men feel calm, cool, and collected when they finally pop the question, no matter how secure they are in their relationship. First, there's the question of whether or not she'll say yes. Even if she's been hinting at it for years, you may have a tiny, nagging doubt in the back of your mind that makes you wonder, "Can such an incredible woman actually want to spend the rest of her life with me?"

As you've come to know each other over the past months and years, you hopefully have talked about the important aspects of your future together, including your views about money, lifestyle, health, existing families and custody issues, ex-spouses, debt, future children, careers, schooling, politics, work styles, and other elements that powerfully affect any relationship. You should fully explore these issues, but it isn't wise to do so during the proposal.

We have a dinner every year to celebrate the anniversary of our first date. That year, we wanted to do a dinner cruise from the Hudson River to the East River with a stop in front of the Statue of Liberty. That's when I proposed. She couldn't run away, because she was on a boat!

— *Kevin, lawyer*

Once you propose, you set a whole series of events in motion, many of which will change your life in ways you may not have expected. A marriage is a legal, spiritual, and financial union — and more. It impacts not only the way you spend your time on a daily basis, but also the people you spend it with and the surroundings you spend it in. Marriage is wonderful, meaningful, and fun . . . and it is also a serious commitment.

If you're reading this book, you've most likely found the woman of your dreams and intend to commit to her. Even before you get down on one knee to propose, you may want to take a look at ways you can help partner with your wife in a successful marriage. See Chapter 6 for some of the issues that couples should address prior to the wedding.

Research proves that people in successful marriages address problems early on and negotiate their decisions with flexibility, mutual tolerance, and humor. Happy couples work toward agreement about important issues, such as how to handle finances, children, and other lifestyle issues. Ideally, by the time you propose, you will have explored your future with your wife-to-be and will be well on your way to protecting what will soon be your greatest asset — your marriage.

Asking Permission, or Not

In times past, marriage often involved dowries and other financial settlements, as parents wanted to ensure their daughter's and any children's financial future. A man was expected to ask permission to marry from the bride's father. However, today, the average American guy does not feel the need to ask a father for his daughter's hand. If a man does ask, it's generally out of a desire to follow tradition or as a sign of respect for his future in-laws.

Whether or not you ask formal permission, it's a good idea to spend some time getting to know your bride's parents and letting them get to know you. Above all, tell them how much you love, respect, and care for their daughter.

The Perfect Proposal

How comfortable do you feel with the romantic stuff? Maybe you're a success at your career, playing poker, or answering questions on Jeopardy. Maybe you're good at fixing the car, taking out the trash, or painting the bathroom. But when it comes to

Wise people know that each partner gives not 50 but 150 percent in any good relationship. So, when it comes to creating your proposal, it's important to get outside of your head and inside of your bride's head. Your proposal doesn't have to be fancy or cost a lot of money. But it should celebrate the sense of connection between the two of you. Make it romantic. What you want to focus on are the areas and interests that you share.

romance, you may feel pressured to perform. You know she's expecting that big, romantic proposal, the kind of creative, sensitive, loving gesture that will make her heart beat wildly — one that she'll remember for the rest of her life.

Do a search on the Internet, and you'll get plenty of ideas promising you creative ways to pop the question. There are books that tell the stories of how other men have proposed. There are puzzles you can buy that, when they are assembled, will ask the question for you. You can even buy a silver arrow that contains a hidden scroll onto which the proposal can be scribed.

Great though these ideas and suggestions are, they come up short in one key area. What's missing in all of the ideas is — you, and your personal touch. To make your proposal truly unique and romantic, all you need to do is take a good look at who you are, who your future bride is, and what makes your relationship so special and unique. Then follow a few basic guidelines, and you're on your way to creating your own unforgettable scenario.

CREATING YOUR PROPOSAL BLUEPRINT

Following are some questions to ask yourself that can help you shape a proposal that's just right for the two of you.

Are there any hobbies the two of you share?
For example, if you both love hiking, plan a proposal around a hike. Do you both like to fish? Have her "reel" in your proposal. Does she love old, black-and-white film noir movies? It's cheap enough to have a friend videotape you. Your Humphrey Bogart cannot fail to charm, no matter how corny.

Is she a public or private person?
Do you have close friends in common? If so, tell them ahead of time you plan to propose and make arrangements for them to come in at the final moment to share your joy and perhaps film the results. Is she a private person? Then keep the proposal exclusively between the two of you until she accepts, and the two of you can discuss how you want to announce it to the world.

What is her favorite flower, candy, color?
All of these can be used to dress up your message. If she's a comic book fan, buy one you think she'll enjoy, white out the balloons, and write your own happy ending.

Does she love animals?
Maybe her golden retriever can use a new collar — one embroidered with those magic words.

Does she like poetry?
Ask your local librarian to help you pick out a poem or write one yourself. You can read her the poem before proposing. Or, you can have a calligrapher write it on a card, get it framed, and give it to her while telling her: "This poem describes how I feel about you. I want to spend the rest of our lives together. Will you marry me?"

I proposed one week before Valentine's Day. While it was pretty much expected that we would get married, I wanted to surprise her. Valentine's Day would have been too obvious.

— *Rob, bookstore manager*

Is she the artistic type?

See if a local art gallery or museum can help you dream up a proposal. One of the most important parts of any proposal is the message, so give some thought to what you want to say. If you are truly tongue-tied and want some help crafting a proposal, try finishing the following sentences:

(Her Name)_____ :
When I first met you, I thought_____ . We have spent time together doing_____ , going to_____ , and talking about_____. I came to love you because_____. In future years, I can see us_____. You are truly _____ _____ (List her great qualities).
     (Her Name)_____ , will you marry me?

But remember, your partner loves you because of who you are. Making an effort is important, but you need to be genuine. You should never feel you have to act out a role. A simple, heartfelt proposal that tells your girlfriend you know who she is and you love her for it is what will truly win her heart.

Unique Proposal Ideas

- Engrave a silver box.

- Ask a confectioner to create a candy egg to hold the ring.

- Hire a skywriter at the beach.

- Appliqué letters to a kite.

- Have someone embroider a T-shirt on a Teddy Bear asking her to marry you and present it to her.

- Put a message in a bottle and go treasure hunting.

- Write a message and enclose it in a silver locket.

- Ask a jeweler to attach letter charms to a charm bracelet to spell out M-A-R-R-Y M-E.

- Make a video or DVD starring you and slip it into a video box one Saturday night.

Buying the Engagement Ring

No bridal garment, accessory, or physical adornment resonates with as much meaning, or elicits as much interest, as that slender circle of commitment, the engagement ring. The ring is a token of the promises you have made, and will continue to make, to each other throughout your lives.

Given that the engagement ring is such an important part of the marriage proposal, the following section covers common questions many grooms have when buying it.

How Much Money Should I Spend?

The diamond industry recommends that the groom spend two months' salary on the ring, but this is by no means a hard-and-fast rule (and consider the source!). What's more important is how much of a ring you can reasonably afford. You don't want to run up debt before you're married, especially when you may want to buy a home in the near future. If you don't have a lot of money, perhaps there is a family ring that you can give to your bride. Or perhaps you can give her an inexpensive ring now with the promise to buy her something more elaborate in the future. One groom I know even gave his wife a ring from a candy machine, with the promise that he would get her a fancier ring once his career took off.

WHAT IS THE CLASSIC ENGAGEMENT RING?

About 75 percent of engagement rings sold in the United States today are diamond rings. Tiffany introduced today's classic engagement ring, a solitaire elevated in a six-prong setting, in 1886. Tiffany certifies its diamonds in its own gem laboratory. Other jewelers sell rings that are referred to as "Tiffany-style."

Some brides prefer old-fashioned rose diamond cuts, pearls, or colored gemstones to the traditional diamonds. Green emeralds, said to break at the moment of marital infidelity, are considered more valuable than fancy-colored diamonds, for example. An alternative three-stone engagement ring is sometimes worn both as engagement ring and wedding band.

A platinum setting is the most durable and expensive. White gold is a less expensive alternative to platinum. Eighteen carat gold is popular with those who prefer Renaissance or old-fashioned ring styles. Metal can be worked a number of ways — delicate filigree, pavé ("paved" or set with fine, tiny stones), set with ancient-looking beading, hand-tooled, cast designed, and more.

How Can I Be Sure She'll Like It?

Take a close look at the jewelry she wears, especially any pieces she tells you she especially likes. "Borrow" a piece of jewelry she is fond of, if you can do it without her knowing about it. Or take some snapshots of some of her favorite pieces from her jewelry box. Bring these visual clues to the jeweler, who can help you choose something with the same feel.

Ask her mother, sister, or a close friend whose taste you know she shares to help you narrow the selection. (But the final choice should be your own! Choose from among the candidates at another time, so your bride will be the first to see the actual ring.)

Head to the mall and go window-shopping with your girlfriend. Walk slowly and casually. Make sure you pass by one or more jewelry store. It wouldn't hurt if, in addition to a modern chain jeweler, there was an antique store specializing in vintage jewelry or, if your bride likes crafts, an artisan jeweler. Pay close attention if and when your bride mentions that she likes a particular ring.

Ask her to shop for a ring with you. However, don't buy it when she's with you. Even if you buy the ring she picks out, if you get it when she's not around and surprise her with it over a romantic dinner or on a special occasion, it will heighten her excitement at getting it.

Recently, controversy has arisen around diamonds mined in areas that do not adhere to United Nations resolutions. If your bride is sensitive to global conflict and related political issues, you may want to ensure the diamond you buy comes from a source willing to guarantee the diamond is "conflict free."

How can I be sure I'm buying a quality stone?

Read about diamonds. Pricescope, a consumer advocate site for gemstones, has a proposal forum and lots of tools and links. (See "Resources" on p. 110 for suggestions.)

A number of independent gem laboratories provide grading reports that will give you an independent expert's opinion on a diamond's characteristics and the quality of its cut. Each lab has its own system, so the grading reports will vary, depending on the lab.

What if the ring doesn't fit?

If the ring runs on the large side, the jeweler you bought it from should be able to size the ring for you. Keep in mind, though, that sizing, no matter how carefully it's done, causes small, physical changes to the ring. Therefore, it's best to find out your bride's size if you can.

In some cases — for example, when you are giving your bride an old family ring — resizing may be inevitable. If that's the case, it's important to understand what constitutes a quality sizing job. The jeweler should be able to explain exactly what changes you can expect in a sized, repaired, or reconstructed ring.

If the ring is old, the jeweler may not be able to match the exact texture of the metal's surface. Reworking can be costly, so make sure you go over the process in as much detail as possible before proceeding. Another

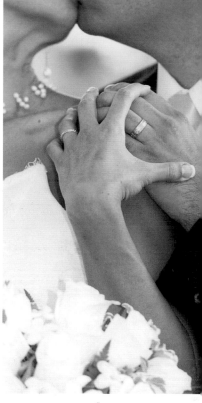

Strategy: Put some effort into the proposal. It shows you care.

I put together a romantic weekend getaway for the two of us at a fancy historic hotel. After a fun day visiting museums and taking a walk around beautiful gardens, I proposed to her over a candlelight dinner, with champagne and roses.

— *Rich, engineer*

alternative — although some feel it's a less attractive one — is to ask your jeweler to install an adjustable shank.

Most contemporary settings can be purchased in a variety of ring finger sizes. The jeweler can then put a stone of your choice in the setting. Ask the jeweler about return policies and whether the setting lends itself to this option.

As is the case with buying any item, the more time you spend researching your purchase, the more comfortable you will feel about your ability to judge quality, and the more confidence you will have when it comes to purchasing a stone.

The Four "Cs" of a Diamond

CUT — The 'cut' of a diamond refers to the shape of the diamond, i.e., how it's cut from the rough stone. How a diamond is cut determines how much sparkle it has. The goal is to allow the maximum amount of light through the top of the stone and to reflect it back through the diamond's top facets.

CARAT — A carat is a measurement of weight. One carat is equal to 1/5 of a gram.

CLARITY — The number of flaws or inclusions in the stone is indicated by the following terms:

FL (flawless)

IF (Internally flawless with minor surface imperfections)

VVS1-2 (very, very slightly imperfect)

VS1-2 (very slightly imperfect)

SI1-2 (slightly imperfect)

I1-2-3 (Imperfect — inclusions visible with the naked eye)

COLOR — Traditionally, the whiter the stone, the better. However, colored diamonds are increasing in value. Pink diamonds are especially rare.

D, E, F = colorless	G, H, I = near colorless
J, K, L, M = faint yellow	N, O, P, Q, R = very light yellow
S, T, U, V, W, X, Y, Z = light yellow	

Can I buy a loose diamond online?

The Internet has become an increasingly popular source for many consumer goods, and diamonds are no exception. Numerous sites have popped up to educate consumers about purchasing either loose diamonds or diamond engagement rings online; most also sell them or have links to site sponsors that sell diamonds.

No transaction over the Internet is entirely safe, but many people have successfully and safely purchased items online by taking these precautions:

◆ Make sure there is a phone number and, preferably, a company address on the Web site. Call the phone number and verify the address.

◆ Ask if you can obtain a grading report and then have the stone sent to an independent appraiser. Then have the appraiser send the stone to you. Make sure the stone is insured during shipping.

◆ Exercise caution with online auctions — typically, the responsibility is on the seller to disclose what the item is, as well as to provide an accurate description. Even if the seller makes an honest mistake, you don't want to have the stress of returning the item.

◆ Make a one-time only purchase, so your account information will not automatically appear the next time you bring up the page.

◆ Don't enter any "optional" information.

◆ Never share your password with anyone, including someone claiming to call from the site/store.

◆ Before clicking the "Buy" button, print out any pages describing or picturing your purchase.

◆ Use a credit card, NOT a debit card, when making an online purchase. If you use a credit card, the issuer can make a charge back against the seller if there is an issue or a fraudulent transaction. That's not the case with debit cards, which also transfer the money almost immediately from your account to the seller's.

◆ Be sure the online store utilizes the standard for secure online processing, which is 128-bit encryption. Look for a yellow padlock or a key symbol on the browser window and "https" instead of "http" in the address bar at the top of the page. Also, the online store should have a posted security policy that states that it uses 128-bit encryption.

◆ Before purchasing, read any notices, especially the return policy, paying extra attention to the fine print. Can you return the item for a full refund if you're not satisfied?

◆ Verify when your order will arrive. A Federal Trade Commission (FTC) rule requires merchants to ship items within 30 days after the order date if no specific date is promised.

◆ Print the transaction receipt or confirmation page.

◆ After you make the purchase, completely log off the site. (Click "back" to see if you can recall the previous page. If you can, you are not logged off.)

Engagement Ring Worksheet

Use this worksheet (or copy if you need more than one) and fill out the information for each ring you are seriously considering. Once you make your final purchase, attach your receipts and make sure that you get everything in writing.

Jeweler Name										
Address										
Telephone / Fax										
E-mail			Web site							
Contact Name			Phone							
Item ID			Cost							
Shape										
(circle one below)	Asscher	Cushion	Emerald	Heart		Marquise	Oval			
	Pear	Princess	Radiant	Round		Trilliant				
Other (explain)										
Carat Size										
Clarity (circle one)	FL	IF	VVS1-2	VS1-2	SI1-2	I1-2-3				
Color (circle one)	D	E	F	G	H	I	J	K	L	M
	N	O	P	Q	R	S	T	U	V	W	X	Y	Z
Cut (circle one)	Premium	Ideal	Excellent	V. Good	Good	Fair				
Comments										

Spreading the News

Once your fiancée has said "yes," it will probably be very difficult to keep the exciting news to yourselves! The following section provides some insight into announcing the engagement.

ANNOUNCING YOUR ENGAGEMENT TO YOUR FAMILIES

How should you two tell your families that you are engaged? Even if you tell them first in a phone call, it's a good idea to invite them for a get-together.

Before you meet, you might want to think first about what to say to your parents and future in-laws. Each of you should think of a few nice words to say about your soon-to-be in-laws, or at the very least, about how much you love your fianceé. At this first meeting, you and your bride will want to bring up the wedding planning process itself, if you have agreed on certain basics, such as a date, style, or location. But don't go overboard. The goal is to celebrate and then to set another date for an actual planning meeting.

Some mothers dream of the day they will be able to plan their daughter's wedding. If that's the case, consider following up the first meeting with a handwritten note thanking her for her efforts and letting her know that you will be happy to assist.

THE NEWSPAPER ANNOUNCEMENT

As it is typically the bride's mother's responsibility, ask her if she plans to submit an announcement to the newspaper; if so, offer to type up any relevant information to make that task easy for her.

Sample newspaper announcement

- Full names
- Hometown, states
- High schools attended
- Colleges, universities, or professional school(s) attended, and degrees received
- Any additional professional affiliations
- Occupations and employers
- Parents' full names, including any appropriate titles, the town and state they live in, and their occupations

GETTING STARTED

GETTING STARTED

When, where, how much, and who

❖ Getting Organized
❖ The Groom's Role
❖ The Groom's Countdown
❖ Budgets and Finances

A survey of bridal magazines indicates that today's more balanced partnerships have blurred the line between the groom's duties and the bride's duties, with many couples planning and paying for their weddings together, without the help of parents. Preparation is the key to planning the perfect wedding. Traditionally, the groom's role was to show up at the altar, but there's more. How much more? Few grooms know just what to expect when planning a wedding, so this chapter provides you with a starting point. Read on for how to begin the wedding planning process, including an outline of the groom's traditional wedding responsibilities and real-life strategies to help you get organized.

Getting Organized

Every year, millions of excited couples make plans to walk down the aisle and say "I do." For most couples, the easy part is accepting the proposal. The harder part is planning the big event.

Between finding a venue, creating the guest list, and choosing a wedding party, life can become very hectic. So how can today's busy couples stay organized? Following are our recommendations for the most effective tried-and-true organization ideas. You may decide to buy a wedding organizer to help you keep track of the wedding planning process. You'll want to review this book together even alongside the wedding organizer. See "Resources" on page 110 for our suggestions, and use this valuable tool in tandem with one or more of the ideas below.

Use Web Sites

Many Web sites feature tools that can assist couples in planning a wedding. However, you don't need to purchase software to get some technological tools of your own. Most computers today are uploaded with a suite of general office software. A spreadsheet can help you keep track of your budget. Project software can help you keep track of your wedding timeline. And, with database software, you can create a database that will help you keep track of your guest lists, invitation responses, gifts, and thank-you notes.

Are you artistic? You can use photo or illustration software to design and print your own invitations and program books. Most office supply stores carry elegant blank invitations that you can personalize.

If you like designing Web sites and know a bit of HTML, you can design and host a wedding Web site to keep guests and participants apprised of your wedding plans as they progress and get them the information they need to do their parts. You can even direct invitees to RSVP via your wedding Web site.

HIRE A WEDDING PLANNER

A wedding planner is a professional who can help you plan your wedding using his or her expertise and contacts. A wedding planner is an adviser, coordinator, supervisor, mediator, and financial planner.

With today's hectic, career-oriented lifestyles, many couples and their families do not have the time for the detailed planning and work that results in a beautiful wedding. A wedding planner, working with you, can handle all of the details, some of the details, or just a few, depending upon how much you want to be involved. I've listed some wedding planner resources on page 110. Professional associations for wedding planners can put you in touch with a planner in your area.

As mentioned previously, your role as groom may expand considerably from the traditional role. You may be expected to investigate and book just a few of the services. Or you may end up planning the wedding every step of the way, side-by-side with your fiancée. As soon as possible after the proposal, therefore, you need to get down to business.

The first thing to do is meet with your bride to decide what type of wedding you want and what you can do to make it a reality. You may have had a lot of discussions about getting married and can pretty well guess what type of wedding you as a couple would like to have. Even so, you need to confirm with your fiancée that your impressions are correct. Schedule a first "official" planning meeting for just the two of you.

FIND YOUR WEDDING STYLE

Today, many couples find that there are so many wedding looks, fashions, and styles that appeal to them that just narrowing it down is a huge challenge! Finding your style is imperative to planning your wedding. Having someone else's style form the basis of your event leaves very little embedded in your guests' minds to cherish and savor. Flavor your event with your style. Your unique vision should be imprinted on each and every detail to offer your guests an event rich in the essence of you.

Starting off the wedding planning process with a sweet gesture will help keep things calm and romantic and create an ambience that will foster positive discussions and reduce stress. Even though both of you love and are prepared to commit to each other, there is no doubt that you will be greatly challenged by planning this event. Chances are, like many couples today, you will have to deal with something — parents from different cultures or faiths, stepfamilies or second marriages, financial issues, vendors who promise things but don't deliver, scheduling difficulties, family politics, and so on. These challenges are best negotiated in an atmosphere of relaxation and fun.

Before you meet (with your bride-to-be)

- Think about the weddings you've attended — what you liked about them and what you didn't like about them.

- Ask yourself — are you suave and sophisticated or just a simple, laid-back kind of guy? Knowing who you are will help you to give clear input on the kind of wedding you want.

- You may want to buy a wedding organizer, if you haven't already done so. (If you want one that coordinates with this book, check out *The Bride's Year Ahead: The Ultimate Month by Month Wedding Planner* by the same author.)

- Bring a calendar for the next one to two years.

WEDDING STYLE QUESTIONNAIRE

(Note — this is just a starting point. You'll refine your answers to the questions below, as you get input from your families and start to visit wedding vendors to get ballpark wedding costs.)

*What size of wedding are you imagining? (Big or small; the total number of guests.)*_____

*What type of ceremony? Religious or civil? If religious and you are not of the same faith, what spiritual tradition — yours, hers, or both?*_____

*What style? A formal affair, a casual one, or a theme wedding revolving around one of your interests or hobbies?*_____

_____

*Do you have a location in mind? (Town or country, in your or the bride's hometown, at the school where you met, equidistant between families, a specific reception hall?)*_____

*On what date — or, at the very least — month — of the year would you prefer to hold the wedding? Remember to give yourself as much time as you can, between 1 and 1½ years.*_____

*What part (if any) will her parents (and yours) play in the wedding planning process?*_____

Who will be involved in paying for and planning the wedding?

_____

_____

*Will you follow the common path of getting assistance from the bride's family, or will the two of you be contributing together?*_____

*Will your family help out?*_____

If you are expected to contribute, or if the two of you plan to pay for the wedding yourselves, how much money can you reasonably afford, while remaining fiscally responsible?

What would the ideal wedding planning process look like — a meeting once a week, every two weeks, each month? Who should be present at each meeting? The timeline on pages 10–12 of this book should give you some perspective on what needs to get done, and when to schedule things.

If you are expected to do more than the duties on the groom's traditional short list, review the timeline and determine with your fiancée what you can best assist with. You can put a "B" in the

Do's and Don'ts of Choosing a Venue

The success of any social event depends upon following through with the details. To make sure you select the perfect venue for your ceremony and/or reception:

- **Do** visit the place before booking. Ask to sample food and see a photo album of receptions previously held there, so you can study sample set-ups.
- **Do** ask for brochures with detailed descriptions and pricing. Take them home to study. Don't be pressured into making an instant decision.
- **Don't** take anyone's word for anything.
- **Do** get everything in writing.
- **Don't** sign paperwork without reading it carefully.
- **Do** review all contracts looking for hidden costs such as gratuities, taxes, and miscellaneous fees (such as valet parking or bottle uncorking fees).
- **Do** keep in frequent contact with vendors.
- **Do** keep copies of contracts in a safe place.

margin next to the things your bride has agreed to take care of and a "G" next to your tasks. You may want to make notes in pencil, though — your roles may shift over subsequent planning meetings!

The Groom's Role

In today's modern relationships, most couples work outside the home and have plenty of responsibilities that make it necessary for the bride and groom to work together to plan the wedding. No longer is the groom on the periphery; he is now an equal partner in the planning, decision-making, and budgeting process. This section is devoted to the modern responsibilities of the groom, both those that are financial and those that are focused on planning and decision-making.

Craft the wedding proposal and purchase the engagement ring

Book the services of the officiant or celebrant
- You will be responsible for booking the officiant's time for the ceremony. Your fiancée will usually be involved with this, and your chosen celebrant may wish to get to know you both before the ceremony.

Select the best man, groomsmen, and ushers

Buy the wedding ring

Choose formal wear for the male members of the wedding party and arrange for wedding attire to be collected after the wedding

Compile the guest list
- The groom is responsible for putting together his side of the guest list. The number of guests should be flexible to accommodate the budget.
- After the wedding, arrange for your wedding clothes to be returned to the tuxedo store, if necessary.

Plan, book, and pay for the honeymoon

Arrange transportation to and from the ceremony and reception sites

Order the buttonnieres for the groomsmen.

- These may be ordered with the other flowers and collected from the bride's home on the morning of the wedding by the best man. Alternatively, have them delivered and give to the best man for distribution. It is also traditional for the groom to pay for the bride's bouquet, the bridesmaids' flowers, and corsages for the mothers.

Buy gifts

- For the best man and ushers
- For your bride
- Perhaps for your new mother-in-law or parents-in-law

Write your speech for the rehearsal and reception

Attend the wedding rehearsal

Pack for your honeymoon

Get the marriage license and schedule blood tests

- The groom is responsible for making the appointment for a wedding license and arranging for blood tests if the state requires it.

Your wedding planning process will no doubt end up being as unique as the love you share, but most likely you will be expected to do certain tasks that the groom is traditionally assigned to do. As a "heads up," a detailed overview of these tasks is provided.

The Groom's Countdown

18 Months to 2 Years Ahead
- Plan the proposal and decide on an engagement ring.
- Pop the question.

12 to 18 Months Ahead
- Have a brainstorming session with your bride about your mutual dreams for the celebration, its style (religious or secular, formal or informal), and your budget and financial obligations.
- Meet with both sets of parents to get their input and assistance.
- Decide on an officiant.
- Accompany your fiancée to all reception sites being seriously considered.
- If applicable, assist with booking the reception site and ceremony location.
- Select a wedding date and time with your bride-to-be.
- Select your groomsmen. (You'll need one usher per 50 guests. Your bride may ask you to include some of her family members.)
- Decide on an engagement ring for your bride — if you haven't already presented her with one.
- Begin compiling a guest list — check with bride for estimated numbers and get input from your parents.
- Begin your honeymoon plans — either as a surprise for your bride or with her.
- Discuss your housing situation with your future wife.
- Determine all financial arrangements and responsibilities.

STRATEGY:
Give Yourself Plenty of Time. Start planning as far in advance as possible, because if you wait, it limits your choices, especially if you are getting married in a popular month. We got married in May, which may be the second most popular month.

— *Russ, computer programmer*

11 Months Ahead
- Choose your best man.
- Discuss and book the music, photographer, and videographer.

10 to 9 Months Ahead
- Discuss and shop for invitations, decorations, and favors.

8 Months Ahead
- Shop for your tuxedo and ushers' attire.

7 Months Ahead

- Secure a florist if you are buying the flowers.
- Help choose a wedding cake.

6 Months Ahead

- Together with your fiancée, register for gifts.

5 Months Ahead

- Get a passport if traveling abroad.
- Attend to any legal matters, such as insurance policies, wills, joint checking accounts, trusts, custody issues, health insurance and other employment benefits, prenuptial agreements associated with any children from a former marriage, business issues.

4 Months Ahead

- Look for a new home or apartment, if appropriate.
- Find accommodations for out-of-town guests.
- Take dance lessons.
- Order wedding attire for your attendants — be sure to get everyone's correct size, shoe sizes, too!
- Shop for wedding rings.
- Make final honeymoon arrangements.

3 Months Ahead

- Finalize the guest list, ensuring that names, titles, and addresses are included.
- Order your wedding rings. Choose an inscription to engrave inside the rings.

2 Months Ahead

- Help plan the rehearsal dinner.
- Get blood tests if applicable.
- Apply for a marriage license.
- Pick up the wedding rings.
- Choose a gift for your bride.
- Choose gifts for your groomsmen.

1 Month Ahead

- Review vendor contracts and confirm dates and details.
- Help your parents finalize plans for the rehearsal dinner.
- Arrange your transportation for your wedding day.
- Pick up your rings and try them on for size.

2 Weeks Before

- Pick up the marriage license.
- Review the wedding day itinerary with your groomsmen.
- Host a bachelor dinner or attend a bachelor party.
- Write and practice your toasts.

- Pick up your rental attire and remind your groomsmen to collect their attire.
- Get a haircut.
- Make sure honeymoon plans are on course.
- Assist with giving final instructions to vendors and officiant.
- Pack luggage for honeymoon.
- Pick up all necessary tickets for honeymoon.
- Try on all wedding-day attire.

1 Day Before
- Attend the rehearsal and rehearsal dinner.
- Review the wedding day itinerary with your groomsmen for the last time.

- Give gifts to groomsmen.
- Think of a nice, romantic gesture to do for your bride.

Day of the Ceremony
- Give the bride's ring to your best man.
- Remember to take your marriage license to the ceremony.
- Prepare the officiant's fee and give to best man.
- Don't skip any meals.
- Take your time and enjoy your day!

Probably the most important thing to know is how soon to start planning. We thought we started planning early, but it turns out that we were on the edge of starting too late. Don't ever think you're starting too early! We learned this lesson over and over again with the reception hall, vendors, DJs, photographers, the quartet — and we started more than a year in advance.

— *Kevin, lawyer*

Who Pays for What?

The traditional expenses of the groom are:

◆ The marriage license

◆ The officiant fee

◆ Tips for altar boys, if there are any

◆ The bachelor dinner

◆ The bride's engagement ring

◆ The bride's wedding ring

◆ The groom's medical exam and blood test

◆ The bride's bouquet

◆ Boutonnieres for the groomsmen

◆ Mothers' corsages

◆ His own attire

◆ The ushers' ties, gloves, and other accessories

◆ Gifts for the ushers, the bride, and his groomsmen

◆ Transportation from the wedding to the honeymoon

◆ The honeymoon

◆ Hotel rooms for his best man and ushers if needed

The traditional expenses of the groom's family are:

◆ Their clothes

◆ The rehearsal dinner

◆ Often, bar and liquor costs at the reception

The traditional expenses of the bride's family are:

◆ The engagement party

◆ The invitations and announcements, including postage costs

◆ The ceremony site fees

◆ The cost to transport the bridal party from the bride's house to the ceremony and between the ceremony location to the reception

◆ The bride's wedding attire, including headpiece, shoes, gloves, and accessories

◆ The bridesmaids' bouquets and for large, formal weddings, attendants' dresses

◆ The attire for the mother and father of the bride

◆ The grandmothers' corsages

◆ The birdseed shower

◆ The flowers for the ceremony and reception

◆ The decorative props and other rentals for the ceremony and reception

◆ The reception itself, including programs, location, food, drinks, caterer, favors, chairs and tables

◆ The photography, videography, music for the ceremony and reception

◆ The wedding cake

◆ The lodging costs for out of-town members of the wedding party and, sometimes, guests

◆ A generous gift to the couple upon their marriage

◆ The bridal shower

◆ The after-the-ceremony wedding brunch or open house

Budgets and Finances

For vendors, a wedding is a cash cow; in fact, many photographers, musicians, and hotels would not survive if they did not have a substantial wedding business.

Most couples, on the other hand, are stunned to find out just how expensive a "not very lavish" wedding can cost and, moreover, how little opportunity there is to trim their wedding

expenses. Almost every wedding venue prices its services as a package, leaving very little room for price negotiation.

But it's not all business greed that causes weddings to be expensive. Many couples find themselves spending money in order to satisfy social expectations. Parents of the couple may feel strongly that the wedding of their son or daughter must compare favorably to those hosted by their friends. Family and social obligations may require the couple to substantially enlarge their guest list. It all sounds a bit grim, but take heart. This section will show you what you can do to control your wedding destiny (financial, anyway).

If you are helping to pay for or plan the wedding, consider opening a separate but joint checking account for wedding expenses and gift money. Everyone contributing to the wedding — including parents — can deposit money into the account, too. This will help you keep track of all wedding expenses and funds to date.

TIPPING

Originally, tips were sums of money given to service people "to insure prompt service (TIPS)." Today, most service people regard tips as part of the fees charged, rather than an option. The event hosts should prepay any tipping. Wedding guests should never be required to tip, and you should place a sign at appropriate areas, such as the bar, to indicate so.

Musicians' tips range from $25 per member of a wedding band up to $75 for a church organist. Check with local laws and governmental policies about whether you can tip your civil officiant. Clergy usually accept a "donation" of between $75 and $200.

If your contract does not state that a service fee or gratuity has been included, then you would tip waiters and bartenders between 15 and 20 percent, as you would at a restaurant. However, most banquet halls automatically tack on a minimum 15 percent service charge (and sometimes as much as 20 percent) to the bill and, on top of that, suggest (although not require) the customer add another gratuity. The additional, expected gratuity is less than the typical 15-20 percent tip in a restaurant and is usually calculated by figuring $1 to $2 dollars per guest. A headwaiter or hostess maybe tipped between 1 and 2 percent of the bill as well.

Other attendants who typically expect gratuities are restroom, coat check, and valet parking attendants; tip between $1 and $2 per coat or car. Tip limousine drivers between 15 percent and 20 percent of the bill.

If they are truly exceptional, tip DJs, bakers, florists, photographers, and videographers between 15 percent and 20 percent of the bill.

Wedding Budget Overview

Money Facts and Figures: (The average wedding costs $19,000.) Here is a typical breakdown of a wedding budget.

- Invitations and printed matter — 5%
- Clothing — 15%
- Reception and ceremony — 45%
- Alcohol and wait staff — 10%
- Music — 10%
- Flowers — 5%
- Photography/videography — 8%

- Other (transportation, favors, gifts) — 2%
- Note: Reception halls typically offer packages at a fixed price per "head." If you ask them to change the package, the cost is likely to skyrocket.
- The same package can cost $150 per person in a big city and $50 per person in a small town.

Compiling The Guest List

If yours is a traditional wedding scenario, that is, if the parents of the bride are paying for the majority of the wedding, you will have to confirm the number of seats reserved for your guests with the bride's family (assuming they are the ones paying for the reception). The reception is the most expensive part of a wedding, with an average per-person cost of $50-$75. While there's nothing to prevent you from inviting more people to the actual ceremony than to the reception, the ones who are not invited to the reception might feel a bit left out. If you feel strongly about inviting more people than your mother-in-law assigns to you, another possibility is that you can offer to bear some of the cost for the reception (as long as the reception site has adequate room).

While it's tempting to invite everyone at work, on your softball team, investment club, and poker league, you don't have to. You can limit invitees to your closest friends, and simply treat the others to a round of beer in honor of your engagement or marriage.

RSVP, Please

It's unlikely that everyone on your invitation list will be able to come. Assume between 10 and 20 percent will send regrets. In addition, you don't have to allow everyone invited to the wedding to bring a guest. To deliver this message, address the invitation to one person and refrain from adding "and guest." You can also cut down your list by deciding not to invite anyone you haven't socialized with in the past year, as well as young children.

THE
PLAYERS

THE PLAYERS

A wedding who's who

- ❖ **Lead Roles and Supporting Cast**
- ❖ **It's All in the Family**
- ❖ **Wardrobe and Formal Wear Timeline**

In this chapter, I'll cover every role for the typical wedding. I will also provide you with advice on dealing with various family issues, choosing formal wear for your big day, and buying the wedding rings. If yours is the typical American wedding, you will promise to love and cherish each other not only in front of an officiant, but also before friends and family members, many of whom will take part in the actual wedding ceremony itself. This chapter will provide guidance on how to keep track of the roles and responsibilities traditionally assigned to wedding party members.

Lead Roles and Supporting Cast

What follows is a list of the players in a typical American wedding and what they're expected to do. These roles may vary, depending on whether you are having a religious or civil ceremony, the size and location of the wedding, and the cultural traditions of your families.

Best Man

If you have a brother, traditionally he's your best man. If you don't have a brother, it's your best friend. He is someone you can depend on to:

- Plan the bachelor party
- Help with last-minute organizing
- Help coordinate limos and other transportation
- Assist with getting you dressed
- Pay fees and take care of tips (you'll give him the money)
- Coordinate the ushers
- Stand next to you at the altar
- Hold the wedding rings
- Immediately after the ceremony, serve as a witness and sign the marriage certificate
- Appear in wedding photos taken after the ceremony and prior to the reception
- Sit at the head table, on the bride's right
- Deliver the first toast at the reception (to the bride)
- Dance with maid of honor during the first dance
- Organize the getaway, including storing the luggage in the car
- Return your tuxedo and any other rentals after the wedding

Groomsmen and Ushers

Ushers are responsible for seating the guests at the ceremony. They are usually male but can also be female. You should have at least one usher for every 40 to 50 guests. Groomsmen can be friends, brothers, or cousins from your side or your fiancée's side. Most grooms choose groomsmen to equal the number of bridesmaids in the wedding party. Groomsmen and ushers sometimes overlap. Groomsmen's responsibilities include:

- Seating guests upon arrival. This involves reviewing the seating plan (i.e., reserved areas for family members) and ensuring the bride's family sits on the left and the groom's on the right, with the mother of the bride in the first row on the left and the mother of the groom in the first row on the right.

- Unrolling a runner (aisle covering) along the aisle prior to the processional, as well as row ribbons (see page 83)

- Walking in pairs prior to the processional to stand next to the best man at the altar

- Assisting with the ceremony, perhaps doing a reading during the ceremony

- Escorting the bridesmaids down the aisle at the recessional

- After the ceremony, removing the row ribbons and rolling up the aisle runner

- Appearing in wedding photos taken after the ceremony and prior to the reception

- Sitting at either end of the head table next to the designated bridesmaid

- Dancing with a specific bridesmaid at the reception during the formal dance introducing the wedding party

- Keeping track of the gifts

- Returning formal wear rented for the groomsmen

THE PARENTS OF THE GROOM

- Arrive at ceremony prior to other bridal party members (except groom and ushers)

- Your mother is ushered down the aisle and seated in first row on right. Your father follows her, alone

- Exit church together after recessional

- Appear in wedding photos taken after the ceremony and prior to the reception

- At the entrance to the reception hall, your mother stands next to either the bride's mother or, alternatively, your father in the receiving line

- Your mother sits next to the bride's father and opposite your father at the parents' table

- Your mother dances the first dance with the father of the bride, and your father dances the first dance with the mother of the bride

The Parents of the Bride

◆ On the day of the wedding, the bride's mother is the first to leave the family home, accompanied by the bridesmaids

◆ The bride and her father follow in a separate car

◆ The bride's mother is seated just prior to processional

◆ The bride's father escorts the bride down the aisle, then joins her mother in the first row on the left

◆ The bride's parents exit church together after recessional

◆ Appear in wedding photos taken after the ceremony and prior to the reception

◆ The bride's mother stands first in the receiving line, next to either your mother or the bride's father

◆ The bride's mother is seated next to your father and opposite the bride's father at the table

◆ The bride's father's first dance is with your mother and her mother dances first with your father

Maid or Matron of Honor

The maid of honor is the bride's chief attendant. Usually she is the bride's sister or her best friend. If she is married, she is referred to as the matron of honor.

◆ Helps the bride get dressed

◆ Walks down the aisle before the bride, the flower girl(s), and the ring bearer

◆ Arranges the bride's train and veil before the start of the ceremony

◆ Holds the groom's wedding ring during the ceremony

◆ Holds the bride's bouquet during the wedding vows and exchange of rings

◆ Straightens the bride's train as she turns away from the altar and, with the best man, follows the couple down the aisle

- Signs the marriage certificate as a witness
- Appears in wedding photos taken after the ceremony and prior to the reception
- Arranges the bride's train and veil before she enters the reception
- Stands in the receiving line
- Sits to the groom's left
- Toasts the couple
- Dances with the best man during the first dance
- Helps the bride change for the honeymoon
- Helps keep track of the gifts

BRIDESMAIDS

Bridesmaids are usually chosen by the bride from among her friends and family members, although it's not unusual for the groom's sister to be chosen as a bridesmaid.

- Assists with preparations at the bride's house or in the hospitality suite
- Accepts flowers at the bride's house and passes them out
- Follows the flower girl/ring bearer and precedes the maid of honor down the aisle at the start of the ceremony
- Accompanies the designated groomsman down the aisle after the ceremony
- Appears in wedding photos taken after the ceremony and prior to the reception
- Stands next to the maid of honor in the receiving line
- Sits at either end of the head table next to the designated groomsman
- Dances with the designated groomsman during the first dance

Ring Bearer

In the tradition of a page boy during medieval times, the ring bearer:

◆ Proceeds down the aisle before the flower girl(s) and the bride and her father

◆ Carries the bride's wedding ring (or a symbolic ring) on a pillow down the aisle

◆ Sits in the row occupied by the mother of the bride during the ceremony and recessional

◆ Appears in wedding photos taken after the ceremony and prior to the reception

Flower Girl

In the Middle Ages, flower girls attended the bride and carried sheaves of wheat, symbolizing fertility. In Britain, couples traditionally walked to the village church preceded by flower girls strewing the path with rose petals to ward off evil spirits. The flower girl:

◆ Proceeds down the aisle before the bride and her father, scattering flower petals

◆ Sits in bride's mother's row just before reaching the altar

◆ Follows the newly married couple during the recessional

◆ Appears in wedding photos taken after the ceremony and prior to the reception

It's All in the Family

Weddings bring out the best — and worst — in people. It's not unusual for various family members to snap from time to time under the tension of producing a once-in-a-lifetime event. Sooner or later, as the groom, you'll no doubt be expected to lend support or help deal with some sticky situations or difficult personalities.

> My fiancée's parents are divorced. There were a few uncomfortable moments, but everyone was on his or her best behavior. No one wanted to be the one to ruin the day.
>
> — *Rich, writer and graduate student*

Fortunately, weddings are social institutions, and a good etiquette book can go a long way toward resolving problem scenarios. For example, etiquette dictates that parents who are separated but not divorced should be listed on the wedding invitation, host the wedding, and attend the ceremony and reception together as if they were happily married. A remarried parent may attend the wedding with his or her current spouse. At the ceremony, the stepfather sits beside his wife, the mother of the bride or the groom, in the first row, and the birth father and his current spouse sit a row or two behind them. If the bride issues an invitation, stepparents may attend the reception as guests; otherwise, the birth parent attends the reception alone. If the parents are divorced, whoever gives the reception acts as host or hostess, along with his or her current spouse.

Wardrobe and Formal Wear Timeline

If you are accustomed to attending formal functions, you may own a tuxedo you can wear or know a tailor or expert formal wear retailer you can rely on to help you.

On the other hand, if you're like many men, the last time you wore a tuxedo was at your high school prom. You may vaguely remember selecting a fairly cheap tux, somewhat trendy in style, in an embarrassing shade of pistachio to "blend" with your date's prom dress. If you want to walk down the aisle a man of style, read on.

Groom's guide to wedding wear

TYPE OF OCCASION	TIME OF DAY	FORMAL WEAR DESCRIPTION
Very Formal	After 6 pm	**White Tie:** Black tailcoat with silk-face, classic black trousers with a formal satin side stripe, a white pique (waffle-like fabric) waistcoat, stiffly starched white pleated dress shirt with wing collar and French cuffs, white bow tie and gloves, black patent pumps or plain black oxford shoes and silk socks, pearl cuff links and studs, white or dark red boutonniere, or a sprig from the bride's bouquet, optional silk hat and walking stick.
Formal	After 6 pm	**Black Tie:** Dinner jacket (tuxedo) in black with a single-breasted silk-faced shawl collar or peaked lapels accompanied by a pleated white dress shirt with French cuffs and turned-down collar, black dress trousers, black bow tie, and optional black cummerbund or black suspenders, black oxfords and socks, white or dark red boutonniere or blue cornflower boutonniere.
Semiformal	After 6 pm	Black (in winter) or white (in summer) short-waisted dinner jacket, resembling a tailcoat without the tails; or a suit-length dinner jacket, either single- or double-breasted, worn with white wing collar shirt with pleated bosom or plain white shirt, and matching trousers. Black bow tie, shoes, and socks.
Formal	Daytime	A cutaway (morning suit), consisting of a dark gray coat worn buttoned in the front, which curves away gradually to a tailcoat length in the back; a stiff white shirt with a wing or fold-down collar; gray-striped trousers or black trousers with white pinstripes; black-and-gray tie or ascot; gray, white, or buff waistcoat; white or light gray gloves; silk hat; optional spats, black shoes and socks. Alternatively, a black sack coat with a white collarless shirt.
Semiformal	Daytime	Grey stroller (a short coat that matches the cutaway), with striped trousers, gray vest, four-in-hand tie with white pleated formal shirt. Optional: homburg, gloves.
Informal	Afternoon	Blue, black, or dark gray business suit, white shirt, with turn-down collar, four-in-hand tie, black socks, oxford shoes, white boutonniere, gray or black hat.
Casual	Daytime	Navy blue blazer with white shirt, patterned tie or bow tie, and camel or gray trousers; or, in hot weather, all-white linen suit with a dark tie, four-in-hand, white socks, shoes, and handkerchief.

MILITARY DRESS	GUEST ATTIRE
Formal dress or "mess" dress uniform, typically a dark blue uniform, except that during the summer months, the army and navy men may wear white trousers; decorations instead of boutonniere.	Specify "black tie" on the invitations if it's mandatory and "black tie preferred" if it's optional and a dark suit and tie is acceptable. Note: Black tie doesn't mean everyone has to wear black. Colorful vests, cummerbunds, and ties may be worn with the tuxedo jacket and trousers.
"Mess dress" or dinner dress uniform; no boutonniere.	Same as above
"Class-A" or "service" dress uniform; like the "mess" dress uniforms, these are usually also dark blue.	Specify "formal wear optional" on the invitations.
Service dress uniform; no boutonniere.	Specify "traditional morning attire" on the invitations
Service dress uniform; no boutonniere.	Formal wear optional.
Military: Service dress uniform sometimes with white trousers; no boutonniere.	
Military: Prescribed uniform to military functions as considered appropriate.	

Shopping for Formal wear

There are several ways to go about getting dressed for your wedding. You can:

Order a custom-made tuxedo

A custom tux is costly, but it will fit you like a glove. If you are a connoisseur of fabric, this is the way to go. Plus, if you choose a style that is classic and elegant, cut from a fabric such as a tropical-weight wool which can be worn all year round, you can wear it again and again — provided your weight doesn't fluctuate! Plus, you can specify a hand-sewn interfacing (see below).

Buy it

Buying a tuxedo off the rack in a store or through an online supplier gives you the option of taking it along on your honeymoon. Many cruises have formal dinners, as do fine hotels and charity events. This is a possibility if you are a conservative guy who goes for a traditional or classic look. Look for a jacket with a hand-sewn interfacing. The most expensive and durable jackets have one or more layers of interfacing between the exterior fabric and the jacket lining made from canvas or horsehair for the purpose of reinforcing the lapel, shoulder, and chest. Stitched by hand, this layer of reinforce-

I knew I wanted to go with a vest . . . it looks nicer, and you have flexibility in terms of color — it needs to coordinate with bridesmaid's colors and flowers to make sure that nothing clashes. I didn't have anything to do with picking out the colors — although the vest color was more my choice, but she had to make sure that my choice didn't clash with anything.

— Kevin, lawyer

ment floats with the garment, allowing for an elegant drape. Less expensive jackets are reinforced with a synthetic mesh attached, or "fused" to the exterior fabric by heat. This layer can later cause the garment to pucker if it shrinks during dry cleaning.

Rent a tuxedo

Probably the most popular option, this is a good choice if you don't plan to attend any formal parties in the next few years or you enjoy dressing in trendy styles and are concerned that your wedding look may go out of style quickly.

No matter which option you choose, don't wait until the last minute to start shopping. Styles and sizes can get sold out quickly, especially during the popular wedding months. Fittings and subsequent alterations, which are usually necessary, take time. Your choice sets the tone for your attendants' wedding day look, too, and getting your men lined up could take awhile.

GETTING THE RIGHT FIT

A tuxedo can be altered, but the fewer alterations that have to be made, the better. You might start by trying on an expensive suit if you can. Even if you don't have the money to purchase one, it will give you an idea of what a good fit feels like. Another option is to take a look at the designer of your favorite suit. Many designers have expanded their lines to include tuxedos.

Choose a jacket silhouette that flatters your figure. Double-breasted jackets tend to widen the torso; avoid them if you are heavy set, along with center vents and obvious patterns. (A tone-on-tone texture is okay, though.) The most flattering jacket for all body types is a single-breasted jacket that closes with one to three buttons. The jacket should be proportional to your body height. If you are short, choose a shorter jacket to lengthen you.

> Because members of the wedding party live around the country, we considered getting tuxes from an online vendor or a store with locations throughout the country.
>
> — *Kevin, lawyer*

The Trendsetting Nonconformist

If you are a man who sets his own style, consider a tuxedo with a mandarin or Nehru collar. Or try one of the newer tuxedo designs that dispense with lapels and buttons down the front altogether — this approach is truly elegant in its simplicity.

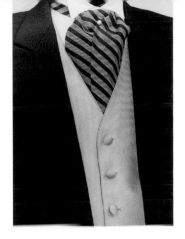

Taking measurements

If your groomsmen live out of town, you can have the retailer in question send them the store's measurement form, which they can take to any professional tailor to fill out (or you can copy the one on page 63).

Measurements are best left to professionals. If your groomsmen can't get into the formal wear retailer, a local professional tailor may fill out the form as an industry courtesy.

If you find yourself ordering online or needing to take measurements on your own due to unforeseen circumstances, the Chart of Standard Sizes on the following page will provide guidelines. Keep in mind, though, that this is only a guide, and you will probably end up needing some alterations.

Chart of Standard Sizes

Men's	XS	S	M	L	XL
Size	30-32	34-36	38-40	42-44	46-48
Chest	30-32	34-36	38-40	42-44	46-48
Waist	24-26	28-30	32-34	36-38	40-42
Hip	30-32	34-36	38-40	42-44	46-48
Neck	13	14	15	16	17

Men's	2XL	3XL	4XL	5XL	
Size	50-52	54-56	58-60	62-64	
Chest	50-52	54-56	58-60	62-64	
Waist	44-46	48-50	52-54	56-58	
Hip	50-52	54-56	58-60	60-62	
Neck	18	19	20	21	

Record of Measurements

You may want to photocopy this chart for each member of the wedding party.

MEASUREMENTS:

Name		Role	
Address			
Phone #		Cell Phone #	
E-mail		Web site	
Height (Foot/In)		Weight	
Shirt Neck		Sleeve Length	
Jacket	S R L XL XXL	Sleeve	
Chest Under		Chest Over	
Trousers Outseam		Hip	
Trousers Inseam		Waist	
Shoe Size		Width	
○ Tie/Ascot	○ Buttons	○ Studs	
○ Gloves	○ Cuff links	○ Belt/Cummerbund	
○ Pocket Square	○ Other		
Notes			

Formal Wear Countdown

1 year ahead

- Together with your bride, choose a wedding style — formal, informal, day, or night.

6 months ahead

- Visit retailers and shop the Internet to investigate designers, jacket and shirt styles, and accessory options.

3 months ahead

- Make your selection. Have the store take your measurements. Send out fitting forms to your groomsmen. Before ordering the merchandise, you will need to provide the store with accurate sizing information. (Exceptions are any children who are members of the wedding party. Take their measurements closer to 3 weeks prior to the wedding.)

6 weeks ahead

- Contact anyone who has not turned in his fitting form and make sure he gets it to the store within the next 2 weeks.

4 to 6 weeks ahead

- Finalize your order.

2 weeks ahead

- Pick up the garments. Arrange for final fittings.

1 week ahead

- After final fittings, pick up your order. Keep in mind that even after the garment arrives, it may need some last-minute adjustments. Picking it up a day or two in advance is cutting it close. You want to have options in case something unfortunate happens and additional adjustments or a replacement garment is required.

The next business day after the wedding

- Return all rented garments and accessories to the store.

PRE-WEDDING EVENTS

PRE-WEDDING EVENTS

It's not just one day of celebration!

❖ **Socializing in Style**
❖ **Toasts and Speeches**
❖ **Party, Party, Party**
❖ **The Wedding Rings**

I hope you like to party. Because not only will you be one of the guests of honor at the big party, chances are you'll be expected to show up at some smaller functions that precede it — the engagement party, the "shower," the rehearsal dinner, and, the most hyped wedding-related event for grooms, the bachelor party.

Although tradition dictates who's supposed to throw the event and who's supposed to attend, today few couples follow the prescribed rules. If your organizing capabilities are tapped for any of these affairs, or for the reception itself, this chapter will provide you what you need to know to host an affair with style.

Socializing in Style

Feel a bit inept when it comes to social graces, etiquette, and toasting? Never fear; we've enrolled you in Mr. Manners 101 and have outlined the basics for the perfect toast so you'll never be without a witty remark.

Mr. Manners 101

*The well-bred man feels at ease in all companies,
is modest without appearing bashful, and self-possessed
without an undue forwardness of manner.*

— From *General Principles Of Good Manners* (1902)

- Be on time and call if you are going to be late.
- Dress for the occasion. Call in advance and ask what's appropriate if you're not sure what to wear.
- Hold the door open for people you're with and let them enter first.
- Offer to carry packages or luggage and offer to hold the umbrella when it rains.
- Introduce a person to a group before introducing a group to the person.
- Wait to talk until you've been formally introduced.
- Don't get drunk.
- Don't drink and drive.
- Help people on and off with their coats.
- Offer to pull out a woman's chair.
- When at a restaurant, signal that you are ready to order by closing your menu and placing it on the table.
- Use the appropriate utensil. If you're uncertain which utensil to use, start with the outermost one first.
- Don't talk with your mouth full.
- Keep your elbows off the table while putting food in your mouth.
- Don't reach for food unless it's directly in front of you.
- Bring your food to your mouth; don't hunch over to reach it.
- Pass food to the right.
- Use a napkin to wipe your hands and face, not your clothes or the back of your hand.
- When escorting a woman, offer her your arm.
- Don't flaunt your money, business, or social position.
- Don't let anyone see you looking at your watch.
- Avoid off-color jokes.
- Avoid talking about politics, sex, or religion in social situations.
- If you smoke, do it outdoors.
- Thank the wait staff.
- Thank the host.
- Write thank-you notes.

Toasts and Speeches

Toasts are an integral part of any wedding celebration. At the engagement party, it's customary for the host — usually, the father of the bride — to order the guests' glasses to be filled, then stand to lift his glass and "propose a toast to the health of" his daughter and future son-in-law. The couple remains seated. The guests then rise, take a sip, and congratulate the couple. At this point, the groom may be called upon to say a few words. The smart groom keeps it short and sweet, thanking everyone for their kind wishes and adding how much he's looking forward to life with his future wife.

The formal bachelor dinner, which was the staid forerunner of today's bachelor party, traditionally included a toast to the bride. As the dinner was winding down, the groom would rise, hold a glass filled with champagne high in the air, and say simply, "To the bride!" The groom's friends would then stand to drink the toast, and smash their glasses, in theory to ensure that the wine glasses would never be used for a less noble sentiment. While toasting the bride is still seen as a lovely gesture, today many frugal-minded grooms skip breaking the glass.

Toasts are also offered at the rehearsal dinner. And then there's the wedding reception itself, a highlight of which is the best man's toast. The host or emcee, if there is one, may remind the best man it's time to stand and deliver the toast. As soon as the guests have been served drinks with their meal (or, if an actual meal isn't being served, with the wedding cake), the glasses are filled in the following order: bride, groom, maid or matron of honor, guests seated at the bride's table, and, finally, the best man. The best man may strike a glass with a piece of silverware to signal the toast is about to begin. Traditionally, the best man toasts the bride, although increasingly, the couple is toasted. The guests touch their glasses to each other's and take a sip. The recipient of the toast remains seated during the toast, leaving his or her glass on the table until everyone else has sipped the drink, at which point he or she may smile, say thanks, and take a sip.

Toasting Tips

- Draft the toast far enough in advance for you to have plenty of time to practice it.

- Be positive. Avoid crude jokes, offensive language, potentially embarrassing stories.

- Limit the length to around 2 to 3 minutes.

- Always stand when delivering a toast.

- Hold the glass in your right hand.

- Look around the room and try to catch the eyes of people in the audience as you speak.

- Before the big day, practice delivering the toast. The goal is to speak slowly and deliberately.

- Hire a speech coach if you're afraid of speaking in public. Or consider joining Toastmasters International (www.toastmasters.org) several months beforehand to get some practice in before the big day.

- If you get nervous, practice deep breathing.

- Get enough sleep the night before, so you aren't jumpy. Avoid drinking too much before delivering the toast.

The Five Keys to a Perfect Toast

Below are the key points of any toast or speech, as well as suggested hints for the five main parts of a toast.

1. The introduction:

- "I'd like to propose a toast to . . . "
- "Please join me in wishing every happiness to . . . "
- "On behalf of myself and my bride, thank you for your kind wishes . . . "

2. Establish your relationship to the honoree(s):

Explain how you know the honoree(s).
"My good friend Kevin . . . " "My sister introduced . . . "
"My daughter became friends with . . . "

3. The anchor:

What brought him/her/them together, or why are he/she/they here now? Imagery or a metaphor can help here. For example, "Everyone knows how I like to play ball, and as soon as I met her, I knew she was a great catch." "Life is a game you can't win without teammates . . . " "You've been with me through . . . " Or consider a romantic poem: "In the words of the poet . . . "

4. The anecdote(s):

One or two personal stories that expand on the anchor, underscoring the wonderful qualities of the honoree(s) and how the relationship has developed through time. Choose one thing that's funny and one thing that's profound or sentimental.

5. The main point:

"Today we've scored our first home run together." "I am so proud to welcome you into our family." "I wish you the best . . . " "May your dreams come true . . . "

Party, Party, Party

There will be many social events before the big day. This is for-
tuitous, as you will be given opportunities to polish your social
style and also get to know the people who will be sharing in your
wedding day celebration.

THE ENGAGEMENT PARTY

The parents of the bride usually host the engagement party. This is where you'll be introduced to the bride's extended family and friends. Your hostess decides whether it will be big, small, or have a theme. Find out what kind of event it is in advance and dress appropriately.

The event itself offers an opportunity for you to reinforce whatever good impression you've made on the bride's parents in the past — or, conversely, mitigate a bad one. Offer to bring a suitable beverage (champagne, if it's a dressy event; imported beer, if it's more casual), or show up with a big bouquet of flowers for mom and something nice for your bride. It's also helpful to prepare a few words to toast your bride and her parents. Your toast doesn't have to be fancy — a few heartfelt words that show how much you're looking forward to the upcoming event and cherish their daughter are all that's needed.

Your parents may also throw a party to introduce their daughter-to-be to your side of the family.

> **STRATEGY: Couples Shower**
>
> There was no engagement party. We did a couples' shower. It was an opportunity to get friends together that wouldn't mesh with the traditional family crowd. Also, it was a chance for me to be involved in getting friends together. When a shower is just the bride and her friends and family, there isn't a chance for her guy friends to attend; similarly, my female friends would not have been able to go to a bachelor party.
>
> — *Kevin, lawyer*

THE SHOWER

The bridal shower was created to help the bride assemble all of the things she would need to set up a new home. The bride's best friend invited women close to the bride's age to her house for an afternoon tea. Each guest brought a household item to "shower" the bride with.

Bridal showers today are quite different from those of the past. The traditional party has expanded to include women of all ages as well as family members and, sometimes, even men. "Couples" showers, attended by the bride and groom and their friends, male and female, are increasingly popular.

Although it was the bride's best friend's responsibility to throw the shower, nowadays it's not uncommon for the party to be hosted by the mother of the bride or even by the couple. If the mother hosts it, it's not unusual to find the event held in a restaurant rather than a home. If the couple is hosting it, it can be held at a less expensive location — such as a cookout at a local park.

No matter who hosts the shower, the wedding's hosts should get the shower guest list. To avoid hurting anyone's feelings, those invited to the shower should also get an invitation to the wedding.

> My mom didn't want to have a lot of influence over our wedding — she made very few demands and no demands about a particular church. My mother-in-law had more of an impact on the list of invitees. She held a separate reception at a nice country club near her for other family friends that we could not afford to invite and paid for that herself
>
> — *Russ, computer programmer*

Registering For Gifts

You should complete your gift registry before these pre-wedding parties, as a courtesy to your guests. Gift registries have come a long way since they were first introduced. Traditional registry items include china, crystal, silver, and linens. For this reason, it used to be that only department and upscale jewelry stores had bridal registries, but today you can find them everywhere, from your favorite mail-order catalog to furniture stores to travel agencies to kitchen specialty stores to hardware stores.

The idea behind the gift registry is to prevent couples from receiving duplicates of gifts or gifts they can't use or don't want. The bridal couple goes to a store where they'd like to register and creates a list of products they'd like. They make their choices, which are typically recorded in the store's computer. Then, when someone wants to buy a wedding gift, the person calls the bridal registry, or visits the store to look at the items the bride and groom

have chosen. The purchaser makes his or her selection, and the registrar crosses the item off the list, so no one else will buy it.

Before you register, have a detailed discussion with your bride about your priorities and goals. You might want to ask a registry for a printout of items or categories that you can take home and study before making your actual selections. If you both have different preferences in terms of colors and styles, or even regarding what you should be registering for, you will need to work out those differences before you register. Don't forget to choose items in a variety of price ranges to suit different budgets.

THE BACHELOR PARTY

Can you trust your best man to have your best interests at heart? I hope so. Your best man is typically the one to arrange the bachelor party. He should consult with you to find out what type of party you'd like to have and then carry out your wishes.

> There was a lot of give and take on china patterns. We wanted different patterns and finally compromised on a pattern that was similar to what each of us had wanted. In most cases, I let my fiancée pick out what she wanted. I wanted more input on luggage and china.
>
> — *Kevin, lawyer*

The bachelor party with attendant stripper and massive hangover is the legendary stuff of B-movies and male magazine cartoons, but all jokes aside, it's a bad idea to let the party get too out of hand, especially if it's scheduled for the night before the wedding. No matter how well-planned, a wedding is an exhausting day, and you need to be up for it.

The good news is that today anything goes. Many men have women friends they'd like to invite, and it's perfectly acceptable to have a co-ed party. If you and your guy friends have a mutual hobby, then that may be an acceptable type of party to suggest. Traditional bachelor parties are fast being replaced by golf outings and other more benign yet still fun male bonding experiences.

The Rehearsal

Unless you, your family, and your friends are Broadway actors, you all are likely to feel a bit nervous as the nuptial day approaches — even if you've been a member of a wedding before. Public speaking rates pretty high on everybody's list of feared activities, and walking down the aisle before a sea of people, no matter how much they wish you well or how well they know you, increases anxiety.

I was really nervous standing in front of all those people, waiting for everything to start. I have a stutter, so I was afraid I'd mess up during the vows. Then, of course, there are those last-minute fears and doubts. All that went away, though, once the music started and my bride came walking down the aisle. I hadn't seen her since the previous night's rehearsal dinner. She was beautiful.

— *Rich, graduate student and writer*

One or two days before the wedding, all members of the wedding party meet at the ceremony location to rehearse the actual ceremony. Although this sounds easy, there are some logistics that need to be taken care of. First, it's important that everybody who is a part of the actual rehearsal be there on time. So you

need to arrange transportation for everyone and make sure they've adjusted their schedules (gotten out of work early, beat rush-hour traffic, etc.) in order to be at the appointed place at least one-half hour in advance.

Before the actual rehearsal, it's a good idea to e-mail each member of the wedding party a list of his or her duties, a copy of the ceremony, and any readings they may be asked to give. If you have a printed program book, make sure you bring copies of it to the rehearsal. It will serve as an actors' script and help take the edge off the rehearsal. Your bride should bring along a fake bouquet and the ring-bearer's pillow, if you have a ring bearer. If you have flower girls, they should have empty baskets to carry so they can practice throwing invisible petals. You may be rehearsing in front of a small crowd of strangers — members of other wedding parties.

Your officiant will let you know beforehand exactly what time you will need to be at the ceremony site and will gesture you to begin proceedings at the time that's been reserved for you. You will run through the main parts of the ceremony quickly. The rehearsal is typically one-third the length of the actual ceremony the following day.

At the end of the rehearsal, you most likely will have only a few minutes to ask any additional questions of your officiant. So, be prepared. Hopefully by now you've gotten all of your answers, but if you've forgotten to ask about anything, it wouldn't hurt to write down your last-minute questions before the rehearsal so you can ask them quickly before you leave.

You are not expected to wear your wedding clothes to the rehearsal. Nevertheless, the solemnity of the occasion dictates that everyone attending the rehearsal take care with his or her attire. At the very least, make sure you are showered and wearing clean, pressed clothes, your shoes are shined, and your fingernails are trimmed and clean. A business suit or sports jacket would not be out of place.

THE REHEARSAL DINNER

It's traditional for the groom's parents to host the rehearsal dinner, which takes place after the wedding rehearsal on the night before the wedding. Because even a small wedding party tends to need a large table, it's best to reserve a private room at a restaurant or banquet hall. (However, if money is an issue, a family member can host it at home.)

The invitation list includes all members of the wedding party, the officiant and his or her spouse, and any close friends or family members who attended the rehearsal. Your officiant may not be able to attend if he or she is rehearsing other wedding parties; all the same, extending the invitation is the courteous thing to do. If the officiant attends, you can give him or her the fee or donation at the end of the dinner; if not, you may pay the officiant at the end of the rehearsal.

During the rehearsal dinner, the bride and groom thank everyone involved in the wedding. Now is the time to give your wedding party members gifts to thank them for their help. Expect your wedding party members and parents to spontaneously toast the bride and groom. You, too, may toast without reservation your bride, her parents, your parents, and your best man.

The Wedding Rings

Most couples go to the jewelry store together to choose wedding rings, those time-honored symbols of commitment, fidelity, and honor. The traditional wedding band is a plain, gold ring worn on the left ring finger. However, if you want something more creative, you won't lack choices. Weddings are big business, and jewelers have responded to the marketplace by introducing new combinations of metals and surface treatments, as well as semiprecious stones and revived artisan techniques.

While gold wedding bands are the standard, platinum, an incredibly durable precious metal that lasts for up to 50 years without wearing thin, is increasing in popularity. In contrast to gold, which is 58 percent pure for 14 carat, platinum has a 90 percent pure standard, which is why many feel that it is a better investment than gold, even though it costs more.

There is no preferred method for choosing ring designs. Some couples prefer to wear the same style of wedding band, sized differently for him and her. Others will choose two completely different bands. For example, a bride often likes a wedding band that complements the design of her engagement ring. In such a case, the groom's band is likely to be much simpler.

Much of what has already been said about choosing an engagement ring applies to buying wedding bands. Work with a reputable jeweler. Ask for an appraisal certificate, so you can insure your rings for the value of their replacement.

Of all the choices you will have to make for your wedding day, choosing the right wedding rings is one decision that will be with you for years to come. To help you with this special choice, we have put together this easy-to-use guide to selecting the perfect wedding rings.

Wedding Ring Worksheet

You may want to make a copy of this sheet for each wedding ring you are considering.

RINGS WE LOOKED AT:

Jeweler Name	
Address	
Telephone/Fax	

E-mail		Web site	
Contact Name		Ext.	

Item ID				
Description		Size		Cost

OUR ORDER:

Jeweler Name	
Address	

E-mail		Web site	
Contact Name		Ext.	

Item ID				
Description		Size		Cost

Ordered on		Deposit		Amount due	
				Pick-up Date	

THE MAIN
EVENT

THE MAIN EVENT

Mark your calendar!

- ❖ **The Ceremony**
- ❖ **The Reception**
- ❖ **Cigars and Celebrations**
- ❖ **Drinks Anyone?**

You and your bride have worked hard for the better part of a year to plan the glorious event that is about to occur. You will shortly be standing at the altar, and the woman you have committed your heart and soul to will walk down the aisle to pledge herself and her love to you. But if you're like most grooms, you may feel a bit nervous now that the big day is actually here and wonder what to expect. Don't worry. You're going to be okay. Here's a play-by-play of the traditional wedding day.

The Ceremony

The big day has arrived! Congratulations on all of your hard work and planning; now you get to reap the wonderful rewards. The "traditional" wedding day for the groom is described below; of course, yours may be quite different based on your type of ceremony and your level of involvement.

DAY OF THE WEDDING

Your best man meets you at your house in the morning. He helps make sure the transportation is scheduled to run smoothly and that your suitcases are packed for the honeymoon. He reviews any tips or payments he's supposed to deliver on your behalf and picks up the wedding ring, which he carefully stows in his pocket.

Your "going-away clothes" should be put into a suit bag and given to the best man, who is charged with making sure it arrives at the reception hall. If you are planning to spend your wedding night at a local hotel, he can act as a go-between, checking your reservations, collecting your luggage, and delivering it to the

hotel. Together with the maid or matron of honor, he may check in for you, obtain your room key, and help decorate your room in preparation for the wedding night.

AT THE CEREMONY SITE

Your best man helps you dress and dresses himself. You'll probably want to get to the ceremony site at least an hour before the wedding, together with your parents.

The ushers arrive at the ceremony location around the same time. One usher should be designated for your

side and another for your bride's. If the ribbons are not already in place, the chief usher should ensure that the first six to twenty rows on either side of the center aisle are cordoned off to indicate the seats reserved for close family members. Your bride's parents sit in the first row on the left, with friends and family members behind them, and your parents sit in the first row on the right, with your friends and family members behind them.

As the guests arrive, the ushers show them to the appropriate side. Guests with pew cards (see "Weddings A to Z," p. 13) or on a printed list are escorted to seats "within the ribbons" on the appropriate side; otherwise, the usher asks which side the guest prefers to sit on and seats the person accordingly.

The bride's mother arrives after the groom, groom's parents, and groomsmen. The bridesmaids arrive next, followed by the bride and her father. Typically, the bride is a bit late, to ensure last-minute guests have time to be seated.

As soon as the entire wedding party is at the location, an usher closes the door. Your mother goes down the aisle first on the arm of an usher, with your father following behind. The usher then returns to offer the bride's mother an arm and escort her to her seat. No one may be seated once the mother of the bride is seated.

Your mother and the mother of the bride may light a family candle after the candle lighters have left the altar area and before the rest of the wedding party enters.

The aisle runner is unrolled. Music begins to play. This is the cue for the officiant to enter.

The ushers walk up the aisle, two by two, followed by the bridesmaids, then the maid or matron of honor alone, then the flower girl(s) and the ring bearer.

Your bride follows on her father's right arm. As the bride comes closer, you may step forward to receive her from her father.

The ceremony begins. The vows are exchanged. When it's time for the ring, the best man takes it from his pocket. You place it on the bride's unadorned left ring; on the day of her wedding, the bride may wear her engagement ring on her right hand or leave it at home. The bride then puts the rings on the groom's finger, you are pronounced husband and wife, and then you may kiss your bride!

At the end of the ceremony, your father escorts your mother-in-law, or other witnesses, to the signing of the register. After the register is signed, the recessional takes place.

Music begins, signaling the recessional. Arm in arm, you and your bride start down the aisle. The maid of honor follows, attending to the bride's train. The bridesmaids and ushers follow after the maid of honor.

As soon as the recessional ends, the ushers return to escort the women seated within the ribboned area in order of importance — your mother-in-law first and then your mother, then the remaining immediate family members. Next, the ushers remove the ribbons, signaling that the remaining guests may leave on their own accord.

The Reception

After pictures, you head to the reception location. The traditional reception includes:

A receiving line. The mothers stand at the head of the receiving line, greeting guests as they enter, while the fathers circulate. Traditionally, the receiving line consists of the wedding party, minus the best man and ushers. Your bride stands to your right, the maid of honor stands on the bride's right, and the bridesmaids stand either half on one side and half on the other or to the right of the maid of honor. Casual weddings may not have a receiving line.

STRATEGY: Dance lessons
Take dancing lessons for the first dance with your bride. Most people aren't used to being on stage, and these days it's recorded on video for posterity. You don't have to remember the dance the day after the wedding; you just have to do it once. Trust me; dance studios get this request all the time.

— *Joe, Writer/IT Consultant*

The first dance. Once all of the guests have been seated, the host or emcee announces the names of the wedding party as they enter the room. You and your bride enter last, to cheers. The first dance takes place, beginning with you and your wife alone. Gradually, the rest of the wedding party joins in. Your mother-in-law dances with you next, while your bride dances with her father. Then your father-in law dances with your mother. Gradually, the guests join in.

The toast: The best man toasts the couple. The groom toasts his bride. Others can follow.

Before you leave the reception, don't forget to . . .

- Thank the bride's father and mother.
- Thank your guests for being there.
- Acknowledge your wife and tell her you love her.
- Visit with guests who traveled far to be at your wedding.
- Spend some time with the oldest guests.
- Thank all those who helped you plan the wedding and took part in it.

The cutting of the cake. After dinner, the host or emcee will announce that it is time to cut the cake. You place your hand over your bride's, and together you slice the wedding cake for the first time. You and your bride may feed each other a piece of cake. Afterwards the caterer wheels the cake away to cut it and serve it to the remaining guests.

The garter toss and bouquet throw. After cutting the cake, you remove your bride's garter and throw it into a cluster of single men. The bride turns her back and tosses her bouquet into a cluster of single women. The man who catches the garter will put it on the leg of the woman who catches the bouquet. Legend has it they'll

be the next to marry — though not necessarily to each other.

Taking leave: You and your bride will sneak away, change into your going-away clothes, bid a final farewell, leave in a shower of rice, birdseed, or flower petals, and drive away in a car with a "just married" sign on the back.

MUSIC MUSCLE

If you are a lover of a certain type of music, you may find it difficult to get used to the idea that you are spending an awful lot of money on a band that most of the time is playing the sort of music you never listen to. But, your wedding guests will be from all age groups, and you do want your guests to enjoy themselves. Still, you can ask the band to play some of the music you like. Be as specific as possible. If you don't detail your expectations, the band's idea of indie rock or jazz standards may be quite different from yours.

Don't forget to ask how long the band plays and how many breaks they take. Make sure the contract details whether transportation to the reception hall is covered, whether you are expected to pay for meals or put the musicians up overnight, what type of clothing you expect the band members to wear, how much playing overtime will cost (and whether the band will even do it), what kind of insurance the band carries, and payment arrangements. If the band is not familiar with the reception location, you should also provide them with a floor plan and information about electrical outlets so they know what is needed to set up their equipment.

Another option for music for the reception is a DJ. A DJ will normally cost less than a full band, but of course the effect is not quite the same. If you are considering a DJ, be sure to check references.

Cigars and Celebrations

For many, a good cigar and a glass of bourbon are the preferred finish to any noteworthy celebration, weddings included. The stag party, the rehearsal dinner, and, of course, the reception, are all opportunities for the cigar lover to indulge in his (and, yes, sometimes, her) favorite extravagance.

A popular trend is to hold the bachelor party at a cigar bar where special ventilation systems allow partygoers to savor cigars without being overwhelmed by clouds of smoke. A cigar tasting, or a workshop on matching cigars to alcohol makes for an enjoyable and sophisticated alternative to a traditional bachelor party.

More grooms are choosing to include a cigar bar at the reception or to give out cigars as wedding favors. Cigar samplers, cases, cutters, lighters (you can even buy themed ones), punches and bullets (devices that cut a small hole in the end of the cigar prior to smoking), tubes (a case that protects a single cigar), finger cases (cases made of a variety of materials that hold up to four cigars), travel humidors (small, humidified storage units that hold up to 20 cigars), and ashtrays (deep and wide enough to hold a cigar level so it can burn evenly) also make appropriate thank-you gifts, provided the recipient shares your taste for tobacco.

If you are a cigar lover, you already know the basics of choosing a cigar, storing a cigar, and pairing it with liquor. But for those of you who are novices and would like to incorporate smokes into some aspect of your celebration — if only to make a hospitable gesture to those of your friends and relations who enjoy a good cigar — here's a down-and-dirty guide on the subject.

> Because the best man lived too far away, I did not have a bachelor party. Instead, after the rehearsal dinner, my groomsmen and I went out to a couple of local bars to eat wings, drink, and talk. We were out until about two in the morning.
>
> — *Rob, bookstore manager*

CIGAR CONSTRUCTION

Cigars are made up of three components:

Filler: The leaves on the inside of the cigar. "Long filler" is made from full tobacco leaves. "Short filler" is made from broken leaves or odds and ends left over from long filler production. The type of tobacco leaf and its country of origin contribute to the cigar's flavor. Jamaica is known for mild tobacco, the Dominican Republic for medium, and Honduras and Nicaragua for strong tobacco.

Binder: Layers of leaves that surround the filler and form it into a circular shape.

Wrapper: The outside sheath of the cigar, made from one layer of a delicate tobacco leaf chosen for its consistency of color and smooth texture. A better cigar wrapper is resilient — firm, but not so stiff that it cracks. In addition to providing a consistent surface to the cigar, the wrapper gives the cigar its color. An entire vocabulary has developed to describe cigar wrappers/colors:

- Claro (light tan)
- Colorado (brown)
- Maduro (deep brown)
- Oscuro (black)

Shade-grown tobacco is protected from direct exposure to the sun by large sheets of fabric, resulting in a paler color wrapper than that grown in direct sunlight. In general, the darker the wrapper, the sweeter and more full-bodied the flavor is thought to be.

A "premium" cigar may be short (less than 5.5 inches) or long (more than 6.5 inches) as long as it is a carefully crafted cigar, involving some handwork. Although its name would suggest otherwise, a hand-rolled cigar isn't necessarily entirely made by hand. The filler is usually assembled by machine. However, unlike machine-made cigars, in which the filler, binder, and wrapper are assembled by a machine, hand-rolled cigars are finished by hand. A *puro* is a cigar that has a filler, binder, and wrapper made from the tobaccos of a single country — as is the case, most famously, with the Cuban cigar.

Physical attributes used to describe cigars include:

Length/ring gauge (cigar's diameter): Cigars are described by two numbers. The first number represents the cigar's length in inches. The second number represents the ring gauge or thickness measured in sixty-fourths of an inch (so a cigar with a gauge of 64 is an inch wide). The larger the ring size, the more variety of tobacco leaves the cigar can contain. A large ring size allows the cigar maker latitude to blend different leaves, thereby achieving more complexity of flavor. Thin is less than 42 ring size; thick is greater than 47.

Cigars can be stored for an indefinite period of time in the following optimum conditions:

- Humidity between 65 and 75 percent
- Temperature of 70 degrees

Connoisseurs prefer an aged cigar to one right out of the box, which is why proper storage conditions are essential.

You'll want to choose your cigar by the length of the event — there's no use lighting up a long-lasting cigar if you have only thirty minutes after dinner to smoke it. To savor the flavor, avoid lighting up with lighter fuels that give off a chemical smell. Butane, which burns cleanly, is the preferred lighter fuel. Look for a lighter that gives off a large, hot flame. There is an art to lighting a cigar. Clip the round end off with a cigar cutter. Hold the end about two inches from the flame; like an alchemist's trick, the flame should leap to the cigar. Carefully coax the heat up, ensuring the end lights evenly. (Don't insert the entire cigar into the flame, which will impart an astringent, charred taste.) Puff and rotate the cigar a quarter of a turn. Repeat until it's evenly lit, then remove the band. Hold the cigar gently in the middle, between your index finger and thumb, and savor it.

See "Resources" on page 110 for further information.

Drinks Anyone?

Not every couple chooses to have alcohol at their wedding. For some, the reason is religious. For others, it's the cost. Alcohol is mighty expensive. And then there are those who are concerned about the drinking getting out of hand. For them, providing plenty of nonalcoholic beverages or limiting the amount and kind of alcohol is simply a stress-control mechanism.

If you choose to limit alcohol at your wedding, that's cool. Consider adding sparkling fruit juices (a champagne alternative), smoothies, nonalcoholic cocktails, or exotic coffees to the regular menu of soft drinks, punch, and tea for a festive touch. If, on the other hand, you plan to have alcohol and have agreed to take charge of planning how much and what kind, read on.

PLANNING YOUR BAR SERVICE

Ensure your caterer has a state liquor license and appropriate insurance. Reception sites typically charge either a flat fee per drink (example: $4.75) or a flat rate per person ($20 or more). Most reception sites offer alcohol packages of varying quality, including the following:

Open Bar: A basic bar with everything — soft drinks, beer, wine, and mixed drinks. Guests can order freely and do not have to pay.

Limited Bar: You choose what kind and how much alcohol is served. Guests typically do not pay as long as they choose from the drinks offered.

Cash Bar: Guests order whatever drinks they like and pay for them one at a time, with their own money.

Wine only: What the name implies. No bar, just wine.

Match your dinner wine to your menu. Traditionally, white wine accompanies white meat or light fare, and red wine is served with dark meat and rich foods.

For fun, ask the bartender to create a signature cocktail in your honor.

It's considered in better taste to have no alcohol at all than to have a cash bar and demand that guests buy drinks themselves; however, a cash bar can reduce your liability.

Be sure the servers are of legal age to serve alcohol.

Ask how excessive drinking is handled.

Ask the facility to post a "Bar Closed" sign when the bar is closed.

Don't let the bartender put out a jar for tips. If anything, a sign that states "no tipping, please," should be placed in a visible area, so guests understand it's your treat.

Nothing spoils a good time like a guest who has too much to drink. Here are some tips on how to prevent alcohol abuse from becoming an issue at your wedding:

- ◆ Notify all bartenders to beware of any friends or relatives who have drinking problems; use photos if necessary.
- ◆ Request the bar staff not to mix strong drinks.
- ◆ Close down the bar an hour before the end of the party and provide a coffee service.
- ◆ Instruct the valet parking staff to refuse car keys to anyone who is clearly tipsy and does not have a designated driver.

In many states the host may be charged with reckless endangerment if he or she allows a guest to depart under the influence. To prevent this from happening at your wedding, appoint a friend or relative to monitor departures for you. Supply them with the name and number of a reliable taxi service and cab fare for guests who need it.

Cutting Costs

- If you have hired the caterer directly, ask if you can purchase the liquor wholesale.

- For the champagne toast, instruct the wait staff to fill only a third of the glass. If someone wants more, they can ask for it.

- Serve beer and wine instead of mixed drinks.

- Opt for domestic brews or sparkling wine instead of imported beer or champagne.

- Choose less expensive "call" or "house pour" brands instead of more expensive "top shelf" or "premium" brands. Consider serving a house wine instead of a name brand.

- Instruct the facility to shut the bar down once the bill reaches a certain limit or to convert to a cash bar.

- Provide wine and one signature drink but require guests to pay for additional alcoholic beverages.

- Tell the bartender not to open any wine or bottles of alcohol until it's necessary. You don't want to pay for something just because it can't be returned to stock.

- Have an open bar for only an hour or two during "cocktails." If anyone wants something beyond the cocktail hour, they can pay for it on their own.

- Choose a place where you can supply your own alcohol.

AFTER THE WEDDING

AFTER THE WEDDING

What do we do now?

❖ **The Honeymoon**
❖ **Write Thank-you Notes**
❖ **Set up House**
❖ **Get Down to Business**
❖ **Protect Your Greatest Asset**

During the months leading up to the wedding, so much needs to be done to plan the ceremony and reception, it's easy to put off thinking about the days that follow. To ensure your marriage gets off to a positive start, this chapter provides tips for planning a honeymoon that's relaxing, romantic, and fun, plus guidelines addressing some of the issues that prove stickiest for many newlyweds.

The Honeymoon

It's easy to understand why most newlyweds want to splurge on a honeymoon. Chances are, they've endured months of stressful preparation for what will probably be the biggest event of their lives. With the planning and the wedding itself behind them, the happy couple looks forward to some much-needed rest and relaxation! A bit of planning and some help from the experts can make the experience a wonderful and romantic prelude to years of wedded bliss.

HONEYMOON TIPS

Your honeymoon is a trip of a lifetime. I've included some helpful tips below to ensure yours is every bit as perfect as you've dreamed.

Booking

◆ Avoid spending the night of the wedding at an airport hotel; hearing jets take off all night long is noisy and not very romantic.

◆ Consider adding a day or two "buffer" before you take off for the honeymoon so you can travel rested.

◆ Avoid booking an early morning flight the day after the wedding.

◆ Don't over-book excursions; keep in mind the purpose of the honeymoon is to relax, unwind, and bond as newlyweds.

◆ Ensure your lodgings offer privacy.

◆ Request a double or king bed; this is especially important if you're taking a cruise.

◆ Avoid locales or resorts that cater to children.

Rental cars

◆ The smaller the car, the cheaper the rate. You may even get a free upgrade if they don't have your model or size in stock.

◆ Many rental car agencies offer reduced rates if you book for an entire week, rather than a few days or a weekend.

◆ Ask your health and/or auto insurance agents whether your policies cover rental cars and automobile injuries. Ask your credit card company whether your card covers you in case of collision, so you can decline collision damage waivers or loss damage waivers, which increase your rental fee.

Travel advisories

◆ Check the National Weather Service for weather warnings, forecasts, and maps.

◆ Check for government advisories, cultural information about foreign destinations, and helpful numbers to contact in case of an emergency.

◆ Consult the U.S. Department of State Web site: www.state.gov. The U.S. Department of State Travel Warnings Hotline is 202-647-5225.

Health

◆ Check with a foreign embassy to ensure any medications you plan to carry abroad aren't illegal there. Keep medicine in its original, clearly labeled container.

◆ Ensure your health insurance provides for overseas coverage and carry your card with you.

◆ Contact the Center for Disease Control for any advisories. The international travel hotline is 1-877-FYI-TRIP; or go to the Web site at www.cdc.gov.

Travel Safety and Security

◆ Keep a list of the contents of your suitcases in your carry-on bag, in case your luggage is lost.

◆ Carry cell phones, cameras, film, travel documents, toiletries, and a change of clothing in your carry-on luggage.

- ◆ Be sure your homeowner's or renter's insurance is up-to-date.
- ◆ Leave a copy of your travel itinerary with family members and friends.
- ◆ Divide up your money so that if your wallet is stolen, you will still have some cash.
- ◆ Don't flash your money or jewelry.
- ◆ Wear a secure money belt with wire reinforcement (tough to cut with a knife).
- ◆ Practice turning to the left when someone taps your right shoulder and vice versa — this is a classic pickpocket technique.
- ◆ Don't accept food or drinks from strangers.

POPULAR DESTINATIONS

After all of the stress of the wedding, it makes sense to choose a honeymoon destination that will allow you both to relax in an intimate setting. Better yet, pick a place where good weather is practically guaranteed. Popular honeymoon venues are geared for just this kind of experience, and most offer "budget" packages, which is why many newlyweds visit them. I have listed some of our favorites here:

If you like sun and fun, consider:

- • The Hawaiian Islands
- • Bermuda
- • The Bahamas
- • Jamaica
- • Las Vegas, Nevada
- • Mexico (Cozumel, Acapulco)
- • Orlando, Florida
- • Puerto Rico
- • The U.S. Virgin Islands

If you like sunny beaches with a bit more exclusivity, consider:

- • St. Barts
- • Anguilla
- • Grand Cayman

> We spent out honeymoon at a spot my bride had visited before and wanted to share with me.
>
> — *Rob bookstore manager*

If you like . . .	Consider
Natural beauty, physical exercise	Australia, Switzerland, Costa Rica
Old-world Europe, art, history, architecture, classical music	Prague, Paris, Rome, Florence
Elegant sophistication, fine dining, history, art, fashion, classical music, nightlife	Paris, Vienna, Milan, Amsterdam, New York, Madrid
Hanging out with the locals, visiting prehistoric ruins, natural beauty, country feasts	Ireland, Tuscany, Canada, Greece
A bit of adventure	A windjammer cruise, African safari, canal boat in France
History, art, music	Venice, New York, Barcelona
La dolce vita	Rome, Naples
A brisk pace, the charm of tradition, and a touch of cozy domesticity	London, New Orleans, San Francisco
Vineyard culture	Napa, Sonoma, Tuscany, New Zealand
Latin romance	Madrid, Buenos Aires
Ocean vistas and sea breezes	A cruise, Greece, Florida, the Caribbean, the Hawaiian Islands

Honeymoon Brainstorming Checklist

Fill out the questionnaire and the budget on the following page and bring it with you to the travel agent; you'll be one step ahead!

My bride and I enjoy:

- ❏ Antiquing
- ❏ Museums
- ❏ Other cultures
- ❏ Hiking
- ❏ Water sports
- ❏ Elegant dining
- ❏ Movies
- ❏ Television
- ❏ Theatre
- ❏ Sporting events
- ❏ Taking classes
- ❏ Music
- ❏ Spa
- ❏ Gym

- ❏ Nature
- ❏ Animals
- ❏ Shopping
- ❏ Biking
- ❏ Rollerblading
- ❏ Snorkeling
- ❏ Diving
- ❏ Sailing
- ❏ Horseback riding
- ❏ Nightlife
- ❏ Boating
- ❏ Jewelry

Other_____

Do you or your fiancée speak any languages besides English? Yes / No

We'd prefer to stay at:

- ❏ An all-inclusive resort (everything is included in a single price)
- ❏ A historic hotel
- ❏ A bed and breakfast
- ❏ A country inn

- ❏ A rental house or apartment
- ❏ On a boat
- ❏ In a tent

Other_____

We'd prefer to:

❏ Travel by ourselves   ❏ Travel with a group

We like to eat _____

What is your fitness level? _____

Do you have any health concerns? _____

When will you travel? _____ **How many days will you travel?** _____

Is temperature/weather an issue for you? _____ **What is your budget?** _____

GET PACKING!

Things You'll Need

- Tickets/rail passes
- Passports: They are available at your local branch of the U.S. Post Office. Credit cards, checks, or money orders are accepted. The standard turn-around time is 6 weeks; expedited delivery is 2 weeks.
- Driver's license
- Itinerary
- Emergency phone numbers
- Names, addresses, phone numbers, and e-mail addresses of family members and friends
- If required for your destination: Visas, proof of inoculations
- Credit card(s)
- List of traveler's checks, credit cards, and checking account numbers (keep this list in a location separate from the actual items)
- Over-the-counter medications and prescriptions, including eyeglasses
- Foreign phrasebook
- Eurorail or other passes/tickets obtained in advance of the trip
- Currency converter
- Travel pillow (for long flights)
- Waterproof luggage with rein forced handles, double stitching, and wheels

Travel Wardrobe

Choose lightweight clothes made of wrinkle-free fabrics such as rayon, polyester, or cotton blends. Your wardrobe choices will vary depending on your destination. Below is a basic men's travel wardrobe.

- 1 waterproof windbreaker
- 1 sport jacket / blazer
- 1 pair dress slacks
- 3 pair casual slacks
- 2 nice dress shirts
- 1 long-sleeved shirt
- 4 short-sleeved sport shirts / polo shirts
- 1 pair walking shoes with rubber soles
- 1 pair casual / dress shoes, such as loafers
- swimsuit
- half-dozen sets of underwear and socks
- 1 hat
- 1 tie
- Pajamas, robe
- 2 pairs of shorts
- Sunglasses
- Umbrella
- Toilet articles ((pack in small, plastic containers or bring trial sizes)
- Sunscreen
- Razor (pack in checked luggage)
- Nail clippers (pack in checked luggage)

Honeymoon Budget Worksheet

	ITEM	LINE ITEM COST	BUDGET $
Car:			
Airfare:			
Train:			
Taxi:			
Tips:			
Subway:			
Other:			
Hotel/Lodging:			
# Nights X			
Rate per night:			
Taxes and Tips:			
Phone/Fax/Video Fees:			
Housekeeping Extras:			
Food/Dining:			
Number of Meals per Day X			
Average Cost per Meal:			
Drinks:			
Entertainment:			
Sightseeing:			
Shopping:			
Museums:			
Day Excursions:			
Travel Insurance:			
Film:			
Other:			
TOTAL COST:			

Write Thank-You Notes

Writing thank-you notes is a chore that is seldom looked forward to by any couple. Some of us get writer's block just thinking about writing them! Even for those of us who enjoy penning notes, writing thank-yous to one hundred or more people can be tiring. However, if people have been kind enough to share in your celebration and give you a wedding gift, the classy response — and truly the proper one — is to send them a thank-you note.

Now all you have to do is provide the final touch — a line or two about the gift, how much you and your wife will enjoy using it, and your personal John Hancock, written in ink on the inside of the card. This will take some time, so prepare to settle in for a night or, if your wedding was very large, even a whole day (perhaps lunch at a nice restaurant will break it up). Or send out for pizza, pour some beer or wine, and create an event around it. Before you know it, it will be done!

Set up House

We've all seen those scenes of newly married life in old movies — the ones where the groom carries his bride over the threshold into a tiny efficiency apartment decorated with a couple of orange crates. In the old days, couples often started out together with nothing.

Today, the average age for first marriages is in the mid-to-late 20s, and both bride and groom have typically been out of school for some time, living on their own, and working for a few years. Both of you undoubtedly have already set up house to some degree and surrounded yourselves with lots of stuff that you plan to bring along into your marital home or apartment. Most likely, you've already developed a personal style, or, at the very least, some preferences relating to décor.

Setting up house together and decorating it can be a big stressor on newlyweds. Here are a few reasons why couples may find setting up house stressful:

◆ One spouse is less of a risk-taker. You may disagree about how much of your finances to commit to an apartment, condo, or house.

◆ One spouse already owns a home, and the other spouse feels like a guest in the house or associates the house with an ex-lover or spouse.

◆ Neither of you is experienced in home repairs or construction, so you are sidelined by the amount of time and energy it takes to keep a house in good order.

◆ You haven't discussed household chores, so one spouse ends up doing more than his/her share.

◆ One spouse prefers a country lifestyle and the other an urban one.

◆ One spouse prefers to live close to his or her family and the other feels the need for some space.

◆ One of you looks at a house as a financial investment — the other, as an emotional one.

◆ One spouse wants a casual, comfortable home and the other wants something more formal.

It's smart to be aware of these potential issues before you move in together, so you can address them before they put unnecessary strain on your relationship. Some simple things you can do to head these issues off at the pass:

• Set aside some time away from home to discuss your preferences.

• Make a list in advance of any ideas or expectations you have. Start by asking your bride what her goals are and what she expects from you.

• Be willing to give in on some points and negotiate others.

• If you can't agree on something important — and neither of you can give in — agree on a third option, or find a third party to help you arrive at a decision.

Keep in mind a home is, for most people, much more than just a financial commitment — it is where you will build a life together. Ideally, your home should support your life goals, provide comfort and refuge from the world, support the romantic aspects of your relationship, and provide visual reminders of your shared experience.

Your house is only one of the big spending decisions you and your bride will have to make together. Below are some tips for handling some of the other responsibilities you will share going forward.

Get Down to Business

As a legal — as well as a spiritual — union, marriage will have far-reaching effects on your financial and legal status. Preferably well before you get married, perhaps even before you propose, you need to have a heart-to-heart talk about all of the business details that will change once you're married.

Studies have shown that money and children are the top two subjects of disagreement among married couples. These topics should be handled with care. To make good decisions, sometimes it helps to get expert advice. Meet together with a tax adviser, financial planner or accountant, insurance expert, and attorney to discuss the options for handling issues such as:

◆ Name changes
◆ Household budgets
◆ Tax returns
◆ Saving for or buying a house
◆ Insurance policies
◆ Independent business ownership
◆ Wills
◆ Property owned prior to marriage
◆ Social Security, Medicare, and disability benefits
◆ Joint checking accounts
◆ Trusts

◆ Credit cards and loans
◆ Government benefits (e.g., veteran's)
◆ Employment benefits (e.g., health insurance)
◆ Parenting and custody issues
◆ Legal benefits and protections provided to spouses
◆ Planning for retirement
◆ Investments
◆ Savings
◆ Emergency cash

Money Management

Since finances are a common source of disagreement between spouses, I have listed some helpful ideas for discussing money and averting potential problems:

◆ Set aside regular time to discuss money, perhaps once a month.

◆ Decide on a maximum amount each person may spend on an item without discussing it with the other spouse first. Items costing more than this amount should be discussed together before a purchase.

◆ Explore your financial dreams, including your home, lifestyle, children, and retirement.

◆ Create a plan to achieve your goals. Create a timeline with achievable milestones, and commit to reviewing your progress regularly. Take into account each other's financial personalities, especially tolerance for risk, when creating your financial plan.

Prenuptial Agreements

If you or your bride have children from a former marriage and want to preserve property for them or have some other extenuating circumstance that needs to be addressed with existing finances, a prenuptial agreement may make sense. If you decide to proceed with a prenuptial agreement, keep in mind that for the prenuptial to be a valid, legal agreement, both parties must be represented by independent legal counsel, preferably trained in matrimonial law, since the main purpose of a prenuptial is to supersede state laws covering division of assets during a divorce.

Protect Your Greatest Asset

Many people seek to protect and grow their financial assets, but they spend little time planning how to protect and grow their relationship with their spouse. The irony is that protecting and growing your personal relationship with your spouse can be one of the most effective ways to protect and grow your other assets — including your financial ones. A lot of work has been done in recent years on preventing divorce and building strong marriages. You and your wife can use this information to create a strong marriage with a financially sound future.

If the previous sections on money and marriage preparation seem like a lot of work, keep in mind that higher commitment levels in married couples have been correlated with fewer thoughts of divorce. Marriage is a challenging endeavor that requires hard work, determination, and discipline. However, as this guide has shown, it also has the potential to be very rewarding and satisfying. Spouses who seek to incorporate positivity, empathy, commitment, acceptance, and mutual love and respect into their relationship are more likely to have a fulfilling marriage.

When people base their marriages on friendship, kindness, fun, and traditions, they usually find joy and happiness in their relationship. Creating a strong and satisfying marriage is possible, and it is definitely worth the effort!

Resources

Web sites

www.romancestuck.com

www.love-sessions.com

www.romantic-lyrics.com

www.pricescope.com

www.consumersgemlab.com

www.diamondhelpers.com

www.Bluenile.com

www.Diamond.com

http://www.gemnation.com

www.toastmasters.org

www.state.gov

Gem laboratories

International Gemological Institute (IGI)

Gemological Institute of America (GIA)

European Gemological Laboratory (EGL)

American Gem Society Laboratories (AGSL)

Accredited Gemologists Association (AGA)

Gübelin Gem Lab.

Wedding Planner Associations

Association for Wedding Professionals International www.afwpi.com

The Association of Bridal Consultants www.bridalassn.com

Association of Certified Professional Wedding Consultants www.acpwc.com

June Wedding, Inc. www.junewedding.com

The National Association of Wedding Professionals, Inc. www.nawp.com

National Black Bridal Association (NBBA) www.nationalbba.com

National Bridal Service www.nationalbridal.com

Weddings Beautiful Worldwide www.weddingsbeautiful.com

Wedding Book Resources

The Bride's Year Head: The Ultimate Month-by-Month Wedding Planner
published by Ronnie Sellers Productions, Inc.

The Mother of the Bride: A Practical Guide & An Elegant Keepsake
published by Ronnie Sellers Productions, Inc.

Telephone numbers

U.S. Department of State Travel Warnings Hotline: 202-647-5225.

Center for Disease Control international travel hotline is 1-877-FYI-TRIP
or www.cdc.gov

Index

Index

D1320394

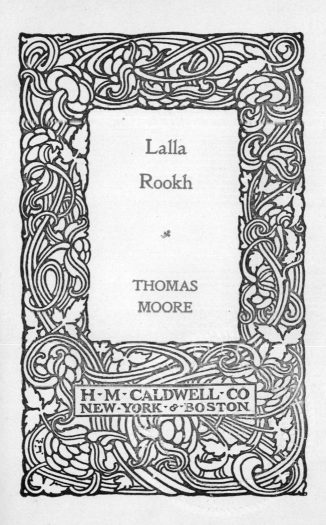

Lalla

Rookh

THOMAS
MOORE

H · M · CALDWELL · CO
NEW · YORK · & · BOSTON

CONTENTS.

PREFACE.

(WRITTEN ORIGINALLY FOR "LALLA ROOKH" IN THE COLLECTED EDITION OF MOORE'S WORKS.)

THE Poem, or Romance, of LALLA ROOKH, having now reached, I understand, its twentieth edition, a short account of the origin and progress of a work which has been hitherto so very fortunate in its course may not be deemed, perhaps, superfluous or misplaced.

It was about the year 1812, that, far more through the encouraging suggestions of friends than from any confident promptings of my own ambition, I conceived the design of writing a Poem upon some Oriental subject, and of those quarto dimensions which Scott's successful publications in that form had then rendered the regular poetical standard. A negotiation on the subject was opened with the Messrs. Longman in the same year ; but, from some causes which I cannot now recollect, led to no decisive result ; nor was it till a year or two after, that any further steps were taken in the matter,—— **their** house being the only one, it is right **to** add, with which, from first to last, I held any communication upon the subject.

On this last occasion, Mr. Perry kindly offered himself as my representative in the treaty ; and, what with the friendly zeal of my negotiator on the one side, and the prompt and liberal spirit with which he was met on the other, there has seldom, I think, occurred any transaction in which Trade and Poesy have shone out so advantageously in each other's eyes. The short discussion that then took place, between the two parties, may be comprised in a very few sentences. "I am of opinion," said Mr. Perry,—enforcing his view of the case by arguments which it is not for me to cite,—"that Mr. Moore ought to receive for his Poem the largest price that has been given, in our day, for such a work." "That was," answered the Messrs. Longman, "three thousand guineas." "Exactly so," replied Mr. Perry, "and no less a sum ought he to receive."

It was then objected, and very reasonably, on the part of the firm, that they had never yet seen a single line of the Poem ; and that a perusal of the work ought to be allowed to them, before they embarked so large a sum in the purchase. But, no ;—the romantic view which my friend Perry took of the matter, was, that this price should be given as a tribute to reputation already acquired, without any condition for a previous perusal of the new work. This high tone, I must confess, not a little startled and alarmed me ; but to the honor and glory of Romance,—as well on the publishers' side as the poet's,—this very generous view of the transaction was, without any difficulty, acceded to, and the firm agreed, before we separated, that I was to receive three thousand guineas for my Poem.

At the time of this agreement, but little of the work, as it stands at present, had yet been written. But the ready confidence in my success shown by others, made up for the deficiency of that requisite feeling within myself ; while a strong desire not wholly to disappoint this "auguring hope" became almost a substitute for inspiration. In the year 1815, therefore, having made some progress in my task, I wrote to report the state of the work to the Messrs. Longman, adding, that I was now most willing and ready, should they desire it, to submit the manuscript for their consideration. Their answer to this offer was as follows : "We are certainly impatient for the perusal of the Poem ; but solely for our gratification. Your sentiments are always honorable.*"

I continued to pursue my task for another year, being likewise occasionally occupied with the Irish Melodies, two or three numbers of which made their appearance during the period employed in writing "Lalla Rookh." At length, in the year 1816, I found my work

* April 10, 1815.

sufficiently advanced to be placed in the hands of the publishers. But the state of distress to which England was reduced, in that dismal year, by the exhausting effects of the series of wars she had just then concluded, and the general embarrassment of all classes, both agricultural and commercial, rendered it a juncture the least favorable that could well be conceived for the first launch into print of so light and costly a venture as "Lalla Rookh." Feeling conscious, therefore, that under such circumstances I should act but honestly in putting it in the power of the Messrs. Longman to reconsider the terms of their engagement with me,—leaving them free to postpone, modify, or even, should such be their wish, relinquish it altogether, I wrote them a letter to that effect, and received the following answer : "We shall be most happy in the pleasure of seeing you in February. We agree with you, indeed, that the times are most inauspicious for 'poetry and thousands ;' but we believe that your poetry would do more than that of any other living poet at the present moment." *

The length of time I employed in writing the few stories strung together in Lalla Rookh will appear, to some persons, much more than was necessary for the production of such easy and "light o' love" fictions. But, besides that I have been, at all times, a far more slow and

* November 9, 1816.

painstaking workman than would ever be
guessed, I fear, from the result, I felt that, in
this instance, I had taken upon myself a more
than ordinary responsibility, from the immense
stake risked b others on my chance of success.
For a long time, therefore, after the agreement
had been concluded, th ugh generally at work
with a view to this ask, I made but very little
real progress in it ; and I have still by me the
beginnings of several stories continued, some
of them, to the length of three or four hundred
lines, which, after in vain endeavoring to mould
them into shape, I threw aside, like the tale of
Cambuscan, "left half-told." One of these
stories, entitled "The Peri's Daughter," was
meant to relate the loves of a nymph of this
aërial extraction with a youth of mortal race,
the rightful Prince of Ormuz, who had been,
from his infancy, brought up in seclusion, on
the banks of the river Amou, by an aged
guardian named Mohassan. The story opens
with the first meeting of these destined lovers,
then in their childhood ; the Peri having wafted
her daughter to this holy retreat, in a bright,
enchanted boat, whose first appearance is thus
described :—

* * * * *

For, down the silvery tide afar.
There came a boat, as swift and bright
  As shines, in heav'n, some pilgrim-star,
That leaves its own high home, at night,
To shoot to distant shrines of light.

"It comes, it comes," young Orian cries,
And panting to Mohassan flies.
Then, down upon the flowery grass
Reclines to see the vision pass ;
With partly joy and partly fear,
To find its wondrous light so near,
And hiding oft his dazzled eyes
Among the flowers on which he lies.

. . . . .

Within the boat a baby slept,
Like a young pearl within its shell ;
    While one, who seem'd of riper years,
    But not of earth, or earth-like spheres,
Her watch beside the slumberer kept ;
Gracefully waving, in her hand,
    The feathers of some holy bird,
    With which, from time to time, she stirr'd
The fragrant air, and coolly fann'd
The baby's brow, or brush'd away
    The butterflies that, bright and blue
As on the mountains of Malay,
    Around the sleeping infant flew.

And now the fairy boat was stopp'd
Beside the bank,—the nymph has dropp'd
Her golden anchor in the stream ;

. . . . .

A song is sung by the Peri in approaching,
of which the following forms a part :—

My child she is but half divine,
Her father sleeps in the Caspian water ;
            Sea-weeds twine
            His funeral shrine,

But he lives again in the Peri's daughter.
Fain would I fly from mortal sight
　To my own sweet bowers of Peristan ;
But, there, the flowers are all too bright
　For the eyes of a baby born of man.
On flowers of earth her feet must tread ;
　So hither my light-wing'd bark hath brought
　　her ;
　　　　Stranger, spread
　　　　Thy leafiest bed,
　To rest the wandering Peri's daughter.

In another of these inchoate fragments, a
proud female saint, named Banou, plays a
principal part ; and her progress through the
streets of Cufa, on the night of a great illuminated festival, I find thus described :—

It was a scene of mirth that drew
A smile from ev'n the Saint Banou,
As, through the hush'd, admiring throng,
She went with stately steps along,
And counted o'er, that all might see,
The rubies of her rosary.
But none might see the worldly smile
That lurk'd beneath her veil, the while :—
Alla forbid ! for, who would wait
Her blessing at the temple's gate,—
What holy man would ever run
To kiss the ground she knelt upon,
If once, by luckless chance, he knew
She look'd and smil'd as others do ?

Her hands were join'd, and from each wrist
By threads of pearl and golden twist
Hung relics of the saints of yore,
And scraps of talismanic lore,—
Charms for the old, the sick, the frail,
Some made for use, and all for sale.
On either side, the crowd withdrew,
To let the Saint pass proudly through;
While turban'd heads of every hue,
Green, white, and crimson, bow'd around,
And gay tiaras touch'd the ground,—
As tulip-bells, when o'er their beds
The musk-wind passes, bend their heads.
Nay, some there were, among the crowd
Of Moslem heads that round her bow'd,
So fill'd with zeal, by many a draught
Of Shiraz wine profanely quaff'd,
That, sinking low in reverence then,
They never rose till morn again.

There are yet two more of these unfinished
sketches, one of which extends to a much
greater length than I was aware of; and, as
far as I can judge from a hasty renewal of my
acquaintance with it, is not incapable of being
yet turned to account.

In only one of these unfinished sketches, the
tale of The Peri's Daughter, had I yet ventured
to invoke that most home-felt of all my inspira-
tions, which has lent to the story of The Fire-
worshippers its main attraction and interest.
That it was my intention, in the concealed
Prince of Ormuz, to shadow out some imper-

sonation of this feeling, I take for granted
from the prophetic words supposed to be addressed to him by his aged guardian :—

> Bright child of destiny ! even now
> I read the promise on that brow,
> That tyrants shall no more defile
> The glories of the Green Sea Isle,
> But Ormuz shall again be free,
> And hail her native Lord in thee !

In none of the other fragments do I find any
trace of this sort of feeling, either in the subject
or the personages of the intended story ; and
this was the reason, doubtless, though hardly
known at the time to myself, that, finding my
subjects so slow in kindling my own sympathies,
I began to despair of their ever touching the
hearts of others ; and felt often inclined to
say :—

> "Oh, no, I have no voice or hand
> For such a song, in such a land."

Had this series of disheartening experiments
been carried on much further, I must have
thrown aside the work in despair. But at last,
fortunately as it proved, the thought occurred
to me of founding a story on the fierce struggle so long maintained between the Ghebers,*
or ancient Fire-worshippers of Persia, and

* Voltaire, in his tragedy of "Les Guèbres," written with a similar undercurrent of meaning, was accused of having transformed his
Fire-worshippers into Jansenists. "Quelques figuristes," he says,
"prétendent que les Guèbres sont les Jansenistes."

their haughty Moslem masters. From that moment, a new and deep interest in my whole task took possession of me. The cause of tolerance was again my inspiring theme ; and the spirit that had spoken in the melodies of Ireland soon found itself at home in the East.

Having thus laid open the secrets of the workshop to account for the time expended in *writing* this work, I must also, in justice to my own industry, notice the pains I took in long and laboriously *reading* for it. To form a store-house, as it were, of illustration purely Oriental, and so familiarize myself with its various treasures, that, as quick as Fancy required the aid of fact, in her spiritings, the memory was ready, like another Ariel, at her "strong bidding," to furnish materials for the spell-work, —such was, for a long while, the sole object of my studies ; and whatever time and trouble this preparatory process may have cost me, the effects resulting from it, as far as the humble merit of truthfulness is concerned, have been such as to repay me more than sufficiently for my pains. I have not forgotten how great was my pleasure, when told by the late Sir James Mackintosh, that he was once asked by Colonel W——s, the historian of British India, "whether it was true that Moore had never been in the East ? " "Never," answered Mackintosh. "Well, that shows me," replied Colonel W——s, "that reading over D'Herbelot is as good as riding on the back of a camel."

I need hardly subjoin to this lively speech, that, although D'Herbelot's valuable work was, of course, one of my manuals, I took the whole range of all such Oriental reading as was accessible to me ; and became, for the time, indeed, far more conversant with all relating to that distant region, than I have ever been with the scenery, productions, or modes of life of any of those countries lying most within my reach. We know that D'Anville, though never in his life out of Paris, was able to correct a number of errors in a plan of the Troad taken by De Choiseul, on the spot ; and for my own very different, as well as far inferior, purposes, the knowledge I had thus acquired of distant localities, seen only by me in my day-dreams, was no less ready and useful.

An ample reward for all this painstaking has been found in such welcome tributes as I have just now cited ; nor can I deny myself the gratification of citing a few more of the same description. From another distinguished authority on Eastern subjects, the late Sir John Malcolm, I had myself the pleasure of hearing a similar opinion publicly expressed ;—that eminent person, in a speech spoken by him at a Literary Fund Dinner, having remarked, that together with those qualities of a poet which he much too partially assigned to me was combined also "the truth of the historian."

Sir William Ouseley, another high authority, in giving his testimony to the same effect, thus

notices an exception to the general accuracy
for which he gives me credit : "Dazzled by
the beauties of this composition,* few readers
can perceive, and none surely can regret, that
the poet, in his magnificent catastrophe, has
forgotten, or boldly and most happily violated,
the precept of Zoroaster, above noticed, which
held it impious to consume any portion of a
human body by fire, especially by that which
glowed upon their altars." Having long lost,
I fear, most of my Eastern learning, I can only
cite, in defence of my catastrophe, an old
Oriental tradition, which relates that Nimrod,
when Abraham refused, at his command, to
worship the fire, ordered him to be thrown
into the midst of the flames.† A precedent so
ancient for this sort of use of the worshipped
element would appear, for all purposes at least
of poetry, fully sufficient.

In addition to these agreeable testimonies, I
have also heard, and need hardly add, with
some pride and pleasure, that parts of this
work have been rendered into Persian, and
have found their way to Ispahan. To this
fact, as I am willing to think it, allusion is
made in some lively verses, written many
years since, by my friend Mr. Luttrell :—

"I'm told, dear Moore, your lays are sung,
    (Can it be true, you lucky man?)

* The Fire-worshippers.
† "Tradunt autem Hebræi hanc fabulam, quod Abraham in ignem
missus sit, quia ignem adorare noluit."—ST. HIERON. in Quæst. in
Genesim.

> By moonlight, in the Persian tongue,
>   Along the streets of Ispahan."

'That some knowledge of the work may have really reached that region appears not improbable from a passage in the Travels of Mr. Frazer, who says, that "being delayed for some time at a town on the shores of the Caspian, he was lucky enough to be able to amuse himself with a copy of 'Lalla Rookh,' which a Persian had lent him."

Of the description of Balbec, in "Paradise and the Peri," Mr. Carne, in his "Letters from the East," thus speaks: "The description in 'Lalla Rookh' of the plain and its ruins is exquisitely faithful. The minaret is on the declivity near at hand, and there wanted only the muezzin's cry to break the silence."

I shall now tax my reader's patience with but one more of these generous vouchers. Whatever of vanity there may be in citing such tribute, they show, at least, of what great value, even in poetry, is that prosaic quality, industry; since, as the reader of the foregoing pages is now fully apprised, it was in a slow and laborious collection of small facts, that the first foundations of this fanciful Romance were laid.

The friendly testimony I have just referred to, appeared, some years since, in the form in which I now give it, and, if I recollect right, in the *Athenæum* :—

"I embrace this opportunity of bearing my individual testimony (if it be of any value) to the extraordinary accuracy of Mr. Moore, in his topographical, antiquarian, and characteristic details, whether of costume, manners, or less changing monuments, both in his 'Lalla Rookh' and in the Epicurean. It has been my fortune to read his Atlantic, Bermudean, and American Odes and Epistles, in the countries and among the people to which and to whom they related; I enjoyed also the exquisite delight of reading his 'Lalla Rookh,' in Persia itself; and I have perused the Epicurean, while all my recollections of Egypt and its still existing wonders are as fresh as when I quitted the banks of the Nile for Arabia:—I owe it, therefore, as a debt of gratitude (though the payment is most inadequate), for the great pleasure I have derived from his productions, to bear my humble testimony to their local fidelity.
"J. S. B."

Among the incidents connected with this work, I must not omit to notice the splendid Divertissement, founded upon it, which was acted at the Chateau Royal of Berlin, during the visit of the Grand Duke Nicholas to that capital, in the year 1822. The different stories composing the work were represented in Tableaux Vivans and songs; and among the crowd of royal and noble personages engaged in the perfomances, I shall mention those only who represented the principal characters, and whom I find thus enumerated in the published account of the Divertissement.*

Besides these and other leading personages, there were also brought into action, under the

---

*Lalla Roûkh, Divertissement mêlés de Chants et de Danses, Berlin, 1822. The work contains a series of colored engravings, representing groups, processions, etc., in different Oriental costumes.

"Fadladin, Grand-Nasir . Comte Haack (Maréchal de Cour).
Aliris, Roi de Bucharie . . S. A. I. le Grand-Duc.
Lalla Roûkh . . . . S. A. I. la Grande-Duchesse.
Aurungzeb, le Grand Mo- ⎰ S. A. R. le Prince Guillaume, frère du Roi.
gol . . . . ⎱
Abdallah, Père d'Aliris. . . S. A. R. le Duc de Cumberland.
La Reine, son épouse . . . S. A. R. la Princesse Louise Radzivill.'

various denominations of Seigneurs et Dames
de Bucharie, Dames de Cachemire, Seigneurs
et Dames dansans à la Fête des Roses, etc.,
nearly 150 persons.

Of the manner and style in which the Tableaux of the different stories are described in
the work from which I cite, the following account of the performance of Paradise and the
Peri will afford some specimen : —

"La décoration représentoit les portes bril-
lantes du Paradis, entourées de nuages. Dans
le premier tableau on voyoit la Péri, triste et
désolée, couchée sur le seuil des portes fermées,
et l'Ange de lumière qui lui adresse des con-
solations et des conseils. Le second repré-
sente le moment où la Péri, dans l'espoir que
ce don lui ouvrira l'entrée du Paradis, recueille
la dernière goutte de sang que vient de verser le
jeune guerrier indien. . . .

"La Péri et l'Ange de lumière répondoient
pleinement à l'image et à l'idée qu'on est tenté
de se faire de ces deux individus, et l'impression
qu'a faite généralement la suite des tableaux
de cet épisode delicat et intéressant est loin de
s'effacer de notre souvenir."

In this grand Fête, it appears, originated the
translation of "Lalla Rookh" into German *
verse, by the Baron de la Motte Fouqué; and
the circumstances which led him to undertake
the task, are described by himself in a Dedi-

* Since this was written, another translation of "Lalla Rookh" into
German verse has been made by Theodor Oelckers (Leipzig, Tauchnitz).

catory Poem to the Empress of Russia, which
he has prefixed to his translation. As soon as
the performance, he tells us, had ended, Lalla
Rookh (the Empress herself) exclaimed, with a
sigh, "Is it, then, all over? Are we now at
the close of all that has given us so much
delight? and lives there no poet who will impart to others, and to future times, some notion
of the happiness we have enjoyed this evening?" On hearing this appeal a Knight of
Cashmere (who is no other than the poetical
Baron himself) comes forward and promises to
attempt to present to the world "the Poem
itself in the measure of the original."—whereupon Lalla Rookh, it is added, approvingly
smiled.

LALLA ROOKH.

In the eleventh year of the reign of Aurung-zebe, Abdalla, King of the Lesser Bucharia, a lineal descendant from the Great Zingis, having abdicated the throne in favor of his son, set out on a pilgrimage to the Shrine of the Prophet ; and, passing into India through the delightful valley of Cashmere, rested for a short time at Delhi on his way. He was entertained by Aurungzebe in a style of magnificent hospital-ity, worthy alike of the visitor and the host, and was afterwards escorted with the same splendor to Surat, where he embarked for Arabia.[1] During the stay of the Royal Pilgrim at Delhi, a marriage was agreed upon between the Prince, his son, and the youngest daughter of the emperor, LALLA ROOKH ;[2]—a Princess de-scribed by the Poets of her time as more beau-tiful than Leila,[3] Shirine,[4] Dewildé,[5] or any of those heroines whose names and loves embel-lish the songs of Persia and Hindostan. It was intended that the nuptials should be celebrated at Cashmere ; where the young King, as soon as the cares of empire would permit, was to meet, for the first time, his lovely bride, and,

2

after a few months' repose in that enchanting
valley, conduct her over the snowy hills into
Bucharia.

The day of LALLA ROOKH's departure from
Delhi was as splendid as sunshine and pageantry could make it.　The bazaars and baths
were all covered with the richest tapestry;
hundreds of gilded barges upon the Jumna
floated with their banners shining in the water;
while through the streets groups of beautiful
children went strewing the most delicious
flowers around, as in that Persian festival
called the Scattering of the Roses; [6] till every
part of the city was as fragrant as if a caravan
of musk from Khoten had passed through it.
The Princess, having taken leave of her kind
father, who at parting hung a cornelian of Yemen round her neck, on which was inscribed
a verse from the Koran, and having sent a
considerable present to the Fakirs, who kept
up the Perpetual Lamp in her sister's tomb,
meekly ascended the palankeen prepared for
her; and, while Aurungzebe stood to take a
last look from his balcony, the procession
moved slowly on the road to Lahore.

Seldom had the Eastern world seen a cavalcade so superb.　From the gardens in the
suburbs to the imperial palace, it was one unbroken line of splendor.　The gallant appearance of the Rajah and Mogul Lords, distinguished by those insignia of the Emperor's
favor, [7] the feathers of the egret of Cashmere
in their turbans, and the small silver-rimmed

kettledrums at the bows of tl. saddles;—the costly armor of their cavaliers, who vied, on this occasion, with the guards of the great Keder Khan,[8] in the brightness of their silver battle-axes and the massiness of their maces of gold;—the glittering of the gilt pine-apples[9] on the tops of the palankeens;—the embroidered trappings of the elephants, bearing on their backs small turrets, in the shape of little antique temples, within which the Ladies of LALLA ROOKH lay as it were enshrined;—the rose-colored veils of the Princess's own sumptuous litter,[10] at the front of which a fair young female slave sat fanning her through the curtains, with feathers of the Argus pheasant's wing;[11]—and the lovely troop of Tartarian and Cashmerian maids of honor, whom the young King had sent to accompany his bride, and who rode on each side of the litter, upon small Arabian horses:—all was brilliant, tasteful, and magnificent, and pleased even the critical and fastidious FADLADEEN, Great Nazir or Chamberlain of the Haram, who was borne in his palankeen immediately after the Princess, and considered himself not the least important personage of the pageant.

FADLADEEN was a judge of everything,—from the pencilling of a Circassian's eyelids to the deepest questions of science and literature; from the mixture of a conserve of rose-leaves to the composition of an epic poem: and such influence had his opinion upon the various

tastes of the day, that all the cooks and **poets of** Delhi stood in awe of him. His political conduct and opinions were founded upon **that** line of Sadi,—"Should the Prince at noon-day say, It is night, declare that you behold **the** moon and stars."—And his zeal for religion, **of** which Aurungzebe was a munificent protector, [12] was about as disinterested as that of the goldsmith who fell in love with the diamond **eyes** of the Idol of Jaghernaut. [13]

During the first days of their journey, LALLA ROOKH, who had passed all her life within **the** shadow of the Royal Gardens of Delhi, [14] found enough in the beauty of the scenery through which they passed to interest her mind, and delight her imagination; and when at evening or in the heat of the day, they turned off from the high-road to those retired and romantic places which had been selected for her encampments, sometimes on the banks of a small rivulet, as clear as the waters of the Lake of Pearl; [15] sometimes under the sacred shade of a Banyan tree, from which the view opened upon a glade covered with antelopes; and often in those hidden, embowered spots, described by one from the Isles of the West, [16] as "places of melancholy, delight, and safety, where all the company around were wild peacocks and turtle-doves;"—she felt a charm in these scenes so lovely and so new to her, which, for a time, made her indifferent to every other amusement. But LALLA ROOKH was young, and the young love variety; nor could the conversation of her Ladies and the Great Chamberlain, FADLADEEN (the only persons of course admitted to her pavilion), sufficiently enliven those many vacant hours, which were devoted neither to the pillow nor the palankeen. There was a little Persian slave who sung sweetly to the Vina, and who, now and then, lulled the Princess to sleep with the ancient ditties of her country, about the loves of Wamak and Ezra,[17] the fair-haired Zal and his mistress Rodahver;[18] not forgetting the combat of Rustam with the terrible White Demon.[19] At other times she was amused by those graceful dancing-girls of Delhi, who had been permitted by the Bramins of the Great Pagoda to attend her, much to the horror of the good Mussulman FADLADEEN, who could see nothing graceful or agreeable in idolaters, and to whom the very tinkling of their golden anklets[20] was an abomination.

But these and many other diversions were repeated till they lost all their charm, and the nights and noon-days were beginning to move heavily, when, at length, it was recollected that, among the attendants sent by the bridegroom, was a young poet of Cashmere, much celebrated throughout the valley for his manner of reciting the Stories of the East, on whom his Royal Master had conferred the privilege of being admitted to the pavilion of the Princess, that he might help to beguile the tediousness of the journey by some of his agreeable recitals.

At the mention of a poet, FADLADEEN elevated his critical eyebrows, and, having refreshed his faculties with a dose of that delicious opium[21] which is distilled from the black poppy of the Thebais, gave orders for the minstrel to be forthwith introduced into the presence.

The Princess, who had once in her life seen a poet from behind the screens of gauze in her Father's hall, and had conceived from that specimen no very favorable ideas of the Caste, expected but little in this new exhibition to interest her;—she felt inclined, however, to alter her opinion on the very first appearance of FERAMORZ. He was a youth about LALLA ROOKH'S own age, and graceful as that idol of women, Crishna,[22]—such as he appears to their young imaginations, heroic, beautiful, breathing music from his very eyes, and exalting the religion of his worshippers into love. His dress was simple, yet not without some marks of costliness; and the Ladies of the Princess were not long in discovering that the cloth which encircled his high Tartarian cap was of the most delicate kind that the shawl-goats of Tibet supply.[23] Here and there, too, over his vest, which was confined by a flowered girdle of Kashan, hung strings of fine pearl, disposed with an air of studied negligence:—nor did the exquisite embroidery of his sandals escape the observation of these fair critics; who, however they might give way to FADLADEEN upon the unimportant topics of

religion and government, had the spirit of
martyrs in everything relating to such moment-
ous matters as jewels and embroidery.

For the purpose of relieving the pauses of
recitation by music, the young Cashmerian held
in his hand a kitar ; —such as, in old times,
the Arab maids of the West used to listen to by
moonlight in the gardens of the Alhambra—
and having premised, with much humility,
that the story he was about to relate was
founded on the adventures of that Veiled
Prophet of Khorassan[24] who, in the year of the
Hegira 163, created such alarm throughout the
Eastern Empire, made an obeisance to the
Princess, and thus began:—

THE VEILED PROPHET OF KHORASSAN.[25]

In that delightful Province of the Sun,
The first of Persian lands he shines upon,
Where all the loveliest children of his beam,
Flow'rets and fruits, blush over every stream,[26]
And, fairest of all streams, the Murga roves
Among Merou's [27] bright palaces and groves ;—
There on that throne, to which the blind belief
Of millions rais'd him, sat the Prophet-Chief,
The Great Mokanna.   O'er his features hung
The Veil, the Silver Veil, which he had flung
In mercy there, to hide from mortal sight
His dazzling brow, till man could bear its light.

For, far less luminous, his votaries said,
Were ev'n the gleams, miraculously shed
O'er Moussa's [28] cheek, [29] when down the Mount
　　he trod,
All glowing from the presence of his God !

　On either side, with ready hearts and hands,
His chosen guard of bold Believers stands ;
Young fire-eyed disputants, who deem their
　　swords,
On points of faith, more eloquent than words ;
And such their zeal, there's not a youth with
　　brand
Uplifted there, but, at the Chief's command,
Would make his own devoted heart its sheath,
And bless the lips that doom'd so dear a
　　death !
In hatred to the Caliph's hue of night, [30]
Their vesture, helms and all, is snowy white ;
Their weapons various—some equipp'd for
　　speed,
With javelins of the light Kathaian reed ; [31]
Or bows of buffalo horn and shining quivers
Fill'd with the stems [32] that bloom on Iran's
　　rivers ; [33]
While some, for war's more terrible attacks,
Wield the huge mace and ponderous battle-
　　axe ;
And as they wave aloft in morning's beam
The milk-white plumage of their helms, they
　　seem
Like a chenar-tree grove, [34] when winter throws
O'er all its tufted heads his feathering snows.

Between the porphyry pillars, that uphold
The rich moresque-work of the roof of gold,
Aloft the Haram's curtain'd galleries rise,
Where, through the silken network, glancing
    eyes,
From time to time, like sudden gleams that
    glow
Through autumn clouds, shine o'er the pomp
    below.—
What impious tongue, ye blushing saints,
    would dare
To hint that aught but Heaven hath placed you
    there?
Or that the loves of this light world could bind,
In their gross chain, your Prophet's soaring
    mind?
No—wrongful thought!—commission'd from
    above
To people Eden's bowers with shapes of love,
(Creatures so bright, that the same lips and
    eyes
They wear on earth will serve in Paradise,)
There to recline among Heaven's native maids,
And crown the Elect with bliss that never
    fades—
Well hath the Prophet-Chief his bidding done;
And every beauteous race beneath the sun,
From those who kneel at Brahma's burning
    founts, [35]
To the fresh nymphs bounding o'er YEMEN'S
    mounts;
From PERSIA'S eyes of full and fawn-like ray
To the small, half-shut glances of KATHAY; [36]

And GEORGIA's bloom, and AZAB's darker smiles,
And the gold ringlets of the Western Isles ;
All, all are there ;—each Land its flower hath
     given,
To form that fair young Nursery for Heaven !

    But why this pageant now ? this arm'd
     array ?
What triumph crowds the rich Divan to-day
With turban'd heads, of every hue and race,
Bowing before that veil'd and awful face,
Like tulip-beds, [87] of different shape and dyes,
Bending beneath the invisible West-wind's
     sighs !
What new-made mystery now, for Faith to
     sign,
And blood to seal, as genuine and divine,
What dazzling mimicry of God's own power
Hath the bold Prophet plann'd to grace this
     hour ?

    Not such the pageant now, though not less
     proud ;
Yon warrior youth, advancing from the crowd,
With silver bow, with belt of broider'd crape,
And fur-bound bonnet of Bucharian shape, [88]
So fiercely beautiful in form and eye,
Like war's wild planet in a summer sky ;
That youth to-day—a proselyte, worth hordes
Of cooler spirits and less practised swords—
Is come to join, all bravery and belief,
The creed and standard of the heaven-sent
     Chief.

Though few his years, the West already
    knows
Young AZIM'S fame; — beyond the Olympian
    snows,
Ere manhood darken'd o'er his downy cheek,
O'erwhelm'd in fight and captive to the Greek,[39]
He linger'd there, till peace dissolv'd his
    chains; —
Oh, who could, even in bondage, tread the plains
Of glorious GREECE, nor feel his spirit rise
Kindling within him? who, with heart and eyes,
Could walk where Liberty had been, nor see
The shining footprints of her Deity,
Nor feel those godlike breathings in the air,
Which mutely told her spirit had been there?
Not he, that youthful warrior, — no, too well,
For his soul's quiet work'd the awakening spell;
And now, returning to his own dear land,
Full of those dreams of good that, vainly grand,
Haunt the young heart, — proud views of
    humankind,
Of men to Gods exalted and refined, —
False views, like that horizon's fair deceit,
Where earth and heaven but *seem*, alas, to
    meet! —
Soon as he heard an Arm Divine was rais'd
To right the nations, and beheld, emblaz'd
On the white flag MOKANNA'S host unfurl'd,
Those words of sunshine, "Freedom to the
    World,"
At once his faith, his sword, his soul obey'd
The inspiring summons; every chosen blade

That fought beneath that banner's sacred text
Seem'd doubly edg'd, for this world and the
next ;
And ne'er did Faith with her smooth bandage
bind
Eyes more devoutly willing to be blind,
In virtue's cause ;—never was soul inspir'd
With livelier trust in what it most desir'd,
Than his, the enthusiast there, who kneeling,
pale
With pious awe, before that Silver Veil,
Believes the form, to which he bends his knee,
Some pure, redeeming angel, sent to free
This fetter'd world from every bond and stain,
And bring its primal glories back again !

Low as young Azim knelt, that motley crowd
Of all earth's nations sunk the knee and bow'd,
With shouts of "Alla !" echoing long and loud;
While high in air, above the Prophet's head,
Hundreds of banners, to the sunbeam spread,
Wav'd, like the wings of the white birds that fan
The flying throne of star-taught Soliman. [40]
Then thus he spoke :—"Stranger, though new
the frame
Thy soul inhabits now, I've track'd its flame
For many an age, [41] in every chance and change
Of that existence, through whose varied
range,—
As through a torch-race, where, from hand to
hand,
The flying youths transmit their shining
brand,—

From frame to frame the unextinguish'd soul
Rapidly passes, till it reach the goal !

 "Nor think 'tis only the gross Spirits, warm'd
With duskier fire and for earth's medium form'd,
That run th:s course ;—Beings, the most divine,
Thus deign through dark mortality to shine.
Such was the Essence that in ADAM dwelt,
To which all Heaven, except the Proud One,
    knelt : [42]
Such the refin'd Intelligence that glow'd
In MOUSSA's [43] frame,—and, thence descending,
    flow'd
Through many a Prophet's breast ; [44]—in ISSA [45]
    shone,
And in MOHAMMED burn'd ; till, hastening on,
(As a bright river that, from fall to fall
In many a maze descending, bright through all,
Finds some fair region where, each labyrinth
    past,
In one full lake of light it rests at last !)
That Holy Spirit, settling calm and free
From lapse or shadow, centres all in me ! "

 Again, throughout the assembly, at these
    words,
Thousands of voices rung : the warriors' swords
Were pointed up to heaven ; a sudden wind
In the open banners play'd, and from behind
Those Persian hangings, that but ill could
    screen
The Haram's loveliness, white hands were
    seen

Waving embroider'd scarves, whose motion
    gave
A perfume forth ;—like those the Houris wave
When beck'ning to their bowers the immortal
    Brave.

"But these," pursued the Chief, "are truths
    sublime,
That claim a holier mood and calmer time
Than earth allows us now ;—this sword must
    first
The darkling prison-house of Mankind burst
Ere Peace can visit them, or Truth let in
Her wakening daylight on a world of sin.
But then, celestial warriors, then, when all
Earth's shrines and thrones before our banner
    fall ;
When the glad Slave shall at these feet lay
    down
His broken chain, the tyrant Lord his crown,
The Priest his book, the Conqueror his wreath,
And from the lips of Truth one mighty breath
Shall, like a whirlwind, scatter in its breeze
That whole dark pile of human mockeries ;—
Then shall the reign of mind commence on
    earth,
And starting fresh, as from a second birth,
Man, in the sunshine of the world's new
    spring,
Shall walk transparent, like some holy thing !
Then, too, your Prophet from his angel brow
Shall cast the Veil that hides his splendors
    now,

And gladden'd Earth shall, through her wide
    expanse,
Bask in the glories of this countenance !
For thee, young warrior, welcome !—thou hast
    yet
Some tasks to learn, some frailties to forget,
Ere the white war-plume o'er thy brow can
    wave ;—
But, once my own, mine all till in the grave ! "

The pomp is at an end—the crowds are
    gone—
Each ear and heart still haunted by the tone
Of that deep voice, which thrill'd like ALLA's
    own !
The Young all dazzled by the plumes and
    lances,
The glittering throne, and Haram's half-caught
    glances ;
The Old deep pondering on the promis'd reign
Of peace and truth ; and all the female train
Ready to risk their eyes, could they but gaze
A moment on that brow's miraculous blaze !

But there was one, among the chosen maids,
Who blush'd behind the gallery's silken shades,
One, to whose soul the pageant of to-day
Has been like death : —you saw her pale dis-
    may,
Ye wondering sisterhood, and heard the burst
Of exclamation from her lips, when first
She saw that youth, too well, too dearly known,
Silently kneeling at the Prophet's throne.

Ah ZELICA ! there *was* a time, when bliss
Shone o'er thy heart from every look of his ;
When but to see him, hear him, breathe the
    air
In which he dwelt, was thy soul's fondest
    prayer ;
When round him hung such a perpetual spell,
Whate'er he did none ever did so well.
Too happy days ! when, if he touch'd a flower
Or gem of thine, 'twas sacred from that hour ;
When thou didst study him till every tone
And gesture and dear look became thy own,—
Thy voice like his, the changes of his face
In thine reflected with still lovelier grace :
Like echo, sending back sweet music, fraught
With twice the aërial sweetness it had brought !
Yet now he comes,—brighter than even he
E'er beam'd before,—but, ah ! not bright for
    thee ;
No—dread, unlook'd for, like a visitant
From the other world, he comes as if to haunt
Thy guilty soul with dreams of lost delight,
Long lost to all but memory's aching sight :—
Sad dreams ! as when the Spirit of our Youth
Returns in sleep, sparkling with all the truth
And innocence once ours, and leads us back,
In mournful mockery, o'er the shining track
Of our young life, and points out every ray
Of hope and peace we've lost upon the way !

Once happy pair ;—in proud BOKHARA'S
    groves,
Who had not heard of their first youthful loves ?

Born by that ancient flood,⁴ which from its
    spring
In the dark Mountains swiftly wandering,
Enrich'd by every pilgrim brook that shines
With relics from BUCHARIA'S ruby mines,
And lending to the CASPIAN half its strength,
In the cold Lake of Eagles sinks at length ;—
There, on the banks of that bright river born,
The flowers, that hung above its wave at morn,
Bless'd not the waters, as they murmur'd by,
With holier scent and lustre, than the sigh
And virgin-glance of first affection cast
Upon their youth's smooth current, as it pass'd !
But war disturb'd this vision,—far away
From her fond eyes summon'd to join the
    array
Of PERSIA's warriors on the hills of THRACE,
The youth exchang'd his sylvan dwelling-place
For the rude tent and war-field's deathful clash ;
His ZELICA's sweet glances for the flash
Of Grecian wild-fire, and Love's gentle chains
For bleeding bondage on BYZANTIUM's plains.

    Month after month, in widowhood of soul
Drooping, the maiden saw two summers roll
Their suns away—but ah ! how cold and dim
Even summer suns, when not beheld with him !
From time to time ill-omen'd rumors came,
Like spirit-tongues mutt'ring the sick man's
    name,
Just ere he dies :—at length those sounds of
    dread
Fell withering on her soul, "AZIM is dead !"

3

Oh Grief, beyond all other griefs, when fate
First leaves the young heart lone and desolate
In the wide world, without that only tie
For which it lov'd to live or fear'd to die ;—
Lorn as the hung-up lute, that ne'er hath
    spoken
Since the sad day its master-chord was broken !
Fond maid, the sorrow of her soul was such,
Even reason sunk,—blighted beneath its touch :
And though, ere long, her sanguine spirit rose
Above the first dead pressure of its woes,
Though health and bloom return'd, the delicate
    chain
Of thought, once tangled, never clear'd again.
Warm, lively, soft as in youth's happiest day,
The mind was still all there, but turn'd astray;—
A wand'ring bark, upon whose pathway shone
All stars of heaven, except the guiding one !
Again she smil'd, nay, much and brightly
    smil'd,
But 'twas a lustre, strange, unreal, wild ;
And when she sung to her lute's touching
    strain,
'Twas like the notes, half ecstasy, half pain,
The bulbul [47] utters, ere her soul depart,
When, vanquish'd by some minstrel's powerful
    art,
She dies upon the lute whose sweetness broke
    her heart !

    Such was the mood in which that mission
    found
Young ZELICA,—that mission, which around

The Eastern world, in every region blest
With woman's smile, sought out its loveliest,
To grace that galaxy of lips and eyes
Which the Veil'd Prophet destin'd for the
    skies :—
And such quick welcome as a spark receives
Dropp'd on a bed of Autumn's wither'd leaves,
Did every tale of these enthusiasts find
In the wild maiden's sorrow-blighted mind.
All fire at once the madd'ning zeal she caught ;—
Elect of Paradise ! blest, rapturous thought !
Predestin'd bride, in heaven's eternal dome,
Of some brave youth—ha ! durst they say
    "of *some ?* "
No—of the one, one only object trac'd
In her heart's core too deep to be effac'd ;
The one whose memory, fresh as life, is twin'd
With every broken link of her lost mind ;
Whose image lives, though Reason's self be
    wreck'd,
Safe 'mid the ruins of her intellect !

Alas, poor ZELICA ! it needed all
The fantasy which held thy mind in thrall,
To see in that gay Haram's glowing maids
A sainted colony for Eden's shades ;
Or dream that he,—of whose unholy flame
Thou wert too soon the victim,—shining came
From Paradise, to people its pure sphere
With souls like thine, which he hath ruin'd
    here !
No—had not Reason's light totally set,
And left thee dark, thou hadst an amulet

In the lov'd image, graven on thy heart,
Which would have sav'd thee from the temp-
    ter's art,
And kept alive, in all its bloom of breath,
That purity, whose fading is love's death !—
But lost, inflamed,—a restless zeal took place
Of the mild virgin's still and feminine grace;
First of the Prophet's favorites,—proudly first
In zeal and charms,—too well the Impostor
    nurs'd
Her soul's delirium, in whose active flame,
Thus lighting up a young, luxuriant frame,
He saw more potent sorceries to bind
To his dark yoke the spirits of mankind,
More subtle chains than hell itself e'er twin'd.
No art was spar'd, no witchery :—all the skill
His demons taught him was employ'd to fill
Her mind with gloom and ecstasy by turns—
That gloom, through which Frenzy but fiercer
    burns ;
That ecstasy, which from the depth of sadness
Glares like the maniac's moon, whose light is
    madness.

'Twas from a brilliant banquet, where the
    sound
Of poesy and music breath'd around,
Together picturing to her mind and ear
The glories of that heaven, her destin'd
    sphere,
Where all was pure, where every stain that
    lay
Upon the spirit's light should pass away,

ZELICA.

And, realizing more than youthful love
E'er wish'd or dream'd, she should forever
    rove
Through fields of fragrance by her Azim's side,
His own bless'd, purified, eternal bride !—
'Twas from a scene, a witching trance like this,
He hurried her away, yet breathing bliss,
To the dim charnel-house ;—through all its
    steams
Of damp and death, led only by those gleams
Which foul Corruption lights, as with design
To show the gay and proud, *she* too can
    shine !—
And, passing on through upright ranks of Dead,
Which to the maiden, doubly craz'd by dread,
Seem'd, through the bluish death-light round
    them cast,
To move their lips in mutterings as she
    pass'd—
There, in that awful place, when each had
    quaff'd
And pledg'd in silence such a fearful draught,
Such—oh ! the look and taste of that red bowl
Will haunt her till she dies—he bound her
    soul

By a dark oath, in hell's own language fram'd,
Never, while earth his mystic presence claim'd,
While the blue arch of day hung o'er them
    both,
Never, by that all-imprecating oath,
In joy or sorrow from his side to sever.—
    She swore, and the wide charnel echoed,
    "Never, never !"

From that dread hour, entirely, wildly given
To him and — she believ'd, lost maid! — to
    Heaven;
Her brain, her heart, her passions all inflam'd,
How proud she stood, when in full Haram
    nam'd
The Priestess of the Faith!—how flash'd her
    eyes
With light, alas! that was not of the skies,
When round, in trances, only less than hers,
She saw the Haram kneel, her prostrate wor-
    shippers!
Well might MOKANNA think that form alone
Had spells enough to make the world his
    own :—
Light, lovely limbs, to which the spirit's play
Gave motion, airy as the dancing spray,
When from its stem the small bird wings
    away :
Lips in whose rosy labyrinth, when she smil'd,
The soul was lost; and blushes, swift and
    wild
As are the momentary meteors sent
Across the uncalm, but beauteous firmament.
And then her look—oh! where's the heart so
    wise
Could unbewilder'd meet those matchless eyes?
Quick, restless, strange, but exquisite withal,
Like those of angels, just before their fall;
Now shadow'd with the shames of earth—now
    crost
By glimpses of the heaven her heart had
    lost ;

In ev'ry glance there broke, without control,
The flashes of a bright but troubled soul,
Where sensibility still wildly play'd,
Like lightning, round the ruins it had made!

And such was now young ZELICA — so
    chang'd
From her who, some years since, delighted
    rang'd
The almond groves that shade BOKHARA's tide,
All life and bliss, with AZIM by her side !
So alter'd was she now, this festal day,
When, 'mid the proud Divan's dazzling array,
The vision of that Youth whom she had lov'd,
Had wept as dead, before her breath'd and
    mov'd ;—
When—bright, she thought, as if from Eden's
    track
But half-way trodden, he had wander'd back
Again to earth, glistening with Eden's light—
Her beauteous AZIM shone before her sight.

O Reason ! who shall say what spells renew,
When least we look for it, thy broken clew !
Through what small vistas o'er the darken'd
    brain
Thy intellectual day-beam bursts again ;
And how, like forts, to which beleaguerers
    win
Unhop'd-for entrance through some friend
    within,
One clear idea, waken'd in the breast
By memory's magic, lets in all the rest !

Would it were thus. unhappy girl, with thee !
But though light came. it came but partially ;
Enough to show the maze in which thy sense
Wander'd about,—but not to guide it thence ;
Enough to glimmer o'er the yawning wave,
But not to point the harbor which might save.
Hours of delight and peace, long left behind,
With that dear form came rushing o'er her
    mind ;
But, oh ! to think how deep her soul had gone
In shame and falsehood since those moments
    shone ;
And, then, her oath—*there* madness lay again,
And, shuddering, back she sunk into her chain
Of mental darkness, as if blest to flee
From light, whose every glimpse was agony !
Yet, *one* relief this glance of former years
Brought, mingled with its pain,—tears, floods
    of tears,
Long frozen at her heart, but now like rills
Let loose in spring-time from the snowy hills,
And gushing warm, after a sleep of frost,
Through valleys where their flow had long
    been lost.

    Sad and subdued, for the first time her frame
Trembled with horror, when the summons came
(A summons proud and rare, which all but she,
And she till now, had heard with ecstasy)
To meet MOKANNA at his place of prayer,
A garden oratory, cool and fair,
By the stream's side, where still at close of day
The Prophet of the Veil retir'd to pray ;

Sometimes alone—but, oftener far, with one,
One chosen nymph to share his orison.

Of late none found such favor in his sight
As the young Priestess ; and though, since that
    night
When the death-caverns echoed every tone
Of the dire oath that made her all his own,
The Impostor, sure of his infatuate prize,
Had, more than once, thrown off his soul's
    disguise,
And utter'd such unheavenly, monstrous things,
As even across the desp'rate wanderings
Of a weak intellect, whose lamp was out,
Threw startling shadows of dismay and
    doubt ;—
Yet zeal, ambition, her tremendous vow,
The thought, still haunting her, of that bright
    brow,
Whose blaze, as yet from mortal eye conceal'd,
Would soon, proud triumph ! be to her re-
    veal'd,
To her alone ;—and then the hope, most dear,
Most wild of all, that her transgression here
Was but a passage through earth's grosser fire,
From which the spirit would at last aspire,
Even purer than before,—as perfumes rise
Through flame and smoke, most welcome to
    the skies —
And that when Azim's fond, divine embrace
Should circle her in heaven, no dark'ning trace
Would on that bosom he once lov'd remain,
But all be bright, be pure, be *his* again !—

These were the wildering dreams, whose curst
    deceit
Had chain'd her soul beneath the tempter's
    feet,
And made her think even damning falsehood
    sweet.
But now that Shape, which had appall'd her
    view,
That Semblance—oh, how terrible, if true !—
Which came across her frenzy's full career
With shock of consciousness, cold, deep, severe,
As when, in northern seas, at midnight dark,
An isle of ice encounters some swift bark,
And, startling all its wretches from their sleep,
By one cold impulse hurls them to the
    deep ;—
So came that shock not frenzy's self could bear,
And waking up each long-lull'd image there,
But check'd her headlong soul, to sink it in
    despair !

Wan and dejected, through the evening dusk,
She now went slowly to the small kiosk,
Where, pondering alone his impious schemes,
MOKANNA waited her—too rapt in dreams
Of the fair-rip'ning future's i.. success,
To heed the sorrow, pale and spiritless,
That sat upon his victim's downcast brow,
Or mark how slow her step, how alter'd now
From the quick, ardent Priestess, whose light
    bound
Came like a spirit's o'er the unechoing
    ground,—

From that wild ZELICA, whose every glance
Was thrilling fire, whose every thought a
    trance !

Upon his couch the Veil'd MOKANNA lay,
While lamps around—not such as lend their
    ray,
Glimmering and cold, to those who nightly
    pray
In holy KOOM,[48] or MECCA's dim arcades,—
But brilliant, soft, such lights as lovely maids
Look loveliest in, shed their luxurious glow
Upon his mystic Veil's white glittering flow.
Beside him, 'stead of beads and books of
    prayer,
Which the world fondly thought he mus'd on
    there,
Stood vases, fill'd with KISHMEE's[49] golden
    wine,
And the red weepings of the SHIRAZ vine ;
Of which his curtain'd lips full many a draught
Took zealously, as if each drop they quaff'd,
Like ZEMZEM's Spring of Holiness,[50] had power
To freshen the soul's virtues into flower !
And still he drank and ponder'd—nor could
    see
The approaching maid, so deep his reverie ;
At length, with fiendish laugh, like that which
    broke
From EBLIS at the Fall of Man, he spoke :—
" Yes, ye vile race, for hell's amusement given,
Too mean for earth, yet claiming kin with
    heaven ;

God's images, forsooth !—such Gods as he
Whom INDIA serves, the monkey deity ; [51]—
Ye creatures of a breath, proud things of
    clay,
To whom if LUCIFER, as grandams say,
Refus'd, though at the forfeit of heaven's light,
To bend in worship. LUCIFER was right ! [52]—
Soon shall I plant this foot upon the neck
Of your foul race, and without fear or check,
Luxuriating in hate, avenge my shame,
My deep-felt, long-nurst loathing of man's
    name ;
Soon at the head of myriads, blind and fierce
As hooded falcons, through the universe
I'll sweep my dark'ning, desolating way,
Weak man my instrument, curst man my prey !

    " Ye wise, ye learn'd, who grope your dull
      way on
By the dim twinkling gleams of ages gone,
Like superstitious thieves, who think the light
From dead men's marrow guides them best at
   night [53]—
Ye shall have honors—wealth,—yes, Sages,
    yes—
I know, grave fools, your wisdom's nothing-
    ness ;
Undazzled it can track yon starry sphere,
But a gilt stick, a bauble blinds it here.
How I shall laugh, when trumpeted along,
In lying speech, and still more lying song,
By these learn'd slaves, the meanest of the
    throng ;

" E'er wish'd, or dream'd, she should forever rove
Through fields of fragrance, by her Azim's side."

Their wits brought up, their wisdom shrunk so
    small,
A sceptre's puny point can wield it all !

" Ye too, believers of incredible creeds,
Whose faith enshrines the monsters which it
    breeds ;
Who, bolder even than NEMROD, think to rise,
By nonsense heap'd on nonsense, to the skies ;
Ye shall have miracles, ay, sound ones too,
Seen, heard, attested, ev'ry thing—but true.
Your preaching zealots, too inspir'd to seek
One grace of meaning for the things they speak ;
Your martyrs, ready to shed out their blood
For truths too heavenly to be understood ;
And your State Priests, sole vendors of the lore
That works salvation ;—as, on AVA'S shore,
Where none *but* priests are privileg'd to trade
In that best marble of which Gods are made ; "
They shall have mysteries—ay, precious stuff
For knaves to thrive by—mysteries enough ;
Dark, tangled doctrines, dark as fraud can
    weave,
Which simple votaries shall on trust receive,
While craftier feign belief, till they believe.
A Heaven too ye must have, ye lords of dust,—
A splendid Paradise,—pure souls, ye must :
That Prophet ill sustains his holy call,
Who finds not heavens to suit the tastes of all ;
Houris for boys, omniscience for sages,
And wings and glories for all ranks and ages.
Vain things !—as lust or vanity inspires,
The Heaven of each is but what each desires,

And, soul or sense, whate'er the object be,
Man would be man to all eternity !
So let him—EBLIS ! grant this crowning curse,
But keep him what he is, no Hell were worse."

   "Oh my lost soul ! " exclaim'd the shudder-
     ing maid,
Whose ears had drunk like poison all he said :—
MOKANNA started—not abash'd, afraid,—
He knew no more of fear than one who dwells
     eath the tropics knows of icicles !
   , in those dismal words that reach'd his ear,
   h my lost soul ! " there was a sound so
     drear,
    like that voice, among the sinful dead,
    which the legend o'er Hell's Gate is read,
   at, new as 'twas from her, whom nought
     could dim
   sink till now, it startled even him.

   " Ha, my fair Priestess ! "—thus, with ready
     wile,
The impostor turn'd to greet her—" thou, whose
     smile
Hath inspiration in its rosy beam
Beyond the Enthusiast's hope or Prophet's
     dream !
Light of the faith ! who twin'st religion's zeal
So close with love's, men know not which they
     feel,
Nor which to sigh for, in their trance of heart,
The heaven thou preachest or the heaven thou
     art !

What would I be without thee? without thee
How dull were power, how joyless victory!
Though born of angels, if that smile of thine
Bless not my banner, 'twere but half divine.
But—why so mournful, child? those eyes, that
shone
All life last night—what!—is their glory gone?
Come, come—this morn's fatigue hath made
them pale,
They want rekindling—suns themselves would
fail,
Did not their comets bring, as I to thee,
From light's own fount supplies of brilliancy.
Thou see'st this cup—no juice of earth is here,
But the pure waters of that upper sphere,
Whose rills o'er ruby beds and topaz flow,
Catching the gem's bright color as they go.
Nightly my Genii come and fill these urns—
Nay, drink—in every drop life's essence burns;
'Twill make that soul all fire, those eyes all
light—
Come, come, I want thy loveliest smiles to-
night :—
There is a youth—why start?—thou saw'st him
then ;
Look'd he not nobly? such the godlike men
Thou'lt have to woo thee in the bowers
above ;—
Though _he_, I fear, hath thoughts too stern for
love,
Too rul'd by that cold enemy of bliss
The world calls virtue—we must conquer
this ;—

Nay, shrink not, pretty sage ! 'tis not for thee
To scan the mazes t Heaven's mystery :
The steel must pass through fire, ere it can
    yield
Fit instruments for mighty hands to wield.
This very night I mean to try the art
Of powerful beauty on that warrior's heart.
All that my Haram boasts of bloom and wit,
Of skill and charms, most rare and exquisite,
Shall tempt the boy ;—young MIRZALA's blue
    eyes,
Whose sleepy lid like snow on violets lies ;
AROUYA's cheeks, warm as a spring-day sun,
And lips that, like the seal of SOLOMON,
Have magic in their pressure ; ZEBA's lute,
And LILLA's dancing feet, that gleam and shoot
Rapid and white as sea-birds o'er the deep—
All shall combine their witching powers to steep
My convert's spirit in that soft'ning trance,
From which to heaven is but the next advance ;
That glowing, yielding fusion of the breast,
On which Religion stamps her image best.
But hear me, Priestess !—though each nymph
    of these
Hath some peculiar, practis'd power to please,
Some glance or step which, at the mirror tried,
First charms herself, then all the world beside ;
There still wants *one*, to make the victory sure.
One who in every look joins every lure ;
Through whom all beauty's beams concentred
    pass,
Dazzling and warm, as through love's burning
    glass ;

Whose gentle lips persuade without a word,
Whose words, ev'n when unmeaning, are
    ador'd,
Like inarticulate breathings from a shrine,
Which our faith takes for granted are divine !
Such is the nymph we want, all warmth and
    light,
To crown the rich temptations of to-night :
Such the refin'd enchantress that must be
This hero's vanquisher,—and thou art she ! "

With her hands clasp'd, her lips apart and
    pale,
The maid had stood, gazing upon the Veil
From which these words, like south winds
    through a fence
Of Kerzrah flowers, came fill'd with pesti-
    lence ; [55]
So boldly utter'd too ! as if all dread
Of frowns from her, of virtuous frowns, were
    fled,
And the wretch felt assur'd that, once plung'd
    in,
Her woman's soul would know no pause in sin !

At first, though mute she listen'd, like a
    dream
Seem'd all he said : nor could her mind, whose
    beam
As yet was weak, penetrate half his scheme.
But when, at length, he utter'd, "Thou art
    she ! "
All flash'd at once, and shrieking piteously,
4

"Oh not for worlds ! " she cried—" Great **God!**
    to whom
I once knelt innocent, is this my doom?
Are all my dreams, my hopes of heavenly bliss,
My purity, my pride then come to this,—
To live, the wanton of a fiend ! to be
The pander of his guilt—oh infamy !
And sunk, myself, as low as hell can steep
In its hot flood, drag others down as deep !
Others—ha ! yes—that youth who came to-
    day—
Not him I lov'd—not him—oh ! do but say,
But swear to me this moment 'tis not he,
And I will serve, dark fiend, will worship even
    thee ! "

"Beware, young raving thing !—in time
    beware,
Nor utter what I cannot, must not bear,
Even from *thy* lips. Go—try thy lute, thy
    voice,
The boy must feel their magic ;—I rejoice
To see those fires, no matter whence they rise.
Once more illuming my fair Priestess' eyes ;
And should the youth, whom soon those eyes
    shall warm,
Indeed resemble thy dead lover's form,
So much the happier wilt thou find thy doom,
As one warm lover, full of life and bloom,
Excels ten thousand cold ones in the tomb.
Nay, nay, no frowning, sweet !—those eyes
    were made
For love, not anger—I must be obey'd. "

"Obey'd!—'tis well—yes, I deserve it all—
On me, on me Heaven's vengeance cannot fall
Too heavily—but AZIM, brave and true
And beautiful—must *he* be ruin'd too?
Must *he* too, glorious as he is, be driven
A renegade like me from Love and Heaven?
Like me?—weak wretch, I wrong him—not
     like me;
No—he's all truth and strength and purity!
Fill up your madd'ning hell-cup to the brim,
Its witch'ry, fiends, will have no charm for him.
Let loose your glowing wantons from their
     bowers,
He loves, he loves, and can defy their powers!
Wretch as I am, in *his* heart still I reign
Pure as when first we met, without a stain!
Though ruin'd—lost—my memory, like a
     charm
Left by the dead, still keeps his soul from harm.
Oh! never let him know how deep the brow
He kiss'd at parting is dishonor'd now;—
Ne'er tell him how debas'd, how sunk is she,
Whom once he lov'd—once—*still* loves dotingly.
Thou laugh'st, tormentor—what! thou'lt brand
     my name?
Do, do—in vain—he'll not believe my shame—
He thinks me true; that nought beneath God's
     sky
Could tempt or change me, and—so once
     thought I.
But this is past—though worse than death my
     lot,
Than hell—'tis nothing while *he* knows it not.

Far off to some benighted land I'll fly,
Where sunbeam ne'er shall enter till I die ;
Where none will ask the lost one whence she
    came,
But I may fade and fall without a name.
And thou—curst man or fiend, whate'er thou
    art,
Who found'st this burning plague-spot in my
    heart,
And spread'st it—oh, so quick !—through soul
    and frame,
With more than demon's art, till I became
A loathsome thing, all pestilence, all flame !—
If when I'm gone——"

                    " Hold, fearless maniac, hold,
Nor tempt my rage—by Heaven, not half so
    bold
The puny bird, that dares with teasing hum
Within the crocodile's stretch'd jaws to come ! [56]
And so thou'lt fly, forsooth ?—what !—give up
    all
Thy chaste dominion in the Haram Hall,
Where now to Love and now to ALLA given,
Half mistress and half saint, thou hang'st as
    even
As doth MEDINA's tomb, 'twixt hell and heaven !
Thou'lt fly !—as easily may reptiles run,
The gaunt snake once hath fix'd his eyes
    upon ;
As easily, when caught, the prey may be
Pluck'd from his loving folds, as thou from
    me.

LALLA ROOKH.

No, no, 'tis fix'd—let good or ill betide,
Thou'rt mine till death, till death MOKANNA'S
    bride !
Hast thou forgot thy oath?"—

                At this dread word,
The Maid, whose spirit his rude taunts had
    stirr'd
Through all its depth, and rous'd an anger
    there,
That burst and lighten'd ev'n through her
    despair—
Shrunk back, as if a blight were in the breath
That spoke that word, and stagger'd, pale as
    death.

    "Yes, my sworn bride, let others seek in
    bowers
Their bridal place—the charnel vault was ours !
Instead of scents and balms, for thee and me
Rose the rich steams of sweet mortality ;
Gay, flickering death-lights shone while we
    were wed,
And, for our guests, a row of goodly Dead,
(Immortal spirits in their time, no doubt,)
From reeking shrouds upon the rite look'd out !
That oath thou heard'st more lips than thine
    repeal—
That cup—thou shudd'rest, Lady,—was it
    sweet?
That cup we pledg'd, the charnel's choicest
    wine,
Hath bound thee—ay, body and soul all mine;

Bound thee by chains that, whether blest or
      curst
No matter now, not hell itself shall burst !
Hence, woman, to the Haram, and look gay,
Look wild, look—anything but sad ; yet stay—
One moment more—from what this night hath
      pass'd,
I see thou know'st me, know'st me *well* at last.
Ha ! ha ! and so, fond thing, thou thought'st
      all true,
And that I love mankind ?—I do, I do—
As victims, love them ; as the sea-dog doats
Upon the small, sweet fry that round him
      floats,
Or, as the Nile-bird loves the slime that gives
That rank and venomous food on which she
      lives ! [57]—

      " And, now thou see'st my *soul's* angelic
      hue,
'Tis time these *features* were uncurtain'd too ;—
This brow, whose light—oh rare celestial
      light !
Hath been reserv'd to bless thy favor'd sight ;
These dazzling eyes, before whose shrouded
      might
Thou'st seen immortal Man kneel down and
      quake—
Would that they *were* heaven's lightnings for
      his sake !
But turn and look—-then wonder, if thou wilt,
That I should hate, should take revenge, by
      guilt,

Upon the hand, whose mischief or whose mirth
Sent me thus maim'd and monstrous upon
    earth ;
And on that race who, though more vile they
    be
Than mowing apes, are demi-gods to me !
Here—judge if hell, with all its power to damn,
Can add one curse to the foul thing I am ! "

He rais'd his veil—the Maid turn'd slowly
    round,
Look'd at him—shriek'd—and sunk upon the
    ground !

On their arrival, next night, at the place of
encampment, they were surprised and delighted
to find the groves all around illuminated ; some
artists of Yamtcheou [58] having been sent on
previously for the purpose. On each side of
the green alley, which led to the Royal Pavilion, artificial sceneries of bamboo-work [59] were
erected, representing arches, minarets, and
towers, from which hung thousands of silken
lanterns, painted by the most delicate pencils
of Canton. Nothing could be more beautiful
than the leaves of the mango-trees and aca-
cias, shining in the light of the bamboo-scenery,
which shed a lustre round as soft as that of the
nights of Peristan.

Lalla Rookh, however, who was too much
occupied by the sad story of Zelica and her
lover, to give a thought to anything else,

except, perhaps, him who related it, hurried on
through this scene of splendor to her pavilion,—
greatly to the mortification of the poor artists of
Yamtcheou,—and was followed with equal
rapidity by the Great Chamberlain, cursing, as
he went, that ancient Mandarin, whose parental
anxiety in lighting up the shores of the lake,
where his beloved daughter had wandered and
been lost, was the origin of these fantastic
Chinese illuminations. [60]

Without a moment's delay, young FERAMORZ
was introduced, and FADLADEEN, who could
never make up his mind as to the merits of a
poet till he knew the religious sect to which he
belonged, was about to ask him whether he
was a Shia or a Sooni, when LALLA ROOKH
impatiently clapped her hands for silence, and
the youth, being seated upon the musnud near
her, proceeded :—

PREPARE thy soul, young AZIM !—thou hast
    brav'd
The bands of GREECE, still mighty though
    enslav'd ;
Hast faced her phalanx, arm'd with all its fame,
Her Macedonian pikes and globes of flame ;
All this hast fronted, with firm heart and brow,
But a more perilous trial waits thee now,—
Woman's bright eyes, a dazzling host of eyes
From every land where woman smiles or sighs ;
Of every hue, as Love may chance to raise
His black or azure banner in their blaze ;

And each sweet mode of warfare, from the
    flash
That lightens boldly through the shadowy lash,
To the sly, stealing splendors, almost hid,
Like swords half-sheath'd, beneath the down-
    cast lid :—
Such, AZIM, is the lovely, luminous host
Now led against thee ; and, let conquerors
    boast
Their fields of fame, he who in virtue arms
A young, warm spirit against beauty's charms,
Who feels her brightness, yet defies her thrall,
Is the best, bravest conqueror of them all.

Now, through the Haram chambers, moving
    lights
And busy shapes proclaim the toilet's rites ;—
From room to room the ready handmaids hie,
Some skill'd to wreathe the turban tastefully,
Or hang the veil, in negligence of shade,
O'er the warm blushes of the youthful maid,
Who, if between the folds but *one* eye shone,
Like SEBA's Queen could vanquish with that
    one : [61]—
While some bring leaves of Henna, to imbue
The fingers' ends with a bright roseate hue,[62]
So bright, that in the mirror's depth they seem
Like tips of coral branches in the stream ;
And others mix the Kohol's jetty dye,
To give that long, dark languish to the eye,[63]
Which makes the maids, whom kings are
    proud to cull
From fair Circassia's vales, so beautiful.

All **is** in motion ; rings and plumes **and**
    pearls
Are shining everywhere :—some younger girls
Are gone by moonlight to the garden beds,
To gather fresh, cool chaplets for their
    heads ;—
Gay creatures ! sweet, though mournful, 'tis to
    see
How each prefers a garland from that tree
Which brings to mind her childhood's **innocent**
    day,
And the dear fields and friendships far **away.**
The maid of INDIA, blest again to hold
In her full lap the Champac's leaves of gold,[64]
Thinks of the time when, by the GANGES' flood,
Her little playmates scatter'd many a bud
Upon her long black hair, with glossy gleam
Just dripping from the consecrated stream ;
While the young Arab, haunted by the smell
Of her own mountain flowers, as by a spell,—
The sweet Elcaya,[65] and that courteous tree
Which bows to all who seek its canopy,[66]
Sees, call'd up round her by these magic **scents,**
The well, the camels, and her father's tents :
Sighs for the home she left with little pain
And wishes even its sorrows back again !

    Meanwhile, through vast illuminated **halls,**
Silent and bright, where nothing but the **falls**
Of fragrant waters, gushing with cool sound
From many a jasper fount, is heard around,
Young AZIM roams bewilder'd,—nor can **guess**
What means this maze of light and loneliness.

Here, the way leads, o'er tesselated floors
Or mats of CAIRO, through long corridors,
Where, ranged in cassolets and silver urns.
Sweet wood of aloe or of sandal burns ;
And spicy rods, such as illume at night
The bowers of TIBET, [67] send forth odorous
    light,
Like Peris' wands, when pointing out the
    road
For some pure Spirit to its blest abode :—
And here, at once, the glittering saloon
Bursts on his sight, boundless and bright as
    noon ;
Where, in the midst, reflecting back the rays
In broken rainbows, a fresh fountain plays
High as the enamell'd cupola, which towers
All rich with Arabesques of gold and flowers ;
And the mosaic floor beneath shines through
The sprinkling of that fountain's silv'ry dew,
Like the wet, glistening shells, of every dye,
That on the margin of the Red Sea lie.

Here, too, he traces the kind visitings
Of woman's love in those fair, living things
Of land and wave, whose fate—in bondage
    thrown
For their weak loveliness—is like her own !
On one side gleaming with a sudden grace
Through water, brilliant as the crystal vase
In which it undulates, small fishes shine,
Like golden ingots from a fairy mine ;—
While, on the other, latticed lightly in
With odoriferous woods of COMORIN, [68]

Each brilliant bird that wings the air is seen ;—
Gay, sparkling loories, such as gleam between
The crimson blossoms of the coral tree [69]
In the warm Isles of India's sunny sea :
Mecca's blue sacred pigeon, [70] and the thrush
Of Hindostan, [71] whose holy warblings gush,
At evening, from the tall pagoda's top ;—
Those golden birds that, in the spice-time,
    drop
About the gardens, drunk with that sweet
    food [72]
Whose scent hath lur'd them o'er the summer
    flood ; [73]
And those that under Araby's soft sun
Build their high nests of budding cinnamon : [74]
In short, all rare and beauteous things, that
    fly
Through the pure element, here calmly lie
Sleeping in light, like the green birds [75] that
    dwell
In Eden's radiant fields of asphodel !

So on, through scenes past all imagining,
More like the luxuries of that impious King, [76]
Whom Death's dark angel, with his lightning
    torch,
Struck down and blasted even in Pleasure's
    porch,
Than the pure dwelling of a Prophet sent,
Arm'd with Heaven's sword, for man's enfran-
    chisement—
Young Azim wander'd, looking sternly round,
His simple garb and war-boots' clanking sound

But ill according with the pomp and grace
And silent lull of that voluptuous place.

"Is this, then," thought the youth, "is this
    the way
To free man's spirit from the dead'ning sway
Of worldly sloth,—to teach him, while he
    lives,
To know no bliss but that which virtue gives,
And, when he dies, to leave his lofty name
A light, a landmark on the cliffs of fame?
It was not so, Land of the generous thought
And daring deed, thy godlike sages taught ;
It was not thus, in bowers of wanton ease,
Thy Freedom nurs'd her sacred energies ;
Oh! not beneath the enfeebling, withering
    glow
Of such dull luxury did those myrtles grow,
With which she wreath'd her sword, when she
    would dare
Immortal deeds ; but in the bracing air
Of toil, —of temperance, — of that high, rare,
Ethereal virtue, which alone can breathe
Life, health, and lustre into Freedom's wreath.
Who, that surveys this span of earth we press,—
This speck of life in time's great wilderness,
This narrow isthmus 'twixt two boundless seas,
The past, the future, two eternities!
Would sully the bright spot, or leave it bare,
When he might build him a proud temple
    there,
A name, that long shall hallow all its space,
And be each purer soul's high resting-place?

But no—it cannot be, that one, whom God
Hath sent to break the wizard Falsehood's
    rod,—
A Prophet of the Truth, whose mission draws
Its rights from Heaven, should thus profane its
    cause
With the world's vulgar pomp;—no, no,—I
    see—
He thinks me weak—this glare of luxury
Is but to tempt, to try the eaglet gaze
Of my young soul—shine on, 'twill stand the
    blaze!"

  So thought the youth;—but, ev'n while he
    defied
This witching scene, he felt its witchery glide
Through ev'ry sense. The perfume breathing
    round,
Like a pervading spirit;—the still sound
Of falling waters, lulling as the song
Of Indian bees at sunset, when they throng
Around the fragrant NILICA, and deep
In its blue blossoms hum themselves to sleep;"
And music, too—dear music! that can touch
Beyond all else the soul that loves it much—
Now heard far off, so far as but to seem
Like the faint, exquisite music of a dream;
All was too much for him, too full of bliss,
The heart could nothing feel, that felt not
    this;
Soften'd he sank upon a couch, and gave
His soul up to sweet thoughts, like wave on
    wave

Succeeding to smooth seas, when storms are
    laid ;
He thought of ZELICA, his own dear maid,
And of the time when, full of blissful sighs,
They sat and look'd into each other's eyes,
Silent and happy—as if God had given
Nought else worth looking at on this side
    heaven.

"Oh, my lov'd mistress, thou, whose spirit still
Is with me, round me, wander where I will—
It is for thee, for thee alone I seek
The paths of glory ; to light up thy cheek
With warm approval—in that gentle look
To read my praise, as in an angel's book,
And think all toils rewarded, when from thee
I gain a smile worth immortality !
How shall I bear the moment when restor'd
To that young heart where I alone am Lord,
Though of such bliss unworthy,—since the best
Alone deserve to be the happiest ;—
When from those lips, unbreath'd upon for
    years,
I shall again kiss off the soul-felt tears,
And find those tears warm as when last they
    started,
Those sacred kisses pure as when we parted ?
O my own life !—why should a single day,
A moment, keep me from those arms away ?"

While thus he thinks, still nearer on the
    breeze
Come those delicious, dream-like harmonies.

Each note of which but adds new, downy links
To the soft chain in which his spirit sinks.
He turns him tow'rd the sound, and far away
Through a long vista, sparkling with the play
Of countless lamps,—like the rich track which
    Day
Leaves on the waters, when he sinks from us,
So long the path, its light so tremulous ;—
He sees a group of female forms advance,
Some chain'd together in the mazy dance
By fetters, forged in the green sunny bowers,
As they were captives to the King of Flowers ;[78]
And some disporting round, unlink'd and free,
Who seem'd to mock their sisters' slavery ;
And round and round them still, in wheeling
    flight,
Went, like gay moths about a lamp at night ;
While others walk'd, as gracefully along
Their feet kept time, the very soul of song,
From psaltery, pipe, and lutes of heavenly thrill,
Or their own youthful voices, heavenlier still.
And now they come, now pass before his eye,
Forms such as Nature moulds, when she would
    vie
With Fancy's pencil, and give birth to things,
Lovely beyond its fairest picturings.
Awhile they dance before him, then divide,
Breaking, like rosy clouds at even-tide
Around the rich pavilion of the sun,—
Till silently dispersing, one by one
Through many a path, that from the chamber
    leads
To gardens, terraces, and moonlight meads,

Their distant laughter comes upon the wind,
And but one trembling nymph remains behind,
Beck'ning them back in vain, for they are gone,
And she is left in all that light alone ;
No veil to curtain o'er her beauteous brow,
In its young bashfulness more beauteous now ;
But a light golden chain-work round her hair,⁷⁹
Such as the maids of YEZD ⁸⁰ and SHIRAS wear,
From which, on either side, gracefully hung
A golden amulet, in the Arab tongue
Engraven o'er with some immortal line
From Holy Writ, or bard scarce less divine ;
While her left hand, as shrinkingly she stood,
Held a small lute of gold and sandal-wood,
Which, once or twice, she touch'd with hurried
     strain,
Then took her trembling fingers off again.
But when at length a timid glance she stole
At AZIM, the sweet gravity of soul
She saw through all his features calm'd her fear,
And, like a half-tam'd antelope, more near,
Though shrinking still, she came ;—then sat
     her down
Upon a musnud's ⁸¹ edge, and, bolder grown,
In the pathetic mode of ISFAHAN ⁸²
Touch'd a preluding strain, and thus began :

There's a bower of roses by BENDEMEER's
     stream,
     And the nightingale sings round it all the
          day long ;
     5

In the time of my childhood 'twas like a sweet
      dream,
   To sit in the roses and hear the bird's song.

That bower and its music I never forget,
   But oft when alone in the bloom of the
      year,
I think—is the nightingale singing there yet?
   Are the roses still bright by the calm
      BENDEMEER?

No, the roses soon wither'd that hung o'er the
      wave,
   But some blossoms were gather'd, while
      freshly they shone,
And a dew was distill'd from their flowers, that
      gave
   All the fragrance of summer, when summer
      was gone.

Thus memory draws from delight, ere it dies,
   An essence that breathes of it many a year;
Thus bright to my soul, as 'twas then to my
      eyes,
   Is that bower on the banks of the calm
      BENDEMEER.

"Poor maiden!" thought the youth, "if
      thou wert sent,
With thy soft lute and beauty's blandishment,
To wake unholy wishes in this heart,
Or tempt its truth, thou little know'st the art.

For though thy lip should sweetly counsel
    wrong,
Those vestal eyes would disavow its song.
But thou hast breath'd such purity, thy lay
Returns so fondly to youth's virtuous day,
And leads thy soul—if e'er it wander'd thence—
So gently back to its first innocence,
That I would sooner stop the unchain'd dove,
When swift returning to its home of love,
And round its snowy wings new fetters twine,
Than turn from virtue one pure wish of thine!"

Scarce had this feeling pass'd, when, spark-
    ling through
The gently open'd curtains of light blue
That veil'd the breezy casement, countless
    eyes,
Peeping ike stars through the blue evening
    skies
Look'd laughing in, as if to mock the pair
That sat so still and melancholy there :—
And now the curtains fly apart, and in
From the cool air, 'mid showers of jessamine
Which those without fling after them in play,
Two lightsome maidens spring,—lightsome as
    they
Who live in the air on odors,—and around
The bright saloon, scarce conscious of the
    ground,
Chase one another, in a varying dance
Of mirth and languor, coyness and advance,
Too eloquently like love's warm pursuit :—
While she, who sung so gently to the lute

Her dream of home, steals timidly away,
Shrinking as violets do in summer's ray,—
But takes with her from AZIM's heart that sigh
We sometimes give to forms that pass us by
In the world's crowd, too lovely to remain,
Creatures of light we never see again !

Around the white necks of the nymphs who
　　danc'd
Hung carcanets of orient gems, that glanc'd
More brilliant than the sea-glass glittering o'er
The hills of crystal on the Caspian shore ; [84]
While from their long, dark tresses, in a fall
Of curls descending, bells as musical
As those that, on the golden-shafted trees
Of EDEN, shake in the eternal breeze, [85]
Rung round their steps, at every bound more
　　sweet,
As 'twere the ecstatic language of their feet.
At length the chase was o'er, and they stood
　　wreath'd
Within each other's arms ; while soft there
　　breath'd
Through the cool casement, mingled with the
　　sighs
Of moonlight flowers, music that seem'd to rise
From some still lake, so liquidly it rose ;
And, as it swell'd again at each faint close,
The ear could track, through all that maze of
　　chords
And young sweet voices, these impassion'd
　　words :

A Spirit there is, whose fragrant sigh
  Is burning now through earth and air :
Where cheeks are blushing, the Spirit is nigh ;
  Where lips are meeting, the Spirit is there !

His breath is the soul of flowers like these,
  And his floating eyes—oh ! *they* resemble [86]
Blue water-lilies, [87] when the breeze
  Is making the stream around them tremble.

Hail to thee, hail to thee, kindling power !
  Spirit of Love, Spirit of Bliss !
Thy holiest time is the moonlight hour,
  And there never was moonlight so sweet as
    this

        By the fair and brave
          Who blushing unite,
        Like the sun and wave,
          When they meet at night;

        By the tear that shows
          When passion is nigh,
        As the rain-drop flows
          From the heat of the sky;

        By the first love-beat
          Of the youthful heart,
        By the bliss to meet,
          And the pain to part ;

        By all that thou hast
          To mortals given,
        Which—oh, could it last,
          This earth were heaven !

We call thee hither, entrancing Power !
   Spirit of Love ! Spirit of Bliss !
Thy holiest time is the moonlight hour,
   And there never was moonlight so sweet as
      this.

————

Impatient of a scene whose luxuries stole,
Spite of himself, too deep into his soul,
And where, 'midst all that the young heart
   loves most—
Flowers, music, smiles—to yield was to be
   lost,
The youth had started up, and turn'd away
From the light nymphs, and their luxurious
   lay,
To muse upon the pictures that hung round,[88]—
Bright images, that spoke without a sound ;
And views, like vistas into fairy ground.
But here again new spells came o'er his sense:—
All that the pencil's mute omnipotence
Could call up into life, of soft and fair,
Of fond and passionate, was glowing there ;
Nor yet too warm, but touch'd with that fine
   art
Which paints of pleasure but the purer part ;
Which knows even Beauty when half-veil'd is
   best,
Like her own radiant planet of the west,
Whose orb when half-retir'd looks loveliest.[89]
There hung the history of the Genii-King,
Traced through each gay, voluptuous wander-
   ing

With her from SABA's bowers, in whose bright
    eyes
He read that to be blest is to be wise; [90]—
Here fond ZULEIKA [91] woos with open arms
The Hebrew boy, who flies from her young
    charms,
Yet, flying, turns to gaze, and, half undone,
Wishes that Heaven and she could *both* be won;
And here MOHAMMED, born for love and guile,
Forgets the Koran in his MARY's smile;—
Then beckons some kind angel from above
With a new text to consecrate their love. [92]

With rapid step, yet pleas'd and ling'ring eye,
Did the youth pass these pictur'd stories by,
And hasten'd to a casement, where the light
Of the calm moon came in, and freshly bright
The fields without were seen, sleeping as still
As if no life remain'd in breeze or rill.
Here paus'd he, while the music, now less near,
Breath'd with a holier language on his ear,
As though the distance, and that heavenly ray
Through which the sounds came floating, took
    away
All that had been too earthly in the lay.

Oh! could he listen to such sounds unmov'd,
And by that light—nor dream of her he lov'd?
Dream on, unconscious boy! while yet thou
    may'st;
'Tis the last bliss thy soul shall ever taste.
Clasp yet awhile her image to thy heart,
Ere all the light, that made it dear, depart.

Think of her smiles as when thou saw'st them
      last,
Clear, beautiful, by nought of earth o'ercast;
Recall her tears, to thee at parting given,
Pure as they weep, *if* angels weep, in Heaven.
Think, in her own still bower she waits thee
      now,
With the same glow of heart and bloom of brow,
Yet shrin'd in solitude—thine all, thine only,
Like the one star above thee, bright and lonely.
Oh! that a dream so sweet, so long enjoy'd,
Should be so sadly, cruelly destroy'd!

      The song is hush'd, the laughing nymphs are
            flown,
And he is left, musing of bliss, alone ;—
Alone ?—no, not alone—that heavy sigh,
That sob of grief, which broke from some one
      nigh—
Whose could it be?—alas! is misery found
Here, even here, on this enchanted ground?
He turns, and sees a female form, close veil'd,
Leaning, as if both heart and strength had
      fail'd,
Against a pillow near ;—not glittering o'er
With gem and wreaths, such as the others wore,
But in that deep-blue, melancholy dress,[98]
BOKHARA's maidens wear in mindfulness
Of friends or kindred, dead or far away ;—
And such as ZELICA had on that day
He left her—when, with heart too full to speak,
He took away her last warm tears upon his
      cheek.

A strange emotion stirs within him,—more
Than mere compassion ever wak'd before;
Unconsciously he opes his arms, while she
Springs forward, as with life's last energy,
But, swooning in that one convulsive bound,
Sinks, ere she reach his arms, upon the
    ground ;—
Her veil falls off—her faint hands clasp his
    knees—
'Tis she herself!—'tis ZELICA he sees!
But, ah, so pale, so chang'd—none but a lover
Could in that wreck of beauty's shrine discover
The once ador'd divinity—even he
Stood for some moments mute, and doubtingly
Put back the ringlets from her brow, and gaz'd
Upon those lids, where once such lustre blaz'd,
Ere he could think she was *indeed* his own,
Own darling maid, whom he so long had
    known
In joy and sorrow, beautiful in both ;
Who, even when grief was heaviest—when loth
He left her for the wars—in that worst hour
Sat in her sorrow like the sweet night-flower,[91]
When darkness brings its weeping glories out,
And spreads its sighs like frankincense about.

    "Look up, my ZELICA—one moment show
Those gentle eyes to me, that I may know
Thy life, thy loveliness is not all gone,
But *there*, at least, shines as it ever shone.
Come, look upon thy AZIM—one dear glance,
Like those of old, were heaven! whatever
    chance

Hath brought thee here, oh, 'twas a blessed
    one !
There—my lov'd lips—they move—that kiss
    hath run
Like the first shoot of life through every vein,
And now I clasp her, mine, all mine again.
Oh the delight—now, in this very hour,
When had the whole rich world been in my
    power,
I should have singled out thee, only thee,
From the whole world's collected treasury—
To have thee here—to hang thus fondly o'er
My own, best, purest ZELICA once more !"

It was indeed the touch of those fond lips
Upon her eyes that chas'd their short eclipse ;
And, gradual as the snow, at Heaven's breath,
Melts off and shows the azure flowers beneath,
Her lids unclos'd, and the bright eyes were seen
Gazing on his—not, as they late had been,
Quick, restless, wild, but mournfully serene ;
As if to lie, even for that tranced minute,
So near his heart, had consolation in it ;
And thus to wake in his belov'd caress
Took from her soul one half its wretchedness.
But, when she heard him call her good and
    pure,
Oh, 'twas too much—too dreadful to endure !
Shudd'ring she broke away from his embrace,
And, hiding with both hands her guilty face,
Said, in a tone whose anguish would have riven
A heart of very marble, "Pure ! — oh,
    Heaven ! "—

That tone—those looks so chang'd—the
   withering blight
That sin and sorrow leave where'er they light;
The dead despondency of those sunk eyes,
Where once, had he thus met her by surprise,
He would have seen himself, too happy boy,
Reflected in a thousand lights of joy;
And then the place,—that bright, unholy place,
Where vice lay hid beneath each winning grace
And charm of luxury, as the viper weaves
Its wily covering of sweet balsam leaves,[95]—
All struck upon his heart, sudden and cold
As death itself ;—it needs not to be told—
No, no—he sees it all, plain as the brand
Of burning shame can mark—whate'er the
   hand,
That could from Heaven and him such bright-
   ness sever
'Tis done—to Heaven and him she's lost for-
   ever !
It was a dreadful moment ; not the tears,
The lingering, lasting misery of years
Could match that minute's anguish—all the
   worst
Of sorrow's elements in that dark burst
Broke o'er his soul, and, with one crash of
   fate,
Laid the whole hopes of his life desolate.

   "Oh ! curse me not," she cried, as wild he
      toss'd
His desperate hand tow'rd Heaven—"though
   I am lost,

Think not that guilt, that falsehood made me
    fall :
No, no—'twas grief, 'twas madness did it all !
Nay, doubt me not—though all thy love hath
    ceas'd—
I know it hath—yet, yet believe, at least,
That every spark of reason's light must be
Quench'd in this brain, ere I could stray from
    thee.
They told me thou wert dead—why, Azim, why
Did we not, both of us, that instant die
When we were parted? Oh ! couldst thou but
    know
With what deep devotedness of woe
I wept thy absence—o'er and o'er again
Thinking of thee, still thee, till thought grew
    pain,
And memory, like a drop that, night and day,
Falls cold and ceaseless, wore my heart away.
Didst thou but know how pale I sat at home,
My eyes still turn'd the way thou wert to
    come,
And, all the long, long night of hope and
    fear,
Thy voice and step still sounding in my ear—
O God ! thou wouldst not wonder that, at last,
When every hope was all at once o'ercast,
When I heard frightful voices round me say,
Azim is dead !—this wretched brain gave way,
And I became a wreck, at random driven,
Without one glimpse of reason or of Heaven—
All wild—and even this quenchless love within
Turn'd to foul fires to light me into sin !—

Thou pitiest me—I knew thou wouldst—that
    sky
Hath nought beneath it half so lorn as I.
The fiend who lur'd me hither—hist! come
    near,
Or thou too, *thou* art lost, if he should hear—
Told me such things—oh! with such devilish
    art
As would have ruin'd even a holier heart—
Of thee, and of that ever-radiant sphere,
Where bless'd at length, if I but serv'd *him*
    here,
I should forever live in thy dear sight,
And drink from those pure eyes eternal light.
Think, think how lost, how madden'd I must
    be,
To hope that guilt could lead to God or thee!
Thou weep'st for me—do weep—oh, that I
    durst
Kiss off that tear! but, no—these lips are curst,
They must not touch thee ;—one divine caress,
One blessed moment of forgetfulness
I've had within those arms, and *that* shall lie,
Shrin'd in my soul's deep memory till I die ;
The last of joy's last relics here below,
The one sweet drop, in all this waste of woe,
My heart has treasur'd from affection's spring,
To soothe and cool its deadly withering !
But thou—yes, thou must go—forever go ;
This place is not for thee—for thee ! oh no !
Did I but tell thee half, thy tortur'd brain
Would burn like mine, and mine grow wild
    again !

Enough, that Guilt reigns here—that hearts,
once good,
Now tainted, chill'd, and broken, are his food.—
Enough, that we are parted—that there rolls
A flood of headlong fate between our souls,
Whose darkness severs me as wide from thee
As hell from heaven, to all eternity ! "

"ZELICA, ZELICA ! " the youth exclaim'd,
In all the tortures of a mind inflam'd
Almost to madness—" by that sacred Heaven,
Where yet, if prayers can move, thou'lt be for-
    given,
As thou art here—here, in this writhing heart,
All sinful, wild, and ruin'd as thou art !
By the remembrance of our once pure love,
Which, like a churchyard light, still burns above
The grave of our lost souls—which guilt in thee
Cannot extinguish, nor despair in me !
I do conjure, implore thee to fly hence—
If thou hast yet one spark of innocence,
Fly with me from this place——"
                    "With thee ! oh bliss !
'Tis worth whole years of torment to hear this.
What ! take the lost one with thee ?—let her
    rove
By thy dear side, as in those days of love,
When we were both so happy, both so pure—
Too heavenly dream ! if there's on earth a cure
For the sunk heart, 'tis this—day after day
To be the blest companion of thy way ;
To hear thy angel eloquence—to see
Those virtuous eyes forever turn'd on me ;

And, in their light re-chasten'd silently,
Like the stain'd web that whitens in the sun,
Grow pure by being purely shone upon !
And thou wilt pray for me—I know thou wilt—
At the dim vesper hour, when thoughts of guilt
Come heaviest o'er the heart, thou'lt lift thine
    eyes,
Full of sweet tears, unto the dark'ning skies,
And plead for me with Heaven, till I can dare
To fix my own weak, sinful glances there ;
Till the good angels, when they see me cling
Forever near thee, pale and sorrowing,
Shall for thy sake pronounce my soul forgiven,
And bid thee take thy weeping slave to
    Heaven !
Oh yes, I'll fly with thee——"

              Scarce had she said
These breathless words, when a voice deep and
    dread
As that of MONKER, waking up the dead
From their first sleep—so startling 'twas to
    both—
Rung through the casement near, "Thy oath !
    thy oath !"
Oh Heaven, the ghastliness of that Maid's
    look !—
"'Tis he," faintly she cried, while terror shook
Her inmost core, nor durst she lift her eyes,
Though through the casement, now, nought
    but the skies
And moonlit fields were seen, calm as before—
"'Tis he, and I am his—all, all is o'er—

Go—fly this instant, or thou'rt ruin'd too—
My oath, my oath, O God ! 'tis all too true,
True as the worm in this cold heart it is—
I am MOKANNA'S bride—his, AZIM, his—
The Dead stood round us, while I spoke that
    vow ;
Their blue lips echo'd it—I hear them now !
Their eyes glar'd on me, while I pledg'd that
    bowl :
'Twas burning blood—I feel it in my soul !
And the Veil'd Bridegroom—hist ! I've seen to-
    night
What angels know not of—so foul a sight,
So horrible—oh ! never may'st thou see
What *there* lies hid from all but hell and me !
But I must hence—off, off—I am not thine,
Nor Heaven's, nor Love's, nor aught that is
    divine—
Hold me not—ha ! think'st thou the fiends that
    sever
Hearts, cannot sunder hands ?—thus, then—
    forever ! "

    With all that strength which madness lends
    the weak,
She flung away his arm ; and, with a shriek,
Whose sound, though he should linger out
    more years
Than wretch e'er told, can never leave his
    ears—
Flew up through that long avenue of light,
Fleetly as some dark, ominous bird of night
Across the sun, and soon was out of sight !

LALLA ROOKH could think of nothing all day
but the misery of these two young lovers.
Her gayety was gone, and she looked pensively
even upon FADLADEEN. She felt, too, without
knowing why, a sort of uneasy pleasure in
imagining that AZIM must have been just such
a youth as FERAMORZ ; just as worthy to enjoy
all the blessings, without any of the pangs,
of that illusive passion which too often, like
the sunny apples of Istkahar,[96] is all sweetness
on one side, and all bitterness on the other.

As they passed along a sequestered river
after sunset, they saw a young Hindoo girl
upon the bank,[97] whose employment seemed to
them so strange that they stopped their palankeens to observe her. She had lighted a small
lamp, filled with oil of cocoa, and, placing it
in an earthen dish, adorned with a wreath of
flowers, had committed it with a trembling
hand to the stream ; and was now anxiously
watching its progress down the current, heed-
less of the gay cavalcade which had drawn up
beside her. LALLA ROOKH was all curiosity ;—
when one of her attendants, who had lived
upon the banks of the Ganges (where this
ceremony is so frequent, that often, in the dusk
of the evening, the river is seen glittering all
over with lights, like the Oton-tala, or Sea of
Stars [98]), informed the Princess that it was the
usual way in which the friends of those who
had gone on dangerous voyages offered up
vows for their safe return. If the lamp sunk
immediately, the omen was disastrous : but if

6

it went shining down the stream, and continued to burn until entirely out of sight, the
return of the beloved object was considered as
certain.

LALLA ROOKH, as they moved on, more than
once looked back to observe how the young
Hindoo's lamp proceeded; and while she saw
with pleasure that it was still unextinguished,
she could not help fearing that all the hopes of
this life were no better than that feeble light
upon the river. The remainder of the journey
was passed in silence. She now, for the first
time, felt that shade of melancholy which
comes over the youthful maiden's heart, as
sweet and transient as her own breath upon a
mirror: nor was it till she heard the lute of
FERAMORZ, touched lightly at the door of her
pavilion, that she waked from the reverie in
which she had been wandering. Instantly her
eyes were lighted up with pleasure; and after
a few unheard remarks from FADLADEEN, upon
the indecorum of a poet seating himself in
presence of a Princess, everything was arranged
as on the preceding evening, and all listened
with eagerness, while the story was thus continued:

WHOSE are the gilded tents that crown the
    way,
Where all was waste and silent yesterday?
This City of War, which, in a few short hours,
Hath sprung up here,[99] as if the magic power

Of Him who, in the twinkling of a star,
Built the high pillar'd halls of CHILMINAR, [100]
Had conjur'd up, far as the eye can see,
This world of tents, and domes, and sun-bright
    armory :
Princely pavilions, screen'd by many a fold
Of crimson cloth, and topp'd with balls of
    gold :—
Steeds, with their housings of rich silver spun,
Their chains and poitrels, glittering in the sun ;
And camels, tufted o'er with Yemen's shells, [101]
Shaking in every breeze their light-ton'd bells !

But yester-eve, so motionless around,
So mute was this wide plain, that not a sound
But the far torrent, or the locust bird [102]
Hunting among the thickets, could be heard ;—
Yet hark ! what discords now, of every kind,
Shouts, laughs, and screams are revelling in
    the wind ;
The neigh of cavalry ;—the tinkling throngs
Of laden camels and their drivers' songs ; [103]—
Ringing of arms, and flapping in the breeze
Of streamers from ten thousand canopies ;—
War music, bursting out from time to time,
With gong and tymbalon's tremendous chime;—
Or, in the pause, when harsher sounds are mute,
The mellow breathings of some horn or flute,
That far off, broken by the eagle note
Of the Abyssinian trumpet, [104] swell and float.

Who leads this mighty army ?—ask ye
    " who ? "
And mark ye not those banners of dark hue,

The Night and Shadow,[105] over **yonder tent?—**
It is the CALIPH's glorious armament.
Roused in his Palace by the dread alarms,
That hourly came, of the false Prophet's **arms,**
And of his host of infidels, who hurl'd
Defiance fierce at ISLAM [106] and the world,—
Though worn with Grecian warfare, and
 behind
The veils of his bright Palace calm reclin'd,
Yet brook'd he not such blasphemy should
 stain,
Thus unreveng'd, the evening of his reign ;
But, having sworn upon the Holy Grave [107]
To conquer or to perish, once more gave
His shadowy banners proudly to the breeze,
And with an army, nurs'd in victories,
Here stands to crush the rebels that o'errun
His blest and beauteous Province of the Sun.

Ne'er did the march of MAHADI display
Such pomp before ;—not even when on his **way**
To MECCA's Temple, when both land and sea
Were spoil'd to feed the Pilgrim's luxury ;[108]
When round him, 'mid the burning sands, **he**
 saw
Fruits of the North in icy freshness thaw,
And cool'd his thirsty lip, beneath the glow
Of MECCA's sun, with urns of Persian snow :[109]—
Nor e'er did armament more grand than that
Pour from the kingdoms of the Caliphat.
First, in the van, the People of the Rock,[110]
On their light mountain steeds, of **royal**
 stock :[111]

Then, chieftains of DAMASCUS, proud to see
The flashing of their swords' rich marque-
    try ;[112]—
Men from the regions near the VOLGA's mouth,
Mix'd with the rude, black archers of the
    South ;
And Indian lancers, in white-turban'd ranks,
From the far SINDE, or ATTOCK's sacred banks,
With dusky legions from the 'land of Myrrh,[113]
And many a mace-arm'd Moor and Mid-sea
    islander.

  Nor less in number, though more new and
    rude
In warfare's school, was the vast multitude
That, fir'd by zeal, or by oppression wrong'd,
Round the white standard of the Impostor
    throng'd.
Beside his thousand of Believers blind,
Burning and headlong as the Samiel wind—
Many who felt, and more who fear'd to feel
The bloody Islamite's converting teel,
Flock'd to his banner ;—Chiefs of the UZBEK
    race,
Waving their heron crests with martial grace ;[114]
TURKOMANS, countless as their flocks, led forth
From the aromatic pastures of the North ;
Wild warriors of the turquoise hills,[115]—and
    those
Who dwell beyond the everlasting snows
Of HINDOO KOSH,[116] in stormy freedom bred,
Their fort the rock, their camp the torrent's
    bed.

But none, of all who own'd the Chief's com-
    mand,
Rush'd to that battle-field with bolder hand,
Or sterner hate, than IRAN's outlaw'd men,
Her Worshippers of Fire[117]—all panting then
For vengeance on the accursed Saracen ;
Vengeance at last for their dear country spurn'd,
Her throne usurp'd, and her bright shrines
    o'erturn'd.
From YEZD's [118] eternal Mansion of the Fire,
Where aged saints in dreams of Heaven expire:
From BADKU, and those fountains of blue flame
That burn into the CASPIAN, [119] fierce they came,
Careless for what or whom the blow was sped,
So vengeance triumph'd, and their tyrants bled.

Such was the wild and miscellaneous host,
That high in air their motley banners tost
Around the Prophet-Chief—all eyes still bent
Upon that glittering Veil, where'er it went,
That beacon through the battle's stormy flood,
That rainbow of the field, whose showers
    were blood.

Twice hath the sun upon their conflict set,
And risen again, and found them grappling
    yet ;
While streams of carnage, in his noontide
    blaze,
Smoke up to Heaven—hot as that crimson
    haze
By which the prostrate Caravan is aw'd, [120]
In the red Desert, when the wind's abroad.

"On, Swords of God!" the panting CALIPH
    calls,—
"Thrones for the living—Heaven for him who
    falls!"
"On, brave avengers, on," MOKANNA cries,
"And EBLIS blast the recreant slave that flies!"
Now comes the brunt, the crisis of the day—
They clash—they strive—the CALIPH'S troops
    give way!
MOKANNA'S self plucks the black Banner down,
And now the Orient World's Imperial crown,
Is just within his grasp—when, hark, that
    shout!
Some hand hath check'd the flying Moslems'
    rout;
And now they turn, they rally—at their head
A warrior, (like those angel youths who led,
In glorious panoply of heaven's own mail,
The Champions of the Faith through BEDER'S
    vale, [121])
Bold as if gifted with ten thousand lives,
Turns on the fierce pursuers' blades, and drives
At once the multitudinous torrent back—
While hope and courage kindle in his track;
And, at each step, his bloody falchion makes
Terrible vistas through which victory breaks!
In vain MOKANNA, 'midst the general flight,
Stands, like the red moon, on some stormy
    night,
Among the fugitive clouds that, hurrying by,
Leave only her unshaken in the sky—
In vain he yells his desperate curses out,
Deals death promiscuously to all about,

To foes that charge and coward friends that fly,
And seems of *all* the Great Arch-enemy.
The panic spreads—"A miracle!" throughout
The Moslem ranks, "a miracle!" they shout,
All gazing on that youth, whose coming seems
A light, a glory, such as breaks in dreams;
And every sword, true as o'er billows dim
The needle tracks the lodestar, following him!

  Right tow'rds MOKANNA now he cleaves his
      path,
Impatient cleaves, as though the bolt of wrath
He bears from Heaven withheld its awful burst
From weaker heads, and souls but half way
      curst,
To break o'er Him, the mightiest and the worst!
But vain his speed—though, in that hour of
      blood,
Had all God's seraphs round MOKANNA stood,
With swords of fire, ready like fate to fall,
MOKANNA'S soul would have defied them all;
Yet now, the rush of fugitives, too strong
For human force, hurries even *him* along;
In vain he struggles 'mid the wedg'd array
Of flying thousands—he is borne away;
And the sole joy his baffled spirit knows,
In this forc'd flight, is—murdering as he goes!
As a grim tiger, whom the torrent's might
Surprises in some parch'd ravine at night,
Turns, even in drowning, on the wretched
      flocks,
Swept with him in that snow-flood from the
      rocks,

And, to the last, devouring on his way,
Bloodies the stream he hath not power to stay.

" Alla illa Alla ! "—the glad shout renew—
" Alla Akbar ! " [122]—the Caliph's in MErou.
Hang out your gilded tapestry in the streets,
And light your shrines and chant your zira-
    leets. [123]
The Swords of God have triumph'd—on his
    throne
Your Caliph sits, and the Veil'd Chief hath flown.
Who does not envy that young warrior now,
To whom the Lord of Islam bends his brow,
In all the graceful gratitude of power,
For his throne's safety in that perilous hour?
Who doth not wonder, when, amidst the
    acclaim
Of thousands, heralding to heaven his name—
'Mid all those holier harmonies of fame,
Which sound along the path of virtuous souls,
Like music round a planet as it rolls,—
He turns away—coldly, as if some gloom
Hung o'er his heart no triumphs can illume ;—
Some sightless grief, upon whose blasted gaze
Though Glory's light may play, in vain it
    plays?
Yes, wretched AzIM ! thine is such a grief,
Beyond all hope, all terror, all relief ;
A dark, cold calm, which nothing now can
    break,
Or warm or brighten,—like that Syrian Lake,[124]
Upon whose surface morn and summer shed
Their smiles in vain, for all beneath is dead !—

Hearts there have been, o'er which this weight
    of woe
Came by long use of suffering, tame and slow;
But thine, lost youth! was sudden—over thee
It broke at once, when all seem'd ecstasy;
When Hope look'd up, and saw the gloomy
    Past
Melt into splendor, and Bliss dawn at last—
'Twas then, even then, o'er joys so freshly
    blown,
This mortal blight of misery came down;
Even then, the full, warm gushings of thy heart
Were check'd—like fount-drops, frozen as they
    start—
And there, like them, cold, sunless relics hang,
Each fix'd and chill'd into a lasting pang.

One sole desire, one passion now remains
To keep life's fever still within his veins,
Vengeance!—dire vengeance on the wretch
    who cast
O'er him and all he lov'd that ruinous blast.
For this, when rumors reach'd him in his flight
Far, far away, after that fatal night,—
Rumors of armies, thronging to the attack
Of the Veil'd Chief,—for this he wing'd him
    back,
Fleet as the vulture speeds to flags unfurl'd,
And, when all hope seem'd desperate, wildly
    hurl'd
Himself into the scale, and saved a world.
For this he still lives on, careless of all
The wreaths that Glory on his path lets fall;

For this alone exists—like li htning-fire,
To speed one bolt of vengeance, and expire !

But safe as yet that Spirit of Evil lives ;
With a small band of desperate fugitives,
The last sole stubborn fragment, left unriven,
Of the proud host that late stood fronting
    Heaven,
He gain'd MEROU—breath'd a short curse of
    blood
O'er his lost throne—then pass'd the JIHON's
    flood,[125]
And gathering all, whose madness of belief
Still saw a Saviour in their down-fall'n Chief,
Rais'd the white banner within NEKSHEB's
    gates,[126]
And there, untam'd, the approaching conqu'ror
    waits.

Of all his Haram, all that busy hive,
With music and with sweets sparkling alive,
He took but one, the partner of his flight,
One—not for love—not for her beauty's light—
No, ZELICA stood withering 'midst the gay,
Wan as the blossom that fell yesterday
From the Alma tree and dies, while overhead
To-day's young flower is springing in its
    stead.[127]
Oh, not for love—the deepest Damn'd must
    be
Touch'd with Heaven's glory, ere such fiends
    as he
Can feel one glimpse of Love's divinity.

But no, she is his victim ; *there* lie all
Her charms for him—charms that can never pall,
As long as hell within his heart can stir,
Or one faint trace of Heaven is left in her.
To work an angel's ruin,—to behold
As white a page as Virtue e'er unroll'd
Blacken, beneath his touch, into a scroll
Of damning sins, seal'd with a burning soul—
This is his triumph ; this the joy accurst,
That ranks him among demons all but first :
This gives the victim, that before him lies
Blighted and lost, a glory in his eyes,
A light like that with which hell-fire illumes
The ghastly, writhing wretch whom it con-
     sumes !

  But other tasks now wait him—tasks that
     need
All the deep daringness of thought and deed
With which the Dives [128] have gifted him—for
     mark,
Over yon plains, which night had else made
     dark,
Those lanterns, countless as the winged lights
That spangle INDIA's fields on shower
     nights, [129]—
Far as th ir formidable gleams they shed,
The mighty tents of the beleaguerer spread,
Glimmering along the horizon's dusky line,
And thence in nearer circles, till they shine
Among the founts and groves, o'er which the
     town
In all its arm'd magnificence looks down.

Yet, fearless, from his lofty battlements
MOKANNA views that multitude of tents;
Nay, smiles to think that, though entoil'd, beset,
Not less than myriads dare to front him yet;—
That friendless, throneless, he thus stands at bay,
Even thus a match for myriads such as they.
"Oh, for a sweep of that dark Angel's wing,
Who brush'd the thousa ds of the Assyrian King [180]
To darkness in a moment, that I might
People Hell's chambers with yon host to-night!
But, come what may, let who will grasp the throne,
Caliph or Prophet, Man alike shall groan;
Let who will torture him—Priest, Caliph, King—
Alike this loathsome world of his shall ring
With victims' shrieks, and howlings of the slave,—
Sounds that shall glad me even within my grave!"
Thus, to himself; but to the scanty train
Still left around him, a far different strain :—
"Glorious Defenders of the sacred Crown
I bear from Heaven, whose light nor blood shall drown,
Nor shadow of earth eclipse;—before whose gems
The paly pomp of this world's diadems,
The crown of GERASHID, the pillar'd throne
Of PARVIZ, [181] and the heron crest that shone, [182]

Magnificent, o'er ALI's beauteous eyes,[138]
Fade like the stars when morn is in the skies:
Warriors, rejoice—the port to which we've
    pass'd
O'er Destiny's dark wave, beams out at last!
Victory's our own—'tis written in that Book
Upon whose leaves none but the angels look,
That ISLAM's sceptre shall beneath the power
Of her great foe fall broken in that hour,
When the moon's mighty orb, before all eyes,
From NEKSHEB's Holy Well portentously shall
    rise!
Now turn and see!"—
            They turn'd, and, as he spoke,
A sudden splendor all around them broke,
And they beheld an orb, ample and bright,
Rise from the Holy Well,[134] and cast its light
Round the rich city and the plain for miles,[135]—
Flinging such radiance o'er the gilded tiles
Of many a dome and fair-roof'd minaret
As autumn suns shed round them when they set.
Instant from all who saw the illusive sign
A murmur broke—"Miraculous! divine!"
The Gheber bow'd, thinking his idol star
Had wak'd and burst impatient through the bar
Of midnight, to inflame him to the war;
While he of MOUSSA's creed saw, in that ray,
The glorious Light which, in his freedom's day,
Had rested on the Ark,[136] and now again
Shone out to bless the breaking of his chain.

"To victory!" is at once the cry of all—
Nor stands MOKANNA loitering at that call;

But instant the huge gates are flung aside,
And forth, like a diminutive mountain-tide
Into the boundless sea, they speed their course
Right on into the MOSLEM's mighty force.
The watchmen of the camp,—who, in their
    rounds,
Had paus'd, and even forgot the punctual
    sounds
Of the small drum with which they count the
    night, [137]
To gaze upon that supernatural light,—
Now sink beneath an unexpected arm,
And in a death-groan give their last alarm.
"On for the lamps, that light yon lofty
    screen, [138]
Nor blunt your blades with massacre so mean;
There rests the CALIPH—speed—one lucky
    lance
May now achieve mankind's deliverance."
Desperate the die—such as they only cast
Who venture for a world, and stake their last.
But Fate's no longer with him—blade for blade
Springs up to meet them through the glimmer-
    ing shade,
And, as the clash is heard, new legions soon
Pour to the spot, like bees of KAUZEROON [139]
To the shrill timbrel's summons,—till, at
    length,
The mighty camp swarms out in all its strength,
And back to NEKSHEB's gates, covering the
    plain
With random slaughter, drives the adventurous
    train;

Among the last of whom the Silver Veil
Is seen glittering at times, like the white sail
Of some toss'd vessel, on a stormy night,
Catching the tempest's momentary light !

And hath not *this* brought the proud spirit
     low ?
Nor dash'd his brow, nor check'd his daring ?
     No.
Though half the wretches, whom at night he
     led
To thrones and victory, lie disgrac'd and dead,
Yet morning hears him, with unshrinking crest,
Still vaunt of thrones and victory to the rest ;—
And they believe him !—oh, the lover may
Distrust that look which steals his soul away ;—
The babe may cease to think that it can play
With Heaven's rainbow ;—alchymists may
     doubt
The shining gold their crucible gives out ;
But Faith, fanatic Faith, once wedded fast
To some dear falsehood, hugs it to the last.

And well the Impostor knew all lures and
     arts
That Lucifer e'er taught to tangle hearts ;
Nor, 'mid these last bold workings of his plot
Against men's souls, is Zelica forgot.
Ill-fated Zelica ! had reason been
Awake, through half the horrors thou hast seen,
Thou never couldst have borne it—Death had
     come
At once, and taken thy wrung spirit home.

But 'twas not so—a torpor, a suspense
Of thought, almost of life, came o'er the intense
And passionate struggles of that fearful night,
When her last hope of peace and heaven took
    flight :
And though, at times, a gleam of frenzy
    broke,—
As through some dull volcano's veil of smoke
Ominous flashings now and then will start,
Which show the fire's still busy at its heart,—
Yet was she mostly wrapp'd in solemn gloom ;
Not such as Azim's, brooding o'er its doom,
And calm without, as is the brow of death,
While busy worms are gnawing underneath.—
But in a blank and pulseless torpor, free
From thought or pain, a seal'd-up apathy,
Which left her oft, with scarce one living
    thrill,
The cold, pale victim of her torturer's will.

Again, as in Merou, he had her deck'd
Gorgeously out, the Priestess of the sect ;
And led her glittering forth before the eyes
Of his rude train, as to a sacrifice,—
Pallid as she, the young, devoted Bride
Of the fierce Nile, when, deck'd in all the
    pride
Of nuptial pomp, she sinks into his tide.[140]
And while the wretched maid hung down her
    head,
And stood, as one just risen from the dead.
Amid that gazing crowd, the fiend would tell
His credulous slaves it was some charm or spell

7

Possess'd her now,—and from that darken d
    trance
Should dawn ere long their Faith's deliverance.
Or if, at times, goaded by guilty shame,
Her soul was rous'd, and words of wildness
    came,
Instant the bold blasphemer would translate
Her ravings into oracles of fate,—
Would hail Heaven's signals in her flashing
    eyes,
And call her shrieks the language of the
    skies !

But vain at length his arts—despair is seen
Gathering around ; and famine comes to glean
All that the sword had left unreap'd :—in va.n
At morn and eve across the northern plain
He looks impatient for the promis d spears
Of the wild Hordes and TARTAR mountaineers ;
They come not—while his fierce beleaguerers
    pour
Engines of havoc in, unknown before, [141]
And horrible as new ; [142]—javelins, that fly
Enwreathed with smoky flames through the
    dark sky,
And red-hot globes, that, opening as they
    mount,
Discharge, as from a kindled Naphtha fount, [143]
Showers of consuming fire o'er all below ;
Looking, as through the illumin'd night they
    go,
Like those wild birds [144] that by the Magians oft,
At festivals of fire, were sent aloft

Into the air, with blazing fagots tied
To their huge wings, scattering **combustion**
    wide.
All night the groans of wretches who expire
In agony, beneath these darts of fire,
Ring through the city—while, descending o'er
Its shrines and domes and streets of syca-
    more,—
Its lone bazaars, with their bright cloths **of**
    gold,
Since the last peaceful pageant left unroll'd,—
Its beauteous marble baths, whose idle jets
Now gush with blood,—and its tall minarets,
That late have stood up in the evening glare
Of the red sun, unhallow'd by a prayer;—
O'er each, in turn, the dreadful flame-bolts **fall,**
And death and conflagration throughout **all**
The desolate city hold high festival!

  Mokanna sees the world is his no more;—
One sting at parting, and his grasp is o'er.
"What! drooping now?"—thus, with unblush-
    ing cheek,
He hails the few, who yet can hear him speak,
Of all those famish'd slaves around him lying,
And by the light of blazing temples dying;—
"What!—drooping now?—now, when **at**
    length we press
Home o'er the very threshold of success;
When Alla from our ranks hath thinn'd **away**
Those grosser branches, that kept out his **ray**
Of favor from us, and we stand at length
Heirs of his light and children of his **strength,**

The chosen few, who shall survive the fall
Of Kings and Thrones, triumphant over all!
Have you then lost, weak murmurers as you
    are,
All faith in him, who was your Light, your Star?
Have you forgot the eye of glory, hid
Beneath this Veil, the flashing of whose lid
Could, like a sun-stroke of the desert, wither
Millions of such as yonder Chief brings hither?
Long have its lightnings slept—too long—but
    now
All earth shall feel the unveiling of this brow!
To-night—yes, sainted men! this very night,
I bid you all to a fair festal rite,
Where—having deep refresh'd each weary limb
With viands, such as feast Heaven's cherubim,
And kindled up your souls, now sunk and dim,
With that pure wine the Dark-eyed Maids above
Keep, seal'd with precious musk, for those they
    love, [145]—
I will myself uncurtain in your sight
The wonders of this brow's ineffable light:
Then lead you forth, and with a wink disperse
Yon myriads, howling through the universe!"

Eager they listen, while each accent darts
New life into their chill'd and hope-sick hearts;
Such treacherous life as the cool draught sup-
    plies
To him upon the stake, who drinks and dies!
Wildly they point their lances to the light
Of the fast sinking sun, and shout "To-
    night!"—

"To-night!" their Chief re-echoes in a voice
Of fiend-like mockery that bids hell rejoice.
Deluded victims!—never hath this earth
Seen mourning half so mournful as their mirth.
Here, to the few, whose iron frames had stood
This racking waste of famine and of blood,
Faint, dying wretches clung, from whom the
    shout
Of triumph like a maniac's laugh broke out :—
There, others, lighted by the smould'ring fire,
Danc'd like wan ghosts about a funeral pyre,
Among the dead and dying, strew'd around ;—
While some pale wretch look'd on, and from
    his wound
Plucking the fiery dart by which he bled,
In ghastly transport wav'd it o'er his head !

    'Twas more than midnight now—a fearful
    pause
Had follow'd the long shouts, the wild ap-
    plause,
That lately from those Royal Gardens burst,
Where the Veil'd demon held his feast accurst,
When ZELICA—alas, poor ruin'd heart,
In every horror doom'd to bear its part !—
Was bidden to the banquet by a slave,
Who, while his quivering lip the summons gave,
Grew black, as though the shadows of the
    grave
Compass'd him round, and, ere he could repeat
His message through, fell lifeless at her feet !
Shuddering she went—a soul-felt pang of fear,
A presage that her own dark doom was near,

Rous'd every feeling, and brought Reason back
Once more, to writhe her last upon the rack.
All round seem'd tranquil—even the foe had
    ceas'd,
As if aware of that demoniac feast,
His fiery bolts ; and though the heavens look'd
    red,
'Twas but some distant conflagration's spread.
But hark—she stops—she listens—dreadful
    tone,
'Tis her Tormentor's laugh—and now a groan,
A long death groan comes with it :—can this be
The place of mirth, the bower of revelry?
She enters—Holy ALLA, what a sight
Was there before her ! By the glimmering light
Of the pale dawn, mix'd with the flare of
    brands
That round lay burning, dropp'd from lifeless
    hands
She saw the board, in splendid mockery spread,
Rich censers breathing—garlands overhead—
The urns, the cups, from which they late had
    quaff'd,
All gold and gems, but—what had been the
    draught ?
Oh ! who need ask, that saw those livid guests,
With their swoll'n heads sunk black'ning on
    their breasts
Or looking pale to Heaven with glassy glare,
As if they sought but saw no mercy there ;
As if they felt, though poison rack'd them
    through,
Remorse the deadlier torment of the two !

While some, the bravest, hardiest of the train
Of their false Chief, who on the battle-plain
Would have met death with transport by his
    side,
Here mute and helpless gasp'd ;—but, as they
    died,
Look'd horrible vengeance with their eyes' last
    strain,
And clench'd the slack'ning hand at him in
    vain.

    Dreadful it was to see the ghastly stare,
The stony look of horror and despair,
Which some of these expiring victims cast
Upon their souls' tormentor to the last ;—
Upon that mocking Fiend whose Veil, now
    rais'd,
Show'd them, as in death's agony they gazed,
Not the long promis'd light, the brow, whose
    beaming
Was to come forth, all conquering, all redeem-
    ing,
But features horribler than Hell e'er trac'd
On its own brood ;—no Demon of the Waste, [146]
No churchyard Ghole, caught lingering in the
    light
Of the blest sun, e'er blasted human sight
With lineaments so foul, so fierce as those
The Impostor, now in grinning mockery,
    shows :—
"There, ye wise Saints, behold your Light,
    your Star—
Ye *would* be dupes and victims, and ye *are.*

Is it enough ? or must I, while a thrill
Lives in your sapient bosoms, cheat you still?
Swear that the burning death ye feel within
Is but the trance with which Heaven's joys
    begin ;
That this foul visage, foul as e'er disgrac'd
Even monstrous man, is—after God's own
    taste ;
And that—but see !—ere I have half-way said
My greetings through, the uncourteous souls
    are fled.
Farewell, sweet spirits ! not in vain ye die,
If Eblis loves you half so well as I.—
Ha, my young bride !—'tis well—take thou
    thy seat ;
Nay, come—no shuddering—didst thou never
    meet
The dead before ?—they grac'd our wedding,
    sweet ;
And these, my guests to-night, have brimm'd so
    true
Their parting cups, that *thou* shalt pledge one
    too.
But—how is this ?—all empty ? all drunk up?
Hot lips have been before thee in the cup,
Young bride,—yet stay—one precious drop
    remains,
Enough to warm a gentle Priestess' veins :—
Here, drink—and should thy lover's conquering
    arms
Speed hither, ere thy lip lose all its charms,
Give him but half this venom in thy kiss,
And I'll forgive my haughty rival's bliss !

" **For** *me*—I too must die—but not like these
Vile, rankling things, to fester in the breeze ;
To have this brow in ruffian triumph shown,
With all Death's grimness added to its own,
And rot to dust beneath the taunting eyes
Of slaves, exclaiming, 'There his Godship lies !'
No—cursed race—since first my soul drew
        breath,
They've been my dupes, and *shall* be e'en in
        death.
Thou see'st yon cistern in the shade—'tis fill'd
With burning drugs, for this last hour distill'd : [147]
There will I plunge me, in that liquid flame—
Fit bath to lave a dying Prophet s frame !—
There perish, all—ere pulse of thine shall
        fail—
Nor leave one limb to tell mankind the tale.
So shall my votaries, whereso'er they rave,
Proclaim that Heaven took back the Saint it
        gave ;—
That I've but vanish'd from this earth awhile,
To come again, with bright, unshrouded smile !
So shall they build me altars in their zeal,
Where knaves shall minister, and fools shall
        kneel ;
Where Faith may mutter o'er her mystic spell,
Written in blood—and Bigotry may swell
The sail he spreads for Heaven with blasts from
        hell !
So shall my banner, through long ages, be
The rallying sign of fraud and anarchy :—
Kings yet unborn shall rue MOKANNA's name,
And, though I die, my spirit, still the same,

Shall walk abroad in all the stormy strife,
And guilt, and blood, that were its bliss in life.
But, hark! their battering engine shakes the
    wall—
Why, *let* it shake—thus I can brave them all.
No trace of me shall greet them, when they
    come,
And I can trust thy faith, for—thou'lt be dumb.
Now mark how readily a wretch like me,
In one bold plunge, commences Deity!"

He sprung and sunk, as the last words were
    said—
Quick clos'd the burning waters o'er his head,
And ZELICA was left—within the ring
Of those wide walls the only living thing;
The only wretched one, still curs'd with breath,
In all that frightful wilderness of death!
More like some bloodless ghost—such as, they
    tell,
In the lone Cities of the Silent [148] dwell,
And there, unseen of all but ALLA, sit
Each by its own pale carcase, watching it.

But morn is up, and a fresh warfare stirs
Throughout the camp of the beleaguerers.
Their globes of fire (the dread artillery lent
By GREECE to conquering MAHADI) are spent;
And now the scorpion's shaft, the quarry sent
From high ballistas, and the shielded throng
Of soldiers swinging the huge ram along,
All speak the impatient Islamite's intent
To try, at length, if tower and battlement

And bastion'd wall be not less hard to win,
Less tough to break down than the hearts
within.
First in impatience and in toil is he,
The burning Azim—oh ! could he but see
The Impostor once alive within his grasp,
Not the gaunt lion's hug, nor boa's clasp,
Could match that gripe of vengeance, or keep
pace
With the fell heartiness of Hate's embrace !

Loud rings the ponderous ram against the
walls ;
Now shake the ramparts, now a buttress falls,
But still no breach—"Once more, one mighty
swing
Of all your beams, together thundering ! "
There—the wall shakes—the shouting troops
exult,
"Quick, quick discharge your weightest cat-
apult
Right on that spot, and Neksheb is our own ! "
'Tis done—the battlements come crashing
down,
And the huge wall, by that stroke riven in two,
Yawning, like some old crater, rent anew,
Shows the dim, desolate city smoking through.
But strange ! no signs of life—nought living
seen
Above, below—what can this stillness mean ?
A minute's pause suspends all hearts and eyes—
" In through the breach ! " impetuous Azim
cries ;

But the cool CALIPH, fearful of some wile
In this blank stillness, checks the troops
    awhile.——
Just then, a figure, with slow step, advanc'd
Forth from the ruin'd walls, and, as there
    glanc'd
A sunbeam over it, all eyes could see
The well-known Silver Veil!—"'Tis He, 'tis He,
MOKANNA, and alone!" they shout around;
Young AZIM from his steed springs to the
    ground—
"Mine, Holy CALIPH! mine," he cries, "the
    task
To crush yon daring wretch—'tis all I ask."
Eager he darts to meet the demon foe,
Who still across wide heaps of ruin slow
And falteringly comes, till they are near;
Then, with a bound, rushes on AZIM's spear,
And, casting off the Veil in falling, shows—
Oh!—'tis his ZELICA's life-blood that flows!

"I meant not, AZIM," soothingly she said,
As on his trembling arm she lean'd her head,
And, looking in his face, saw anguish there
Beyond all wounds the quivering flesh can
    bear—
"I meant not *thou* shouldst have the pain of
    this:—
Though death, with thee thus tasted, is a bliss
Thou wouldst not rob me of, didst thou but
    know
How oft I've pray'd to God I might die so!
But the Fiend's venom was too scant and slow;

To linger on were maddening—and I thought
If once that Veil—nay, look not on it—caught
The eyes of your fierce soldiery, I should be
Struck by a thousand death-darts instantly.
But this is sweeter—oh ! believe me, yes—
I would not change this sad, but dear caress,
This death within thy arms I would not give
For the most smiling life the happiest live !
All, that stood dark and drear before the eye
Of my stray'd soul, is passing swiftly by ;
A light comes o'er me from those looks of love,
Like the first dawn of mercy from above ;
And if thy lips but tell me I'm forgiven,
Angels will echo the blest words in Heaven !
But live, my AZIM ;—oh ! to call thee mine
Thus once again ! *my* AZIM—dream divine!
Live, if thou ever lov'dst me, if to meet
Thy ZELICA hereafter would be sweet,
Oh, live to pray for her—to bend the knee
Morning and night before that Deity,
To whom pure lips and hearts without a stain,
As thine are, AZIM, never breath'd in vain,—
And pray that He may pardon her,—may take
Compassion on her soul for thy dear sake,
And, nought remembering but her love to
    thee,
Make her all thine, all His, eternally !
Go to those happy fields where first we twin'd
Our youthful hearts together—every wind
That meets thee there, fresh from the well-
    known flowers,
Will bring the sweetness of those innocent
    hours

Back to thy soul, and mayst thou feel again
For thy poor ZELICA as thou didst then.
So shall thy orisons, like dew that flies
To Heaven upon the morning's sunshine, rise
With all love's earliest ardor to the skies !
And should they—but, alas, my senses fail—
Oh, for one minute !—should thy prayers pre-
vail—
If pardon'd souls may, from that World of Bliss,
Reveal their joy to those they love in this—
I'll come to thee—in some sweet dream—and
tell—
Oh Heaven—I die—dear love ! farewell, fare-
well ! "

Time fleeted—years on years had pass'd
away,
And few of those who, on that mournful day,
Had stood, with pity in their eyes, to see
The maiden's death and the youth's agony,
Were living still—when, by a rustic grave,
Beside the swift AMOO's transparent wave,
An aged man, who had grown aged there
By that lone grave, morning and night in
prayer,
For the last time knelt down—and, though the
shade
Of death hung darkening over him, there play'd
A gleam of rapture on his eye and cheek,
That brighten'd even Death—like the last streak
Of intense glory on the horizon's brim,
When night o'er all the rest hangs chill and
dim.

His soul had seen a Vision, while he slept ;
She, for whose spirit he had pray'd and wept
So many years, had come to him, all drest
In angel smiles, and told him she was blest !
For this the old man breath'd his thanks, and
　　died. —
And there, upon the banks of that lov'd tide,
He and his Zelica sleep side by side.

THE story of the Veiled Prophet of Khorassan
being ended, they were now doomed to hear
FADLADEEN's criticisms upon it. A series of
disappointments and accidents had occurred
to this learned Chamberlain during the journey.
In the first place, those couriers stationed, as
in the reign of Shah Jehan, between Delhi and
the Western coast of India, to secure a constant
supply of mangoes for the Royal Table, had,
by some cruel irregularity, failed in their duty ;
and to eat any mangoes but those of Mazagong
was, of course, impossible. [149] In the next
place, the elephant, laden with his fine antique
porcelain, [150] had, in an unusual fit of liveliness,
shattered the whole set to pieces :—an irrep-
arable loss, as many of the vessels were so
exquisitely old, as to have been used under the
Emperors Yan and Chun, who reigned many
ages before the dynasty of Tang. His Koran,
too, supposed to be the identical copy between
the leaves of which Mahomet's favorite pigeon
used to nestle, had been mislaid by his Koran-
bearer three whole days ; not without much

spiritual alarm to FADLADEEN, who, though professing to hold with other loyal and orthodox Mussulmans, that salvation could only be found in the Koran, was strongly suspected of believing in his heart, that it could only be found in his own particular copy of it. When to all these grievances is added the obstinacy of the cooks, in putting the pepper of Canara into his dishes instead of the cinnamon of Serendib, we may easily suppose that he came to the task of criticism with, at least, a sufficient degree of irritability for the purpose.

"In order," said he, importantly swinging about his chaplet of pearls, "to convey with clearness my opinion of the story this young man has related, it is necessary to take a review of all the stories that have ever——" — "My good FADLADEEN!" exclaimed the Princess, interrupting him, "we really do not deserve that you should give yourself so much trouble. Your opinion of the poem we have just heard will, I have no doubt, be abundantly edifying, without any further waste of your valuable erudition."—"If that be all," replied the critic,—evidently mortified at not being allowed to show how much he knew about everything but the subject immediately before him,—"if that be all that is required the matter is easily dispatched." He then proceeded to analyze the poem, in that strain (so well known to the unfortunate bards of Delhi) whose censures were an infliction from which few recovered, and whose very praises were like the honey extracted from the bitter flowers of the aloe. The chief personages of the story were, if he rightly understood them, an ill-favored gentleman, with a veil over his face;—a young lady, whose reason went and came, according as it suited the poet's convenience to be sensible or otherwise;—and a youth in one of those hideous Bucharian bonnets, who took the aforesaid gentleman in a veil for a Divinity. "From such materials," said he, "what can be expected?—after rivalling each other in long speeches and absurdities, through some thousands of lines as indigestible as the filberts of Berdaa, our friend in the veil jumps into a tub of aquafortis; the young lady dies in a set speech, whose only recommendation is that it is her last; and the lover lives on to a good old age for the laudable purpose of seeing her ghost, which he at last happily accomplishes, and expires. This, you will allow, is a fair summary of the story; and if Nasser, the Arabian merchant, told no better,[151] our Holy Prophet (to whom be all honor and glory!) had no need to be jealous of his abilities for story-telling."

With respect to the style, it was worthy of the matter;—it had not even those politic contrivances of structure, which make up for the commonness of the thoughts by the peculiarity of the manner, nor that stately poetical phraseology by which sentiments mean in them-

8

selves, like the blacksmith's [152] apron converted
into a banner, are so easily gilt and embroidered into consequence.　Then, as to the
versification, it was, to say no worse of it, ex-
ecrable : it had neither the copious flow of
Ferdosi, the sweetness of Hafez, nor the sen-
tentious march of Sadi ; but appeared to him,
in the uneasy heaviness of its movements, to
have been modelled upon the gait of a very
tired dromedary.　The licenses, too, in which
it indulged, were unpardonable ;—for instance,
this line, and the poem abounded with such :—

Like the faint, exquisite music of a dream.

"What critic that can count," said FADLADEEN,
"and has his full complement of fingers to
count withal, would tolerate for an instant
such syllabic superfluities ? "　He here looked
round, and discovered that most of his audience
were asleep ; while the glimmering lamps
seemed inclined to follow their example.　It
became necessary, therefore, however painful
to himself, to put an end to his valuable an-
imadversions for the present, and he accordingly
concluded, with an air of dignified candor,
thus : "Notwithstanding the observations
which I have thought it my duty to make, it is
by no means my wish to discourage the young
man :—so far from it, indeed, that if he will
but totally alter his style of writing and thinking, I have very little doubt that I shall be
vastly pleased with him."

Some days elapsed after this harangue of the Great Chamberlain, before LALLA ROOKH could venture to ask for another story. The youth was still a welcome guest in the pavilion—to *one* heart, perhaps, too dangerously welcome: —but all mention of poetry was, as if by common consent, avoided. Though none of the party had much respect for FADLADEEN, yet his censures, thus magisterially delivered, evidently made an impression on them all. The Poet himself, to whom criticism was quite a new operation (being wholly unknown in that Paradise of the Indies, Cashmere), felt the shock as it is generally felt at first, till use has made it more tolerable to the patient;—the Ladies began to suspect that they ought not to be pleased, and seemed to conclude that there must have been much good sense in what FADLADEEN said, from its having sent them all so soundly to sleep;—while the self-complacent Chamberlain was left to triumph in the idea of having for the hundred and fiftieth time in his life, extinguished a Poet. LALLA ROOKH alone —and Love knew why—persisted in being delighted with all she had heard, and in resolving to hear more as speedily as possible. Her manner, however, of first returning to the subject was unlucky. It was while they rested during the heat of noon near a fountain, on which some hand had rudely traced those well-known words from the Garden of Sadi,— "Many, like me, have viewed this fountain, but they are gone, and their eyes are closed forever!"—that she took occasion, from the melancholy beauty of this passage to dwell upon the charms of poetry in general. "It is true," she said, "few poets can imitate that sublime bird, which flies always in the air, and never touches the earth: [153]—it is only once in many ages a Genius appears, whose words, like those on the Written Mountain, last forever: [154] but still there are some, as delightful, perhaps, though not so wonderful, who, if not stars over our head, are at least flowers along our path, and whose sweetness of the moment we ought gratefully to inhale, without calling upon them for a brightness and durability beyond their nature. In short," continued she, blushing, as if conscious of being caught in an oration, "it is quite cruel that a poet cannot wander through his regions of enchantment, without having a critic forever, like the old Man of the Sea, upon his back!" [155]—FADLADEEN, it was plain, took this last luckless allusion to himself, and would treasure it up in his mind as a whetstone for his next criticism. A sudden silence ensued; and the Princess, glancing a look at FERAMORZ, saw plainly she must wait for a more courageous moment.

But the glories of Nature, and her wild fragrant airs, playing freshly over the current of youthful spirits, will soon heal even deeper wounds than the dull Fadladeens of this world can inflict. In an evening or two after, they came to the small Valley of Gardens, which

" Oh, you that have the charge of Love,
    Keep him in rosy bondage bound."

had been planted by order of the Emperor, for his favorite sister Rochinara, during their progress to Cashmere, some years before; and never was there a more sparkling assemblage of sweets, since the Gulzar-e-Irem, or Rosebower of Irem. Every precious flower was there to be found that poetry, or love, or religion has ever consecrated; from the dark hyacinth, to which Hafez compares his mistress's hair, [156] to the *Cámalaiá*, by whose rosy blossoms the heaven of Indra is scented. [157] As they sat in the cool fragrance of this delicious spot, and LALLA ROOKH remarked that she could fancy it the abode of that Flower-loving Nymph whom they worship in the temples of Kathay, [158] or of one of those Peris, those beautiful creatures of the air, who live upon perfumes, and to whom a place like this might make some amends for the Paradise they have lost,—the young Poet, in whose eyes she appeared, while she spoke, to be one of the bright spiritual creatures she was describing, said hesitatingly that he remembered a Story of a Peri, which, if the Princess had no objection, he would venture to relate. "It is," said he, with an appealing look to FADLADEEN, "in a lighter and humbler strain than the other;" then, striking a few careless but melancholy chords on his kitar, he thus began :—

PARADISE AND THE PERI

ONE morn a PERI at the gate
Of Eden stood, disconsolate :
And as she listen'd to the Springs
  Of Life within, like music flowing,
And caught the light upon her wings
  Through the half-open portal glowing,
She wept to think her recreant race
Should e'er have lost that glorious place !

"How happy," exclaim'd this child of air,
"Are the holy Spirits who wander there,
  'Mid flowers that never shall fade or fall ;
Though mine are the gardens of earth and sea,
And the stars themselves have flowers for me,
  One blossom of Heaven outblooms them all.

"Though sunny the Lake of cool CASHMERE,
With its plane-tree Isle reflected clear, [159]
  And sweetly the founts of that Valley fall ;
Though bright are the waters of SING-SU-HAY,
And the golden floods that thitherward stray, [160]
Yet—oh, 'tis only the Blest can say
  How the waters of Heaven outshine them
    all !

" Go, wing thy flight from star to star,
From world to luminous world, as far
    As the universe spreads its flaming wall :
Take all the pleasures of all the spheres,
And multiply each through endless years,
    One minute of Heaven is worth them **all !** "

The glorious Angel, who was keeping
The gates of Light, beheld her weeping ;
And, as he nearer drew and listen'd
To her sad song, a tear-drop glisten'd
Within his eyelids, like the spray
    From Eden's fountain, when it lies
On the blue flower, which—Bramins say—
    Blooms nowhere but in Paradise. [161]

" Nymph of a fair but erring line ! "
Gently he said—" One hope is thine.
'Tis written in the Book of Fate,
    𝕿𝖍𝖊 𝕻𝖊𝖗𝖎 𝖞𝖊𝖙 𝖒𝖆𝖞 𝖇𝖊 𝖋𝖔𝖗𝖌𝖎𝖛𝖊𝖓
𝖂𝖍𝖔 𝖇𝖗𝖎𝖓𝖌𝖘 𝖙𝖔 𝖙𝖍𝖎𝖘 𝕰𝖙𝖊𝖗𝖓𝖆𝖑 𝖌𝖆𝖙𝖊
    𝕿𝖍𝖊 𝕲𝖎𝖋𝖙 𝖙𝖍𝖆𝖙 𝖎𝖘 𝖒𝖔𝖘𝖙 𝖉𝖊𝖆𝖗 𝖙𝖔 𝕳𝖊𝖆𝖛𝖊𝖓 !
Go, seek it, and redeem thy sin—
'Tis sweet to let the Pardon'd in."

Rapidly as comets run
To the embraces of the Sun ;—
Fleeter than the starry brands
Flung at night from angel hands, [162]
At those dark and daring sprites
Who would climb the empyreal heights,

Down the blue vault the PERI flies,
   And, lighted earthward by a glance
That just then broke from morning's eyes,
   Hung hovering o'er our world's expanse.

But whither shall the Spirit go
To find this gift for Heaven?—" I know
The wealth," she cries, "of every urn,
In which unnumber'd rubies burn,
Beneath the pillars of CHILMINAR ; [168]
I know where the Isles of Perfume are,
Many a fathom down in the sea,
To the south of sun-bright ARABY ; [164]
I know, too, where the Genii hid
The jewell'd cup of their King JAMSHID, [165]
With Life's elixir sparkling high—
But gifts like these are not for the sky.
Where was there ever a gem that shone
Like the steps of ALLA's wonderful Throne?
And the Drops of Life—oh ! what would they be
In the boundless Deep of Eternity ? "

While thus she mus'd, her pinions fann'd
The air of that sweet Indian land,
Whose air is balm ; whose ocean spreads
O'er coral rocks, and amber beds : [166]
Whose mountains, pregnant by the beam
Of the warm sun, with diamonds teem ;
Whose rivulets are iike rich brides,
Lovely, with gold beneath their tides ;
Whose sandal groves and bowers of spice
Might be a Peri's Paradise !

But crimson now her rivers ran
   With human blood—the smell of death
Came reeking from those spicy bowers
And man, the sacrifice of man,
   Mingled his taint with every breath
Upwafted from the innocent flowers.
Land of the Sun, what foot invades
Thy Pagods and thy pillar'd shades [167]—
Thy cavern shrines, and Idol stones,
Thy Monarchs and their thousand Thrones? [168]

'Tis he of GAZNA [169]—fierce in wrath
   He comes, and INDIA's diadems
Lie scatter'd in his ruinous path.—
   His bloodhounds he adorns with gems,
Torn from the violated necks
   Of many a young and lov'd Sultana; [170]
   Maidens, within their pure Zenana,
   Priests in the very fane he slaughters,
And chokes up with the glittering wrecks
   Of golden shrines the sacred waters!
Downward the PERI turns her gaze,
And, through the war-field's bloody haze,
beholds a youthful warrior stand,
   Alone, beside his native river,—
The red blade broken in his hand,
   And the last arrow in his quiver.
"Live," said the Conqueror, live to "share
The trophies and the crowns I bear!"
Silent that youthful warrior stood—
Silent he pointed to the flood
All crimson with his country's blood,

Then sent his last remaining dart,
For answer, to the Invader's heart.

False flew the shaft, though pointed well,
The Tyrant liv'd, the Hero fell!—
Yet mark'd the PERI where he lay,
    And, when the rush of war was past,
Swiftly descending on a ray
    Of morning light, she caught the last
Last glorious drop his heart had shed,
Before its free-born spirit fled!

"Be this," she cried, as she wing'd her flight,
"My welcome gift at the Gates of Light.
Though foul are the drops that oft distil
    On the field of warfare, blood like this,
    For Liberty shed, so holy is, ¹⁷¹
It would not stain the purest rill
    That sparkles among the Bowers of Bliss!
Oh, if there be, on this earthly sphere,
A boon, an offering Heaven holds dear,
'Tis the last libation Liberty draws
From the heart that bleeds and breaks in her
        cause!"

"Sweet," said the Angel, as she gave
    The gift into his radiant hand,
"Sweet is our welcome of the Brave
    Who die thus for their native Land—
But see—alas!—the crystal bar
Of Eden moves not—holier far

Than even this drop the boon must be,
That opes the Gates of Heaven for thee!"
Her first fond hope of Eden blighted,
   Now among AFRIC's lunar Mountains,[172]
Far to the South the PERI lighted;
   And sleek'd her plumage at the fountains
Of that Egyptian tide—whose birth
Is hidden from the sons of earth
Deep in those solitary woods,
Where oft the Genii of the Floods
Dance round the cradle of their Nile,
And hail the new-born Giant's smile.[173]
Thence over EGYPT's palmy groves,
   Her grots, and sepulchres of Kings,[174]
The exil'd Spirit sighing roves;
And now hangs listening to the doves
In warm ROSETTA's vale[175]—now loves
   To watch the moonlight on the wings
Of the white pelicans that break
The azure calm of MŒRIS' Lake.[176]
'Twas a fair scene—a Land more bright
   Never did mortal eye behold!
Who could have thought, that saw this night,
   Those valleys and their fruits of gold,
Basking in Heaven's serenest light;—
Those groups of lovely date-trees bending
   Languidly their leaf-crown'd heads,
Like youthful maids, when sleep descending
   Warns them to their silken beds;[177]—
Those virgin lilies, all the night
   Bathing their beauties in the lake,
That they may rise more fresh and bright,
   When their beloved Sun's awake;—

Those ruin'd shrines and towers that seem
The relics of a splendid dream ;
  Amid whose fairy loneliness
Nought but the lapwing's cry is heard,
Nought seen but (when the shadows, flitting
Fast from the moon, unsheath its gleam)
Some purple-wing'd Sultana [178] sitting
  Upon a column, motionless
And glittering like an Idol bird !—
Who could have thought, that there, even there,
Amid those scenes so still and fair,
The Demon of the Plague hath cast
From his hot wing a deadlier blast,
More mortal far than ever came
From the red Desert's sands of flame !
So quick, that every living thing
Of human shape, touch'd by his wing,
Like plants where the Simoom hath past,
At once falls black and withering !
The sun went down on many a brow.
  Which, full of bloom and freshness then,
Is rankling in the pest-house now.
  And ne'er will feel that sun again.
And, oh ! to see the unburied heaps
On which the lonely moonlight sleeps—
The very vultures turn away,
And sicken at so foul a prey !
Only the fierce hyæna stalks [179]
Throughout the city's desolate walks [180]
At midnight, and his carnage plies :—
  Woe to the half-dead wretch, who meets
The glaring of those large blue eyes [181]
  Amid the darkness of the streets !

"Poor race of men!" said the pitying Spirit,
  "Dearly ye pay for your primal Fall—
Some flow'rets of Eden ye still inherit,
  But the trail of the Serpent is over them
    all!"

She wept—the air grew pure and clear
  Around her, as the bright drops ran;
For there's a magic in each tear
  Such kindly Spirits weep for man!

Just then beneath some orange trees,
Whose fruit and blossoms in the breeze
Were wantoning together, free,
Like age at play with infancy—
Beneath that fresh and springing bower,
  Close by the Lake, she heard the moan
Of one who, at this silent hour,
  Had thither stolen to die alone.
One who in life, where'er he mov'd,
  Drew after him the hearts of many;
Yet now, as though he ne'er were lov'd,
  Dies here unseen, unwept by any!
None to watch near him—none to slake
  The fire that in his bosom lies,
With even a sprinkle from that lake,
  Which shines so cool before his eyes.
No voice, well known through many a day,
  To speak the last, the parting word,
Which, when all other sounds decay,
  Is still like distant music heard;—
That tender farewell on the shore
Of this rude world, when all is o'er,
Which cheers the spirit, ere its bark
Puts off into the unknown Dark.

Deserted youth! one thought alone
    Shed joy around his soul in death—
That she, whom he for years had known,
And lov'd, and might have call'd his own,
    Was safe from this foul midnight's breath,—
Safe in her father's princely halls,
Where the cool airs from fountain falls,
Freshly perfum'd by many a brand
Of the sweet wood from INDIA's land,
Were pure as she whose brow they fann'd.

But see—who yonder comes by stealth,[162]
    This melancholy bower to seek,
Like a young envoy, sent by Health,
    With rosy gifts upon her cheek?
'Tis she!—far off, through moonlight dim,
    He knew his own betrothed bride,
She, who would rather die with him,
    Than live to gain the world beside!—
Her arms are round her lover now,
    His livid cheek to hers she presses,
And dips, to bind his burning brow,
    In the cool lake her loosen'd tresses.

Ah! once, how little did he think
An hour would come, when he should shrink
With horror from that dear embrace,
    Those gentle arms, that were to him
Holy as is the cradling place
    Of Eden's infant cherubim!
And now he yields—now turns away,
Shuddering as if the venom lay

All in those proffer'd lips alone—
Those lips that, then so fearless grown,
Never until that instant came
Near his unask'd or without shame.
"Oh! let me only breathe the air,
    That blessed air, that's breath'd by thee,
And, whether on its wings it bear
    Healing or death, 'tis sweet to me!
There—drink my tears, while yet they fall—
    Would that my bosom's blood were balm,
And, well thou know'st, I'd shed it all,
    To give thy brow one minute's calm.
Nay, turn not from me that dear face—
    Am I not thine—thy own lov'd bride—
The one, the chosen one, whose place
    In life or death is by thy side?
Think'st thou that she, whose only light,
    In this dim world, from thee hath shone,
Could bear the long, the cheerless night,
    That must be hers when thou art gone?
That I can live, and let thee go,
Who art my life itself?—No, no—
When the stem dies, the leaf that grew
Out of its heart must perish too!
Then turn to me, my own love, turn,
Before, like thee, I fade and burn;
Cling to these yet cool lips, and share
The last pure life that lingers there!"
She fails—she sinks—as dies the lamp
In charnel airs, or cavern damp,
So quickly do his baleful sighs
Quench all the sweet light of her eyes.

One struggle—and his pain is past—
  Her lover is no longer living !
One kiss the maiden gives, one last,
  Long kiss, which she expires in giving !

" Sleep," said the PERI, as softly she stole
The farewell sigh of that vanishing soul,
As true as e'er warm'd a woman's breast—
" Sleep on, in visions of odor rest,
In balmier airs than ever yet stirr'd
The enchanted pile of that lonely bird,
Who sings at the last his own death-lay,[183]
And in music and perfume dies away !"

Thus saying, from her lips she spread
  Unearthly breathings through the place,
And shook her sparkling wreath, and shed
  Such lustre o'er each paly face,
That like two lovely saints they seem'd,
  Upon the eve of doomsday taken
From their dim graves, in odor sleeping ;
While that benevolent PERI beam'd
Like their good angel, calmly keeping
  Watch o'er them till their souls would waken

But morn is blushing in the sky ;
  Again the PERI soars above,
Bearing to Heaven that precious sigh
  Of pure self-sacrificing love.
High throbb'd her heart, with hope elate,
  The Elysian palm she soon shall win,
For the bright Spirit at the gate
  Smil'd as she gave that offering in ;

And she already hears the trees
   Of Eden, with their crystal bells
Ringing in that ambrosial breeze
   That from the throne of ALLA swells;
And she can see the starry bowls
   That lie around that lucid lake,
Upon whose banks admitted Souls
   Their first sweet draught of glory take! [184]

But, ah! even PERIS' hopes are vain :—
Again the Fates forbade, again
The immortal barrier clos'd :—"Not yet,"
The Angel said as, with regret,
He shut from her that glimpse of glory—
"True was the maiden, and her story,
Written in light o'er ALLA's head,
By seraph eyes shall long be read.
But, PERI, see—the crystal bar
Of Eden moves not—holier far
Than even this sigh the boon must be
That opes the Gates of Heaven for thee.'

Now, upon SYRIA's land of roses [185]
Softly the light of Eve reposes,
And, like a glory, the broad sun
Hangs over sainted LEBANON;
   Whose head in wintry grandeur towers,
     And whitens with eternal sleet,
While summer, in a vale of flowers,
   Is sleeping rosy at his feet.

To one, who look'd from upper air
O'er all the enchanted regions there,
  9

How beauteous must have been the glow,
The life, the sparkling, from below!
Fair gardens, shining streams, with ranks
Of golden melons on their banks,
More golden where the sunlight falls ;
Gay lizards, glittering on the walls [186]
Of ruin'd shrines, busy and bright
As they were all alive with light ;
And, yet more splendid, numerous flocks
Of pigeons, settling on the rocks,
With their rich restless wings, that gleam
Variously in the crimson beam
Of the warm West,—as if inlaid
With brilliants from the mine, or made
Of tearless rainbows, such as span
The unclouded skies of PERISTAN.
And then the mingling sounds that come
Of shepherd's ancient reed, [187] with hum
Of the wild bees of PALESTINE, [188]
  Banqueting through the flow'ry vales ;
And, JORDAN, those sweet banks of thine,
  And woods, so full of nightingales. [189]

But nought can charm the luckless PERI ;
Her soul is sad—her wings are weary—
Joyless she sees the Sun look down
On that great Temple, once his own, [190]
Whose lonely columns stand sublime,
  Flinging their shadows from on high,
Like dials, which the wizard, Time,
  Had rais'd to count his ages by !
Yet haply there may lie conceal'd
  Beneath those Chambers of the Sun,

Some amulet of gems anneal'd
In upper fires, some tablet seal'd
  With the great name of SOLOMON,
  Which, spell'd by her illumin'd eyes,
May teach her where, beneath the moon,
In earth or ocean, lies the boon,
The charm, that can restore so soon
  An erring Spirit to the skies.

Cheer'd by this hope she bends her thither;
  Still laughs the radiant eye of Heaven,
  Nor have the golden bowers of Even
In the rich West begun to wither;—
When, o'er the vale of BALBEC winging
  Slowly she sees a child at play,
Among the rosy wild flowers singing,
  As rosy and as wild as they;
Chasing, with eager hands and eyes,
The beautiful blue damsel-flies, [191]
That flutter'd round the jasmine stems,
Like winged flowers or flying gems :—
And, near the boy, who tir'd with play
Now nestling 'mid the roses lay,
She saw a wearied man dismount
  From his hot steed, and on the brink
Of a small imaret's rustic fount [192]
  Impatient fling him down to drink.
Then swift his haggard brow he turn'd
  To the fair child, who fearless sat,
Though never yet hath day-beam burn'd
  Upon a brow more fierce than that,—
Sullenly fierce—a mixture dire,
Like thunder-clouds, of gloom and fire;

In much the PERI's eye could read
Dark tales of many a ruthless deed ;
The ruin'd maid—the shrine profan'd—
Oaths broken—and the threshold stain'd
With blood of guests !—*there* written, **all,**
Black as the damning drops that fall
From the denouncing Angel's pen,
Ere Mercy weeps them out again.

Yet tranquil now that man of crime
(As if the balmy evening time
Soften'd his spirit) look'd and lay,
Watching the rosy infant's play :—
Though still, whene'er his eye by **chance**
Fell on the boy's, its lurid glance
  Met that unclouded joyous gaze,
As torches that have burnt all night
Through some impure and godless **rite,**
  Encounter morning's glorious rays.

But, hark ! the vesper call to prayer,
  As slow the orb of daylight sets,
Is rising sweetly on the air,
  From SYRIA's thousand minarets !
The boy has started from the bed
Of flowers, where he had laid his **head,**
And down upon the fragrant sod
  Kneels, [198] with its forehead to the south
Lisping the eternal name of God
  From Purity's own cherub mouth,
And looking, while his hands and **eyes**
Are lifted to the glowing skies,
Like a stray babe of Paradise,

Just lighted on that flowery plain,
And seeking for its home again.
Oh ! 'twas a sight — that Heaven—that child—
A scene, which might have well beguil'd
Even haughty EBLIS of a sigh
For glories lost and peace gone by!

And how felt *he,* the wretched Man
Reclining there—while memory ran
O'er many a year of guilt and strife,
Flew o'er the dark flood of his life,
Nor found one sunny resting-place,
Nor brought him back one branch of grace!
" There *was* a time," he said, in mild,
Heart-humbled tones—" thou blessed child!
When, young and haply pure as thou,
I look'd and pray'd like thee ; but now—"
He hung his head—each nobler aim,
   And hope, and feeling, which had slept
From boyhood's hour, that instant came
   Fresh o'er him, and he wept—he wept !
Blest tears of soul-felt penitence !
   In whose benign, redeeming flow
Is felt the first, the only sense
   Of guiltless joy that guilt can know.

" There's a drop," said the PERI, " that down
      from the moon
Falls through the withering airs of June
Upon EGYPT'S land,[194] of so healing a power,
So balmy a virtue, that e'en in the hour
The drop descends, contagion dies,
And health re-animates earth and skies !—

Oh, is it not thus, thou man of sin,
    The precious tears of repentance fall?
Though foul thy fiery plagues within,
    One heavenly drop hath dispell'd them all!

And now—behold him kneeling there
By the child's side, in humble prayer,
While the same sunbeam shines upon
The guilty and the guiltless one,
And hymns of joy proclaim through Heaven
The triumph of a Soul Forgiven!
'Twas when the golden orb had set,
While on their knees they linger'd yet,
There fell a light more lovely far
Than ever came from sun or star,
Upon the tear that, warm and meek,
Dew'd that repentant sinner's cheek.
To mortal eye this light might seem
A northern flash or meteor beam—
But well the enraptur'd PERI knew
'Twas a bright smile the Angel threw
From Heaven's gate, to hail that tear
Her harbinger of glory near!

"Joy, joy forever! my task is done—
The Gates are pass'd, and Heaven is won!
Oh! am I not happy? I am, I am—
    To thee, sweet Eden! how dark and sad 195
    And the fragrant bowers of AMBERABAD!
Are the diamonds turrets of SHADUKIAM,
Farewell, ye odors of Earth, that die
Passing away like a lover's sigh;—

My feast is now of the Tooba Tree, [196]
Whose scent is the breath of Eternity !
Farewell, ye vanishing flowers, that shone
    In my fairy wreath, so bright and brief ;—
Oh! what are the brightest that e'er have blown,
To the lote-tree, springing by ALLA's throne, [197]
    Whose flowers have a soul in every leaf !
Joy, joy forever !—my task is done—
The Gates are pass'd, and Heaven is won !"

"AND this," said the Great Chamberlain, " is poetry ! this flimsy manufacture of the brain, which, in comparison with the lofty and durable monuments of genius, is as the gold filigree-work of Zamara besides the eternal architecture of Egypt !" After this gorgeous sentence, which, with a few more of the same kind, FADLADEEN kept by him for rare and important occasions, he proceeded to the anatomy of the short poem just recited. The lax and easy kind of metre in which it was written ought to be denounced, he said, as one of the leading causes of the alarming growth of poetry in our times. If some check were not given to this lawless facility, we should soon be overrun by a race of bards as numerous and as shallow as the hundred and twenty thousand Streams of Basra. [198] They who succeeded in this style deserved chastisement for their very success ; —as warriors have been punished, even after gaining a victory, because they had taken the liberty of gaining it in an irregular or unestab-

lished manner. What, then, was to be said to
those who failed ? to those who presumed, as
in the present lamentable instance, to imitate
the license and ease of the bolder sons of song,
without .ny of that grace or vigor which gave
a dignity even to negligence ;—who, like them,
flung the jereed [199] carelessly, but not like them,
to the mark ;—"and who," said he, raising his
voice, to excite proper degree of wakefulness in
his hearers, " contrive to appear heavy and
constrained in the midst of all the latitude they
allow themselves, like one of those young
pagans that dance before the Princess, who is
ingenious enough to move as if her limbs were
fettered, in a pair of the lightest and loosest
drawers of Masulipatam ! "—

It was but little suitable, he continued, to
the grave march of criticism to follow this fan-
tastical Peri, of whom they had just heard,
through all her flights and adventures between
earth and heaven ; but he could not help
adverting to the puerile conceitedness of the
Three Gifts which she is supposed to carry to
the skies,—a drop of blood, forsooth, a sigh,
and a tear ! How the first of these articles was
delivered into the Angel's "radiant hand" he
professed himself at a loss to discover ; and as
to the safe carriage of the sigh and the tear,
such Peris and such poets were being by far
too incomprehensible for him even to guess
how they managed such matters. "But, in
short " said he, "it is a waste of time and

patience to dwell longer upon a thing so incurably frivolous,—puny even among its own puny race, and such as only the Banyan Hospital [200] for Sick Insects sould undertake."

In vain did LALLA ROOKH try to soften this inexorable critic; in vain did she resort to her most eloquent common-places,—reminding him that poets were a timid and sensitive race, whose sweetness was not to be drawn forth, like that of the fragrant grass near the Ganges, by crushing and trampling upon them; [201]— that severity often extinguished every chance of the perfection which it demanded; and that, after all, perfection was like the Mountain of the Talisman,—no one had ever yet reached its summit. [202] Neither these gentle axioms, nor the still gentler looks with which they were inculcated, could lower for one instant the elevation of FADLADEEN's eyebrows, or charm him into anything like encouragement, or even toleration of her poet. Toleration, indeed, was not among the weaknesses of FADLADEEN:—he carried the same spirit into matters of poetry and of religion, and, though little versed in the beauties or sublimities of either, was a perfect master of the art of persecution in both. His zeal was the same, too, in either pursuit whether the game before him was pagans, (poetasters,—worshippers of cows, or writers epics.

They had now arrived at the splendid c

of Lahore, whose mausoleums and shrines, magnificent and numberless, where Death appeared to share equal honors with Heaven, would have powerfully affected the heart and imagination of LALLA ROOKH, if feelings more of this earth had not taken entire possession of her already. She was here met by messengers, despatched from Cashmere, who informed her that the King had arrived in the Valley, and was himself superintending the sumptuous preparations that were then making in the Saloons of the Shalimar for her reception. The chill she felt on receiving this intelligence,— which to a bride whose heart was free and light would have brought only images of affection and pleasure,—convinced her that her peace was gone forever, and that she was in love, irretrievably in love, with young FERAMORZ. The veil had fallen off in which this passion at first disguises itself, and to know that she loved was now as painful as to love *without* knowing it had been delicious. FERA-MORZ, too,—what misery would be his, if the sweet hours of intercourse so imprudently allowed them should have stolen into his heart the same fatal fascination as into hers ;—if, notwithstanding her rank, and the modest homage he always paid to it, even *he* should have yielded to the influence of those long and happy interviews, where music, poetry, the delightful scenes of nature,—all had tended to bring their hearts close together, and to waken by every means that too ready passion, which often, like the young of the desert-bird, is warmed into life by the eyes alone ! [203] She saw but one way to preserve herself from being culpable as well as unhappy, and this, however painful, she was resolved to adopt. FERAMORZ must no more be admitted to her presence. To have strayed so far into the dangerous labyrinth was wrong, but to linger in it, while the clew was yet in her hand, would be criminal. Though the heart she had to offer to the King of Bucharia might be cold and broken, it should at least be pure ; and she must only endeavor to forget the short dream of happiness she had enjoyed,—like that Arabian shepherd, who, in wandering into the wilderness, caught a glimpse of the Gardens of Irem, and then lost them again forever ! [204]

The arrival of the young Bride at Lahore was celebrated in the most enthusiastic manner. The Rajas and Omras in her train, who had kept at a certain distance during the journey, and never encamped nearer to the Princess than was strictly necessary for her safeguard, here rode in splendid cavalcade through the city, and distributed the most costly presents to the crowd. Engines were erected in all the squares, which cast forth showers of confectionery among the people ; while the artisans, in chariots, [205] adorned with tinsel and flying streamers, exhibited the badges of their respective trades through the streets. Such brilliant displays of life and pageantry among the palaces, and domes, and gilded minarets of Lahore, made the city altogether, like a place of enchantment;—particularly on the day when LALLA ROOKH set out again upon her journey, when she was accompanied to the gate by all the fairest and richest of the nobility, and rode along between ranks of beautiful boys and girls, who kept waving over their heads plates of gold and silver flowers,[206] and then threw them around to be gathered by the populace.

For many days after their departure from Lahore, a considerable degree of gloom hung over the whole party. LALLA ROOKH, who had intended to make illness her excuse for not admitting the young minstrel, as usual to the pavilion, soon found that to feign indisposition was unnecessary;—FADLADEEN felt the loss of the good road they had hitherto travelled, and was very near cursing Jehan-Guire (of blessed memory!) for not having continued his delectable alley of trees,[207] at least as far as the mountains of Cashmere:—while the Ladies, who had nothing now to do all day but to be fanned by peacocks' feathers and listen to FADLADEEN, seemed heartily weary of the life they led, and, in spite of all the Great Chamberlain's criticisms, were so tasteless as to wish for the poet again. One evening, as they were proceeding to their place of rest for the night, the Princess, who, for the freer enjoyment of the air, had mounted her favorite Arabian palfrey, in passing by a small grove, heard the notes of a lute from within its leaves, and a voice, which she but too well knew, singing the following words:—

TELL me not of joys above,
  If that world can give no bliss,
Truer, happier than the Love
  Which enslaves our souls in this.

Tell me not of Houris' eyes;—
  Far from me their dangerous glow,
If those looks that light the skies
  Wound like some that burn below.

Who, that feels what Love is here,
  All its falsehood—all its pain—
Would, for even Elysium's sphere,
  Risk the fatal dream again?

Who, that 'midst a desert's heat
  Sees the waters fade away,
Would not rather die than meet
  Streams again as false as they?

The tone of melancholy defiance in which these words were uttered, went to LALLA ROOKH's heart;—and, as she reluctantly rode on, she could not help feeling it to be a sad but still sweet certainty, that FERAMORZ was to the full as enamoured and miserable as herself.

The place where they encamped that evening was the first delightful spot they had come to since they left Lahore. On each side of them was a grove full of small Hindoo temples, and planted with the most graceful trees of the East; where the tamarind, the cassia, and the silken plantains of Ceylon were mingled in rich contrast with the high fan-like foliage of the Palmyra,—that favorite tree of the luxurious bird that lights up the chambers of its nest with fire-flies.[208] In the middle of the lawn where the pavilion stood there was a tank surrounded by small mango-trees, on the clear cold waters of which floated multitudes of the beautiful red lotus ;[209] while at a distance stood the ruins of a strange and awful-looking tower, which seemed old enough to have been the temple of some religion no longer known, and which spoke the voice of desolation in the midst of all that bloom and loveliness. This singular ruin excited the wonder and conjectures of all. LALLA ROOKH guessed in vain, and the all-pretending FADLADEEN, who had never till this journey been beyond the precincts of Delhi, was proceeding most learnedly to show that he knew nothing whatever about the matter, when one of the Ladies suggested that perhaps FERA-MORZ could satisfy their curiosity. They were now approaching his native mountains, and this tower might perhaps be a relic of some of those dark superstitions which had prevailed in that country before the light of Islam dawned upon it. The Chamberlain, who usually preferred his own ignorance to the best knowledge that any one else could give him, was by no means pleased with this officious reference;

and the Princess, too, was about to interpose a faint word of objection, but, before either of them could speak, a slave was despatched for FERAMORZ, who, in a very few minutes, made his appearance before them—looking so pale and unhappy in LALLA ROOKH's eyes, that she repented already of her cruelty in having so long excluded him.

That venerable tower, he told them, was the remains of an ancient Fire-temple, built by those Ghebers or Persians of the old religion, who, many hundred years since, had fled hither from their Arab conquerors,[210] preferring liberty and their altars in a foreign land to the alternative of apostasy or persecution in their own. It was impossible, he added, not to feel interested in the many glorious but unsuccessful struggles which had been made by these original natives of Persia to cast off the yoke of their bigoted conquerors. Like their own Fire in the Burning Field at Bakou,[211] when suppressed in one place, they had but broken out with fresh flame in another; and, as a native of Cashmere, of that fair and Holy Valley which had in the same manner become the prey of strangers,[212] and seen her ancient shrines and native princes swept away before the march of her intolerant invaders, he felt a sympathy, he owned, with the sufferings of the persecuted Ghebers, which every monument like this before them but tended more powerfully to awaken.

It was the first time that FERAMORZ had ever ventured upon so much *prose* before FADLADEEN, and it may easily be conceived what effect such prose as this must have produced upon that most orthodox and most pagan-hating personage. He sat for some minutes aghast, ejaculating only at intervals, " Bigoted conquerors ! —sympathy with Fire-worshippers ! " [213]—while FERAMORZ, happy to take advantage of this almost speechless horror of the Chamberlain, proceeded to say that he knew a melancholy story, connected with the events of one of those struggles of the brave Fire-worshippers against their Arab masters, which, if the evening was not too far advanced, he should have much pleasure in being allowed to relate to the Princess It was impossible for LALLA ROOKH to refuse ;—he had never before looked so animated ; and when he spoke of the Holy Valley. his eyes had sparkled, she thought, like the talismanic characters on the scimitar of Solomon.   Her consent was therefore most readily granted : and while FADLADEEN sat in unspeakable dismay, expecting treason and abomination in every line. the poet thus began his story of the Fire-worshippers :—

THE FIRE-WORSHIPPERS.

'Tis moonlight over Oman's Sea ; [214]
  Her banks of pearl and balmy isles
Bask in the night-beam beauteously,
  And her blue waters sleep in smiles.
'Tis moonlight in Harmozia's [215] walls,
And through her Emir's porphyry halls,
Where, some hours since, was heard the swell
Of trumpet and the clash of zel, [216]
Bidding the bright-eyed sun farewell ;—
The peaceful sun, whom better suits
  The music of the bulbul's nest,
Or the light touch of lovers' lutes,
  To sing him to his golden rest.
All hush'd—there's not a breeze in motion ;
The shore is silent as the ocean.
If zephyrs come, so light they come,
  Nor leaf is stirr'd nor wave is driven ;—
The wind-tower on the Emir's dome [217]
  Can hardly win a breath from heaven.

Even he, that tyrant Arab, sleeps
Calm, while a nation round him weeps ;
While curses load the air he breathes,
And falchions from unnumber'd sheaths
Are starting to avenge the shame
His race hath brought on Iran's [218] name.

Hard, heartless Chief, unmov'd alike
'Mid eyes that weep, and swords that strike ;—
One of that saintly, murderous brood,
   To carnage and the Koran given,
Who think through unbeliever's blood
   Lies their directest path to heaven ;—
One, who will pause and kneel unshod
   In the warm blood his hand hath pour'd,
To mutter o'er some text of God
   Engraven on his reeking sword ; [219]
Nay, who can coolly note the line,
The letter of those words divine,
To which his blade, with searching art,
Had sunk into its victim's heart !

Just ALLA ! what must be thy look,
   When such a wretch before thee stands
Unblushing, with thy Sacred Book,—
   Turning the leaves with blood-stain'd hands,
And wresting from its page sublime
His creed of lust, and hate, and crime ;
Even as those bees of TREBIZOND,
   Which, from the sunniest flowers that glad
With their pure smile the gardens round,
   Draw venom forth that drives men mad. [220]

Never did fierce ARABIA send
   A satrap forth more direly great ;
Never was IRAN doom'd to bend
   Beneath a yoke of deadlier weight.
Her throne had fallen—her pride was crush'd—
Her sons were willing slaves, nor blush'd,

In their own land,—no more their own,—
To crouch beneath a stranger's throne.
Her towers, where MITHRA once had burn'd,
To Moslem shrines—oh shame !—were turn'd,
Where slaves, converted by the sword,
Their mean, apostate worship pour'd,
And curs'd the faith their sires ador'd.
Yet has she hearts, 'mid all this ill,
O'er all this wreck, high, buoyant still
With hope and vengeance ;—hearts that yet—
   Like gems, in darkness, issuing rays
They've treasur'd from the sun that's set,—
   Beam all the light of long-lost days !
And swords she hath, nor weak nor slow
   To second all such hearts can dare ;
As he shall know, well, dearly know,
   Who sleeps in moonlight luxury there,
Tranquil as if his spirit lay
Becalm'd in Heaven's approving ray.
Sleep on—for purer eyes than thine
Those waves are hush'd, those planets shine ;
Sleep on, and be thy rest unmov'd
   By the white moonbeam's dazzling power ;—
None but the loving and the lov'd
   Should be awake at this sweet hour.

And see—where, high above those rocks
   That o'er the deep their shadows fling,
Yon turret stands ;—where ebon locks,
   As glossy as a heron's wing
   Upon the turban of a king,[221]
Hang from the lattice, long and wild—
'Tis she, that EMIR's blooming child,

All truth and tenderness and grace,
Though born of such ungentle race ;—
An image of Youth's radiant Fountain
Springing in a desolate mountain ! [222]

Oh what a pure and sacred thing
    Is beauty, curtain'd from the sight
Of the gross world, illumining
    One only mansion with her light !
Unseen by man's disturbing eye,—
    The flower that blooms beneath the sea,
Too deep for sunbeams, doth not lie
    Hid in more chaste obscurity.
So, HINDA, have thy face and mind,
Like holy mysteries, lain enshrin'd.
And oh, what transport for a lover
    To lift the veil that shades them o'er !—
Like those who, all at once, discover
    In the lone deep some fairy shore,
    Where mortal never trod before,
And sleep and wake in scented airs
No lip had ever breath'd but theirs.

Beautiful are the maids that glide,
    On summer-eves, through YEMEN's [223] dales
And bright the glancing looks they hide
    Behind their litters' roseate veils ;—
And brides, as delicate and fair
As the white jasmine flowers they wear.
Hath YEMEN in her blissful clime,
    Who, lull'd in cool kiosk or bower, [224]
Before their mirrors count the time, [225]
    And grow still lovelier every hour.

But never yet hath bride or maid
   In ARABY's gay Haram smil'd,
Whose boasted brightness would not fade
   Before AL HASSAN's blooming child.

Light as the angel shapes that bless
An infant's dream, yet not the less
Rich in all woman's loveliness ;—
With eyes so pure, that from their ray
Dark Vice would turn abash'd away,
Blinded like serpents when they gaze
Upon the emerald virgin blaze ; [226]—
Yet fill'd with all youth's sweet desires,
Mingling the meek and vestal fires
Of other worlds with all the bliss,
The fond, weak tenderness of this :
A soul, too, more than half divine,
   Where, through some shades of earthly feel-
     ing,
Religion's soften'd glories shine,
   Like light through summer foliage stealing,
Shedding a glow of such mild hue,
So warm, and yet so shadowy too,
As makes the very darkness there
More beautiful than light elsewhere.

Such is the maid who, at this hour,
   Hath risen from her restless sleep,
And sits alone in that high bower,
   Watching the still and shining deep.
Ah ! 'twas not thus,—with tearful eyes
   And beating heart,—she used to gaze

On the magnificent earth and skies,
　　In her own land, in happier days.
Why looks she now so anxious down
Among those rocks, whose rugged frown
　　Blackens the mirror of the deep?
Whom waits she all this lonely night?
　　Too rough the rocks, too bold the steep,
For man to scale that turret's height!—

So deem'd at least her thoughtful sire,
　　When high, to catch the cool night-air,
After the day-beam's wihtering fire,²²⁷
　　He built her bower of freshness there,
And had it deck'd with costliest skill,
　　And fondly thought it safe as fair:—
Think, reverend dreamer! think so still,
　　Nor wake to learn what Love can dare—
Love, all-defying Love, who sees
No charm in trophies won with ease;
Whose rarest, dearest fruits of bliss
Are pluck'd on Danger's precipice!
Bolder than they who dare not dive
　　For pearls, but when the sea's at rest,
Love, in the tempest most alive,
　　Hath ever held that pearl the best
He finds beneath the stormiest water.
Yes—Araby's unrivall'd daughter,
Though high that tower, that rock-way rude,
　　There's one who, but to kiss thy cheek,
Would climb the untrodden solitude
　　Of Ararat's tremendous peak,²²⁸
And think its steeps, though dark and dread,
Heaven's pathways, if to thee they led!

Even now thou seest the flashing spray,
That lights his oar's impatient way ;—
Even now thou hear'st the sudden shock
Of his swift bark against the rock,
And stretchest down thy arms of snow,
As if to lift him from below !
Like her, to whom at dead of night,
The bridegroom, with his locks of light,²⁸⁵
Came, in the flush of love and pride,
And scal'd the terrace of his bride ;—
When, as she saw him rashly spring,
And midway up in danger cling,
She flung him down her long black hair,
Exclaiming, breathless, "There, love, there !"²⁶
And scarce did manlier nerve uphold
        The hero ZAL in that fond hour,
Than wings the youth who, fleet and bold,
        Now climbs the rocks to HINDA'S bower.
See—light as up their granite steeps
        The rock-goats of ARABIA clamber,²⁹⁰
Fearless from crag to crag he leaps,
        And now is in the maiden's chamber.

She loves—but knows not whom she loves,
        Nor what his race, nor whence he came ;—
Like one who meets, in Indian groves,
        Some beauteous bird without a name,
Brought by the last ambrosial breeze,
From isles in the undiscover'd seas,
To show his plumage for a day
To wondering eyes, and wing away !
Will *he* thus fly—her nameless lover ?
        ALLA forbid ! 'twas by a moon

As fair as this, while singing over
    Seme ditty to her soft Kanoon, ²⁸¹
Alone, at this same witching hour,
    She first beheld his radiant eyes
Gleam through the lattice of the bower,
    Where nightly now they mix their sighs
And thought some spirit of the air
(For what could waft a mortal there?)
Was pausing on his moonlit way
To listen to her lonely lay!
This fancy ne'er hath left her mind:
    And though, when terror's swoon had past,
She saw a youth, of mortal kind,
    Before her in obeisance cast,
Yet often since, when he hath spoken
Strange, awful words,—and gleams have
    broken
From his dark eyes, too bright to bear,—
    Oh! she hath fear'd her soul was given
To some unhallow'd child of air,
    Some erring Spirit cast from heaven,
Like those angelic youths of old,
Who burn'd for maids of mortal mould,
Bewilder'd left the glorious skies,
And lost their heaven for woman's eyes.
Fond girl! nor fiend nor angel he
Who woos thy young simplicity;
But one of earth's impassion'd sons,
    As warm in love, as fierce in ire,
As the best heart whose current runs
    Full of the Day-God's living fire.
But quench'd to-night that ardor seems,
    And pale his cheek, and sunk his brow;—

Never before, but in her dreams,
  Had she beheld him pale as now :
And those were dreams of troubled sleep,
From which 'twas joy to wake and weep ;
Visions, that will not be forgot,
  But sadden every waking scene,
Like warning ghosts, that leave the spot
  All wither'd where they once have been.

"How sweetly," said the trembling maid,
Of her own gentle voice afraid,
So long had they in silence stood,
Looking upon that tranquil flood—
"How sweetly does the moonbeam smile
To-night upon yon leafy isle !
Oft, in my fancy's wanderings,
I've wish'd that little isle had wings,
And we, within its fairy bowers,
  Were wafted off to seas unknown
Where nor a pulse should beat but ours,
  And we might live, love, die alone !
Far from the cruel and the cold,—
  Where the bright eyes of angels only
Should come around us, to behold
  A paradise so pure and lonely.
Would this be world enough for thee ? "—
Playful she turn'd, that he might see
  The passing smile her cheek put on ;
But when she mark'd how mournfully
  His eyes met hers, that smile was gone;
And bursting into heartfelt tears,
"Yes, yes," she cried, " my hourly fears,

My dreams have boded all too right—
We part—forever part—to-night !
I knew, I knew it *could* not last—
'Twas bright, 'twas heavenly, but 'tis past !
Oh ! ever thus, from childhood's hour,
   I've seen my fondest hopes decay ;
I never lov'd a tree or flower,
   But 'twas the first to fade away.
I never nurs'd a dear gazelle,
   To glad me with its soft black eye,
But when it came to know me well,
   And love me, it was sure to die !
Now too—the joy most like divine
   Of all I ever dreamt or knew,
To see thee, hear thee, call thee mine,—
   Oh misery ! must I lose *that* too ?
Yet go—on peril's brink we meet ;—
   Those frightful rocks—that treacherous sea—
No, never come again—though sweet,
   Though heaven, it may be death to thee.
Farewell—and blessings on thy way,
   Where'er thou goest, beloved stranger !
Better to sit and watch that ray,
And think thee safe, though far away,
   Than have thee near me, and in danger !"

"Danger !—oh, tempt me not to boast—"
The youth exclaim'd—" thou little know'st
What he can brave, who, born and nurst
In Danger's paths, has dar'd her worst ;
Upon whose ear the signal word
   Of strife and death is hourly breaking ;

Who sleeps with head upon the **sword**
  His fever'd hand must grasp in **waking.**
Danger !—"
                "Say on—thou fear'st not **then,**
And we may meet—oft meet again ? "

"Oh ! look not so—beneath the **skies**
I now fear nothing but those eyes.
If aught on earth could charm or **force**
My spirit from its destin'd course,—
If aught could make this soul forget
The bond to which its seal is set,
'Twould be those eyes ;—they, onl**y they,**
Could melt that sacred seal away !
But no—'tis fix'd—*my* awful doom
Is fix'd—on this side of the tomb
We meet no more.; why, why did **Heaven**
Mingle two souls that earth has **riven,**
Has rent asunder wide as ours?
O Arab maid, as soon the Powers
Of Light and Darkness may comb**ine,**
As I be link'd with thee or thine !
'l'hy Father——"
                  "Holy ALLA save
  His gray head from that lightning glance**!**
Thou know'st him not—he loves the brave **;**
  Nor lives there under heaven's expanse
One who would prize, would worship the**e**
And thy bold spirit, more than he.
Oft when, in childhood, I have play'd
  With the bright falchion by his **side,**
I've heard him swear his lisping maid
  In time should be a warrior's **bride.**

And still, whene'er at Haram hours
I take him cool sherbets and flowers,
He tells me, when in playful mood,
   A hero shall my bridegroom be,
Since maids are best in battle woo'd,
   And won with shouts of victory !
Nay, turn not from me—thou alone
Art form'd to make both hearts thy own.
Go—join his sacred ranks—thou know'st
   The unholy strife these Persians wage :
Good Heaven, that frown !—even now thou
      glow'st
   With more than mortal warrior's rage,
Haste to the camp by morning's light,
And when that sword is rais'd in fight,
Oh still remember, Love and I
Beneath its shadow trembling lie !
One victory o'er those Slaves of Fire,
Those impious Ghebers, whom my sire
Abhors——"

      " Hold, hold—thy words are death—"
   The stranger cried, as wild he flung
His mantle back, and show'd beneath
   The Gheber belt that round him clung [282]—
" Here, maiden, look—weep—blush to see
All that thy sire abhors in me !
Yes—*I* am of that impious race,
   Those Slaves of Fire, who, morn and even,
Hail their Creator's dwelling-place
   Among the living lights of heaven ; [283]
Yes—*I* am of that outcast few,
To IRAN and to vengeance true,

Who curse the hour your Arabs came
To desolate our shrines of flame,
And swear, before God's burning eye,
To break our country's chains, or die!
Thy bigot sire,—nay, tremble not,—
 He, who gave birth to those dear eyes,
With me is sacred as the spot
 From which our fires of worship rise!
But know—'twas he I sought that night,
 When, from my watch-boat on the sea,
I caught this turret's glimmering light,
 And up the rude rocks desperately
Rush'd to my prey—thou know'st the rest—
I climb'd the gory vulture's nest,
And found a trembling dove within ;—
Thine, thine the victory—thine the sin—
If Love hath made one thought his own,
That Vengeance claims first—last—alone!
Oh! had we never, never met,
Or could this heart e'en now forget
How link'd, how bless'd we might have
  been,
Had fate not frown'd so dark between!
Hadst thou been born a Persian maid,
In neighboring valleys had we dwelt,
Through the same fields in childhood play'd,
 At the same kindling altar knelt,—
Then, then, while all those nameless ties,
In which the charm of Country lies,
Had round our hearts been hourly spun,
Till IRAN's cause and thine were one ;
While in thy lute's awakening sigh
I heard the voice of days gone by,

And saw, in every smile of thine,
Returning hours of glory shine ;—
While the wrong'd Spirit of our Land
    Liv'd, look'd, and spoke her wrongs through
       thee,—
God ! who could then this sword withstand ?
    Its very flash were victory !
But now—estrang'd, divorc'd forever,
Far as the grasp of Fate can sever ;
Our only ties what love has wove,—
    In faith, friends, country, sunder'd wide ;
And then, then only, true to love,
    When false to all that's dear beside !
Thy father, IRAN's deadliest foe—
Thyself perhaps, even now—but no—
Hate never look'd so lovely yet !
    No—sacred to thy soul will be
The land of him who could forget
    All but that bleeding land for thee.
When other eyes shall see, unmov'd,
    Her widows mourn, her warriors fall,
Thou'lt think how well one Gheber lov'd,
    And for *his* sake thou'lt weep for all !
But look——"

             With sudden start he turn'd
    And pointed to the distant wave,
Where lights, like charnel meteors, burn'd
    Bluely, as o'er some seaman's grave ;
And fiery darts, at intervals,[234]
    Flew up all sparkling from the main,
As if each star that nightly falls
    Were shooting back to heaven again.

"My signal lights!—I must away—
Both, both are ruin'd, if I stay.
Farewell—sweet life! thou cling'st in vain—
Now, Vengeance, I am thine again!"
Fiercely he broke away, nor stopp'd
Nor look'd—but from the lattice dropp'd
Down 'mid the pointed crags beneath,
As if he fled from love to death.
While pale and mute young HINDA stood;
Nor mov'd, till in the silent flood
A momentary plunge below
Startled her from her trance of woe ;—
Shrieking she to the lattice flew,
   "I come—I come—if in that tide
Thou sleep'st to-night, I'll sleep there too,
   In death's cold wedlock, by thy side.
Oh! I would ask no happier bed
   Than the chill wave my love lies under :—
Sweeter to rest together dead,
   Far sweeter, than to live asunder!"
But no—their hour is not yet come—
   Again she sees his pinnace fly,
Wafting him fleetly to his home,
   Where'er that ill-starr'd home may lie;
And calm and smooth it seem'd to win
   Its moonlit way before the wind,
As if it bore all peace within,
   Nor left one breaking heart behind!

THE PRINCESS, whose heart was sad enough
already, could have wished that FERAMORZ had
chosen a less melancholy story; as it is only
to the happy that tears are a luxury. He

ladies, however, were by no means sorry that
love was once more the Poet's theme ; for,
whenever he spoke of love, they said, his voice
was as sweet as if he had chewed the leaves of
that enchanted tree which grows over the tomb
of the musician, Tan-Sein. [235]

Their road all the morning had lain through
a very dreary country ;—through valleys,
covered with a low bushy jungle, where, in more
than one place, the awful signal of the bamboo
staff, [236] with the white flag at its top, reminded
the traveller that, in that very spot, the tiger
had made some human creature his victim. It
was, therefore, with much pleasure that they
arrived at sunset in a safe and lovely glen, and
encamped under one of those holy trees whose
smooth columns and spreading roofs seem to
destine them for natural temples of religion.
Beneath this spacious shade, some pious hands
had erected a row of pillars ornamented with
the most beautiful porcelain, [237] which now
supplied the use of mirrors to the young
maidens, as they adjusted their hair in descending from the palankeens. Here, while, as usual,
the Princess sat listening anxiously, with
FADLADEEN in one of his loftiest moods of
criticism by her side, the young Poet, leaning
against a branch of the tree, thus continued
his story :—

THE morn hath risen clear and calm,
   And o'er the Green Sea [238] palely shines,

Revealing BAHREIN's [239] groves of palm,
  And lighting KISHMA's [239] amber vines.
Fresh smell the shores of ARABY,
While breezes from the Indian sea
Blow round SELAMA's [240] sainted cape,
  And curl the shining flood beneath,—
Whose waves are rich with many a grape
  And cocoa-nut and flowery wreath,
Which pious seamen, as they pass'd,
Had tow'rd that holy headland cast—
Oblations to the Genii there
For gentle skies and breezes fair !
The nightingale now bends her flight [241]
From the high trees, where, all the night
  She sung so sweet, with none to listen ;
And hides her from the morning star
  Where thickets of pomegranate glisten
In the clear dawn,—bespangled o'er,
  With dew, whose night drops would not stain
The best and brightest scimitar [242]
That ever youthful Sultan wore
  On the first morning of his reign.

And see—the Sun himself !—on wings
Of glory up the East he springs.
Angel of Light ! who from the time
Those heavens began their march sublime,
Hath first of all the starry choir
Trod in his Maker's steps of fire !
  Where are the days, thou wondrous sphere,
When IRAN, like a sun-flower, turn'd
To meet that eye where'er it burn'd?—
  When, from the banks of BENDEMEER

14

To the nut-groves of SAMARCAND,
Thy temples flam'd o'er all the land?
Where are they? ask the shades of them
   Who, on CADESSIA's [243] bloody plains,
Saw fierce invaders pluck the gem
From IRAN's broken diadem,
   And bind her ancient faith in chains :—
Ask the poor exile, cast alone
On foreign shores, unlov'd, unknown,
Beyond the Caspian's Iron Gates, [244]
Or on the snowy Mossian mountains,
Far from his beaut ous land of dates,
   Her jasmine bowers and sunny fountains :
Yet happier so than if he trod
His own belov'd, but blighted, sod,
Beneath a despot stranger's nod !—
Oh, he would rather houseless roam
   Where Freedom and his God may lead,
Than be the sleekest slave at home
   That crouches to the conqueror's creed !
Is IRAN's pride then gone forever,
   Quench'd with the flame in MITHRA's caves ?—
No—she has sons, that never—never—
   Will stoop to be the Moslem's slaves,
   While heaven has light or earth has graves ;—
Spirits of fire, that brood not long,
But flash resentment back for wrong ;
And hearts where, slow but deep, the seeds
Of vengeance ripen into deeds,
Till, in some treacherous hour of calm,
They burst, like ZEILAN's giant palm, [245]
Whose buds fly open with a sound
That shakes the pigmy forests round !

Yes, Emir ! he, who scal'd that tower,
    And, had he reach'd thy slumbering breast,
Had taught thee, in a Gheber's power
    How safe e'en tyrant heads may rest—
Is one of many, brave as he,
Who loathe thy haughty race and thee ;
Who, though they know the strife is vain,
Who, though they know the riven chain
Snaps but to enter in the heart
Of him who rends its links apart,
Yet dare the issue,—blest to be
E'en for one bleeding moment free,
And die in pangs of liberty !
Thou know'st them well—'tis some moons
        since
    Thy turban'd troops and blood-red flags
Thou satrap of a bigot Prince,
    Have swarm'd among these Green Sea crags ;
Yet here, e'en here a sacred band—
Ay, in the portal of that land
Thou, Arab, dar'st to call thy own—
Their spears across thy path have thrown ;
Here—ere the winds half wing'd thee o'er—
Rebellion brav'd thee from the shore.

Rebellion ! foul, dishonoring word,
    Whose wrongful blight so oft has stain'd
The holiest cause that tongue or sword
    Of mortal ever lost or gain'd.
How many a spirit, born to bless,
    Hath sunk beneath that withering name,
Whom but a day's, an hour's success
    Had wafted to eternal fame !

As exhalations, when they burst
From the warm earth, if chill'd at first,
If check'd in soaring from the plain,
Darken to fogs and sink again ;—
But if they once triumphant spread
Their wings above the mountain-head,
Become enthroned in upper air,
And turn to sun-bright glories there!

And who is he, that wields the might
    Of Freedom on the Green Sea brink,
Before whose sabre's dazzling light 246
    The eyes of YEMEN's warriors wink?
Who comes, embower'd in the spears
Of KERMAN's hardy mountaineers?—
Those mountaineers that truest, last,
    Cling to their country's ancient rites,
As if that God, whose eyelids cast
    Their closing gleam on IRAN's heights,
Among her snowy mountains threw
The last light of his worship too!

'Tis HAFED—name of fear, whose sound
    Chills like the muttering of a charm!—
Shout but that awful name around,
    And palsy shakes the manliest arm.
'Tis HAFED, most accurs'd and dire
(So rank'd by Moslem hate and ire)
Of all the rebel Sons of Fire ;
Of whose malign, tremendous power
The Arabs, at their mid-watch hour,
Such tales of fearful wonder tell,
That each affrighted sentinel

Pulls down his cowl upon his eyes,
Lest HAFED in the midst should rise!
A man, they say, of monstrous birth,
A mingled race of flame and earth,
Sprung from those old, enchanted kings,[247]
   Who in their fairy helms, of yore,
A feather from the mystic wings
   Of the Simoorgh resistless wore;
And gifted by the Fiends of Fire,
Who groan'd to see their shrines expire,
With charms that, all in vain withstood,
Would drown the Koran's light in blood!
Such were the tales, that won belief,
   And such the coloring Fancy gave
To a young, warm, and dauntless Chief, —
   One who, no more than mortal brave,
Fought for the hand his soul ador'd,
   For happy homes and altars free, —
His only talisman, the sword,
   His only spell-word, Liberty!
One of that ancient hero line,
Along whose glorious current shine
Names, that have sanctified their blood;
As LEBANON'S small mountain-flood
Is render'd holy by the ranks
Of sainted cedars on its banks.[248]
'Twas not for him to crouch that knee
Tamely to Moslem tyranny;
'Twas not for him, whose soul was cast
In the bright mould of ages past,
Whose melancholy spirit, fed
With all the glories of the dead,

Though fram'd for Iran's happiest years,
Was born among her chains and tears !—
'Twas not for him to swell the crowd
Of slavish heads, that shrinking bow'd
Before the Moslem, as he pass'd,
Like shrubs beneath the poison-blast—
No,—far he fled—indignant fled
　　The pageant of his country's shame ;
While every tear her children shed
　　Fell on his soul like drops of flame ;
And, as a lover hails the dawn
　　Of a first smile, so welcom'd he
The sparkle of the first sword drawn
　　For vengeance and for liberty !

But vain was valor—vain the flower
Of Kerman, in that deathful hour,
Against Al Hassan's whelming power.—
In vain they met him, helm to helm,
Upon the threshold of that realm
He came in bigot pomp to sway,
And with their corpses block'd his way—
In vain—for every lance they rais'd,
Thousands around the conqueror blaz'd ;
For every arm that lin'd their shore,
Myriads of slaves were wafted o'er,—
A bloody, bold, and countless crowd,
Before whose swarm as fast they bow'd
As dates beneath the locust cloud.
　　There stood—but one short league away
From old Harmozia's sultry bay—
A rocky mountain, o'er the Sea
Of Oman beetling awfully ; [249]

A last and solitary link
 Of those stupendous chains that reach
From the broad Caspian's reedy brink
 Down winding to the Green Sea beach.
Around its base the bare rocks stood,
Like naked giants in the flood,
 As if to guard the Gulf across ;
While, on its peak, that brav'd the sky,
A ruin'd Temple tower'd, so high
 That oft the sleeping albatross 250
Struck the wild ruins with her wing,
And oft from her cloud-rock'd slumbering
Started—to find man's dwelling there
In her own silent fields of air !
Beneath, terrific caverns gave
Dark welcome to each stormy wave
That dash'd, like midnight revellers, in ;—
And such the strange, mysterious din
At times throughout those caverns roll'd,
And such the fearful wonders told
Of restless spirits imprison'd there,
That bold were Moslem, who would dare,
At twilight hour, to steer his skiff
Beneath the Gheber's lonely cliff. 251

On the land side, those towers sublime,
That seem'd above the grasp of Time,
Were sever'd from the haunts of men
By a wide, deep, and wizard glen,
So fathomless, so full of gloom,
 No eye could pierce the void between :
It seem'd a place where Gholes might come
With their foul banquets from the tomb,
 And in its caverns feed unseen.

Like distant thunder, from below,
    The sound of many torrents came,
Too deep for eye or ear to know
If 'twere the sea's imprison'd flow,
    Or floods of ever-restless flame.
For, each ravine, each rocky spire
Of that vast mountain stood on fire;²⁵²
And, though forever past the days
When God was worshipp'd in the blaze
That from its lofty altar shone, —
Though fled the priests, the votaries gone,
Still did the mighty flame burn on,²⁵³
Through chance and change, through good and
    ill,
Like its own God's eternal will,
Deep, constant, bright, unquenchable!
Thither the vanquish'd HAFED led
    His little army's last remains;—
" Welcome, terrific glen!" he said,
" Thy gloom, that EBLIS' self might dread,
    Is Heaven to him who flies from chains!"
O'er a dark, narrow bridge-way, known
To him and to his Chiefs alone,
They cross'd the chasm and gain'd the
    towers, —
" This home," he cried, " at least is ours;—
Here we may bleed, unmock'd by hymns
    Of Moslem triumph o'er our head;
Here we may fall, nor leave our limbs
    To quiver to the Moslem's tread.
Stretch'd on this rock while vultures' beaks
Are whetted on our yet warm cheeks,

Here — happy that no tyrant's eye
Gloats on our torments — we may die!" —
'Twas night when to those towers they came,
And gloomily the fitful flame,
That from the ruin'd altar broke,
Glar'd on his features, as he spoke: —
" 'Tis o'er—what men could do, we've done—
If IRAN *will* look tamely on,
And see her priests, her warriors driven
    Before a sensual bigot's nod,
A wretch, who shrines his lusts in heaven,
    And makes a pander of his God;
If her proud sons, her high-born souls,
    Men, in whose veins — oh last disgrace!
The blood of ZAL and RUSTAM[254] rolls,—
    If they *will* court this upstart race,
And turn from MITHRA'S ancient ray,
To kneel at shrines of yesterday;
If they *will* crouch to IRAN'S foes,
    Why, let them — till the land's despair
Cries out to Heaven, and bondage grows
    Too vile for e'en the vile to bear!
Till shame at last, long hidden, burns
Their inmost core, and conscience turns
Each coward tear the slave lets fall
Back on his heart in drops of gall.
But *here*, at least, our arms unchain'd,
And souls that thraldom never stain'd; —
    This spot, at least, no foot of slave
Or satrap ever yet profan'd;
    And though but few — though fast the
    wave

Of life is ebbing from our veins,
Enough for vengeance still remains.
As panthers, after set of sun,
Rush from the roots of Lebanon
Across the dark sea robber's way, 255
We'll bound upon our startled prey :
And when some hearts that proudest swell
Have felt our falchion's last farewell ;
When Hope's expiring throb is o'er,
And e'en despair can prompt no more,
This spot shall be the sacred grave
Of the last few who, vainly brave,
Die for the land they cannot save ! "

His Chiefs stood round—each shining blade
Upon the broken altar laid—
And though so wild and desolate
Those courts, where once the Mighty sate ;
No longer on those mouldering towers
Was seen the feast of fruits and flowers,
With which of old the Magi fed
The wandering Spirits of their Dead ; 256
Though neither priest nor rites were there,
    Nor charmed leaf of pure pomegranate ; 257
Nor hymn, nor censer's fragrant air,
    Nor symbol of their worshipp'd planet ; 258
Yet the same God that heard their sires
Heard *them*, while on that altar's fires
They swore 259 the latest, holiest deed
Of the few hearts, still left to bleed,
Should be, in Iran's injur'd name,
To die upon that Mount of Flame—

The last of all her patriot line,
Before her last untrampled Shrine !

Brave, suffering souls ! they little knew
How many a tear their injuries drew
From one weak maid, one gentle foe,
Whom love first touch'd with others' woe—
Whose life, as free from thought as sin,
Slept like a lake, till Love threw in
His talisman, and woke the tide,
And spread its trembling circles wide.
Once, Emir ! thy unheeding child,
'Mid all this havoc, bloom'd and smil'd—
Tranquil as on some battle plain
    The Persian lily shines and towers, 260
Before the combat's reddening stain
    Hath fall'n upon her golden flowers.
Light-hearted maid, unaw'd, unmov'd,
While Heaven but spar'd the sire she lov'd,
Once at thy evening tales of blood
Unlistening, and aloof she stood—
And oft, when thou hast pac'd along
    Thy Haram halls with furious heat,
Hast thou not curs'd her cheerful song,
    That came across thee, calm and sweet,
Like lutes of angels, touch'd so near
Hell's confines, that the damn'd can hear !

Far other feelings Love hath brought—
    Her soul all flame, her brow all sadness,
She now has but the one dear thought,
    And thinks that o'er, almost to madness !

Oft does her sinking heart recall
His words—" For *my* sake weep for **all ;**
And bitterly, as day on day
　　Of rebel carnage fast succeeds,
She weeps a lover snatch'd away
　　In every Gheber wretch that bleeds.
There's not a sabre meets her eye,
　　But with his life-blood seems to **swim ;**
There's not an arrow wings the sky,
　　But fancy turns its point to him.
No more she brings with footstep light
　　AL HASSAN's falchion for the fight ;
And—had he look'd with clearer sight,
Had not the mists, that ever rise
From a foul spirit, dimm'd his eyes—
He would have mark'd her shuddering **frame**
When from the field of blood he came,
The faltering speech—the look estrang'd—
Voice, step, and life, and beauty chang'd—
He would have mark'd all this, and **known**
Such change is wrought by Love alone !

Ah ! not the Love that should have **bless'd**
So young, so innocent a breast ;
Not the pure, open, prosperous Love,
That pledg'd on earth and seal'd above,
Grows in the world's approving eyes,
　　In friendship's smile and home's **caress,**
Collecting all the heart's sweet ties
　　Into one knot of happiness !
No. HINDA, no,—thy fatal flame
Is nurs'd in silence, sorrow, shame ;—
　　A passion, without hope or pleasure,

In thy soul's darkness buried deep,
  It lies, like some ill-gotten treasure,—
Some idol, without shrine or name,
O'er which its pale-eyed votaries keep
Unholy watch, while others sleep.

Seven nights have darken'd OMAN'S sea,
  Since last, beneath the moonlight ray,
She saw his light oar rapidly
  Hurry her Gheber's bark away,—
And still she goes, at midnight hour,
To weep alone, in that high bower,
And watch, and look along the deep
For him whose smiles first made her weep;—
But watching, weeping, all was vain,
She never saw his bark again.
The owlet's solitary cry,
The night-hawk flitting darkly by,
  And oft the hateful carrion bird,
Heavily flapping his clogg'd wing,
Which reek'd with that day's banqueting—
  Was all she saw, was all she heard

'Tis the eighth morn—AL HASSAN'S brow
  Is brighten'd with unusual joy—
What mighty mischief glads him now,
  Who never smiles but to destroy?
The sparkle upon HERKEND'S Sea,
When toss'd at midnight furiously, [261]
Tells not of wreck and ruin nigh,
More surely than that smiling eye!
"Up, daughter, up—the KERNA'S [262] breath
Has blown a blast would waken death,

And yet thou sleep'st—up, child, and see
This blessed day for Heaven and me,
A day more rich in Pagan blood
Than ever flash'd o'er OMAN's flood.
Before another dawn shall shine,
His head—heart—limbs—will all be mine;
This very night his blood shall steep
These hands all over ere I sleep !"—
" *His* blood !" she faintly scream'd—her mind
Still singling *one* from all mankind—
"Yes—spite of his ravines and towers,
HAFED, my child, this night is ours.
Thanks to all-conquering treachery,
    Without whose aid the links accurst,
That bind these impious slaves, would be
    Too strong for ALLA's self to burst !
That rebel fiend, whose blade has spread
My path with piles of Moslem dead,
Whose baffling spells had almost driven
Back from their course the Swords of Heaven,
This night, with all his band, shall know
How deep an Arab's steel can go,
When God and Vengeance speed the blow
And—Prophet ! by that holy wreath
Thou wor'st on OHOD's field of death,²⁶³
I swear, for every sob that parts
In anguish from these heathen hearts,
A gem from PERSIA's plunder'd mines
Shall glitter on thy Shrine of Shrines.
But, ha !—she sinks—that look so wild—
Those livid lips—my child, my child,
This life of blood befits not thee,
And thou must back to ARABY.

Ne'er had I risk'd thy timid sex
In scenes that man himself might dread,
Had I not hop'd our every tread
    Would be on prostrate Persian necks—
Curst race, they offer swords instead !
But, cheer thee, maid,—the wind that now
Is blowing o'er thy feverish brow,
To-day shall waft thee from the shore;
And, ere a drop of this night's gore
Have time to chill in yonder towers,
Thou'lt see thy own sweet Arab bowers!

His bloody boast was all too true;
There lurk'd one wretch among the few
Whom HAFED's eagle eye could count
Around him on that fiery mount,—
One miscreant who for gold betray'd
The pathway through the valley's shade
To those high towers where Freedom stood
In her last hold of flame and blood
Left on the field last dreadful night,
When, sallying from their Sacred height,
The Ghebers fought hope's farewell fight,
He lay—but died not withe brave;
That sun, which should have gilt his grave,
Saw him a traitor and a slave;—
And, while the few, who thence return'd
To their high rocky fortress, mourn'd
For him among the matchless dead
They left behind on glory's bed,
He liv'd, and, in the face of morn,
Laugh'd them and Faith and Heaven to
    scorn.

Oh for a tongue to curse the slave,
   Whose treason, like a deadly blight,
Comes o'er the councils of the brave,
   And blasts them in their hour of might!
May Life's unblessed cup for him
Be drugg'd with treacheries to the brim,—
With hopes, that but allure to fly,
   With joys, that vanish while he sips,
Like Dead Sea fruits, that tempt the eye,
   But turn to ashes on the lips! [264]
His country's curse, his children's shame.
Outcast of virtue, peace, and fame.
May he, at last, with lips of flame
On the parch'd desert thirsting die,—
While lakes that shone in mockery nigh, [265]
Are fading off, untouch'd' untasted,
Like the once glorious hopes he blasted!
And, when from earth his spirit flies,
   Just Prophet, let the damn'd one dwell
Full in the sight of Paradise,
   Beholding heaven, and feeling hell!

LALLA ROOKH had, the night before, been
visited by a dream which, in spite of the im-
pending fate of poor HAFED, made her heart
more than usually cheerful during the morning,
and gave her cheeks all the freshened anima-
tion of a flower that the Bidmusk had just
passed over. [266] She fancied that she was
sailing on that Eastern Ocean, where the sea-
gypsies, who live forever on the water, [267] enjoy
a perpetual summer in wandering from isle to

isle, when she saw a small gilded bark
approaching her. It was like one of those
boats which the Maldivian islanders send adrift
at the mercy of winds and waves, loaded with
perfumes, flowers, and odoriferous wood, as an
offering to the Spirit whom they call King of
the Sea. At first, this little bark appeared to
be empty, but, on coming nearer—

She had proceeded thus far in relating the
dream to her Ladies, when FERAMORZ appeared
at the door of the pavilion. In his presence,
of course, everything else was forgotten, and
the continuance of the story was instantly
requested by all. Fresh wood of aloes was set
to burn in the cassolets; the violet sherbets [268]
were hastily handed round, and after a short
prelude on his lute, in the pathetic measure of
Nava, [269] which is always used to express the
lamentations of absent lovers, the Poet thus
continued :—

THE day is lowering—stilly black
Sleeps the grim wave, while heaven's rack,
Dispers'd and wild, 'twixt earth and sky
Hangs like a shatter'd canopy.
There's not a cloud in that blue plain
    But tells of storm to come or past ;—
Here, flying loosely as the mane
Of a young war-horse in the blast ;—
There roll'd in masses dark and swelling,
As proud to be the thunder's dwelling !

12

While some already burst and riven,
Seem melting down the verge of heaven;
As though the infant storm had rent
   The mighty womb that gave him birth,
And, having swept the firmament,
   Was now in fierce career for earth.
On earth 'twas yet all calm around,
A pulseless silence, dread, profound,
More awful than the tempest's sound.
The diver steer'd for ORMUS' bowers,
And moor'd his skiff till calmer hours;
The sea-birds, with portentous screech,
Flew fast to land;—upon the beach
The pilot oft had paus'd, with glance
Turn'd upward to that wild expanse;—
And all was boding, drear, and dark
As her own soul, when HINDA's bark
Went slowly from the Persian shore.—
No music tim'd her parting oar, 270
Nor friends upon the lessening strand
Linger'd, to wave the unseen hand,
Or speak the farewell, heard no more;—
But lone, unheeded, from the bay
The vessel takes its mournful way.
Like some ill-destin'd bark that steers
In silence through the Gate of Tears. 271
And where was stern AL HASSAN then?
Could not that saintly scourge of men
From bloodshed and devotion spare
One minute for a farewell there?
No—close within, in changeful fits
Of cursing and of prayer, he sits

In savage loneliness to brood
Upon the coming night of blood,—
  With that keen second-scent of death,
By which the vulture snuffs his food
  In the still warm and living breath ! [272]
While o'er the wave his weeping daughter
Is wafted from these scenes of slaughter,—
As a young bird of BABYLON, [273]
Let loose to tell of victory won,
Flies home, with wing, ah ! not unstain'd
By the red hands that held her chain'd.

And does the long-left home she seeks
Light up no gladness on her cheeks ?
The flowers she nurs'd — the well-known
      groves,
Where oft in dreams her spirit roves—
Once more to see her dear gazelles
Come bounding with their silver bells ;
Her birds' new plumage to behold,
  And the gay, gleaming fishes count,
She left, all filleted with gold,
  Shooting around their jasper fount ; [274]
Her little garden mosque to see,
  And once again, at evening hour,
To tell her ruby rosary [275]
  In her own sweet acacia bower.—
Can these delights, that wait her now,
Call up no sunshine on her brow :
No,—silent, from her train apart,—
As if e'en now she felt at heart
The chill of her approaching doom,—
She sits, all lovely in her gloom

As a pale Angel of the Grave ;
And o'er the wide, tempestuous wave,
Looks, with a shudder, to those towers,
Where, in a few short awful hours,
Blood, blood, in streaming tides shall run,
Foul incense for to-morrow's sun !
"Where art thou, glorious stranger ! thou,
So loved, so lost, where art thou now ?
Foe—Gheber—infidel—whate'er
The unhallow'd name thou'rt doom'd to bear,
Still glorious—still to this fond heart
Dear as its blood, whate'er thou art !
Yes—ALLA, dreadful ALLA ! yes—
If there be wrong, be crime in this,
Let the black waves that round us roll,
Whelm me this instant, ere my soul,
Forgetting faith—home—father—all—
Before its earthly idol fall,
Nor worship e'en Thyself above him—
For, oh, so wildly do I love him,
Thy Paradise itself were dim
And joyless, if not shared with him !"

Her hands were clasp'd—her eyes upturn'd,
    Dropping their tears like moonlight rain ;
And, though her lip, fond raver ! burn'd
    With words of passion, bold, profane,
Yet was there light around her brow,
    A holiness in those dark eyes,
Which show'd, though wandering earthward
    now,
    Her spirit's home was in the skies.

" Then fare thee well, — I'd rather make
My bower upon some icy lake."

Yes—for a spirit pure as hers
Is always pure, e'en while it errs;
As sunshine, broken in the rill,
Though turn'd astray, is sunshine **still !**

So wholly had her mind forgot
All thoughts but one, she heeded **not**
The rising storm—the wave that cast
A moment's midnight, as it pass'd—
Nor heard the frequent shout, the tread
Of gathering tumult o'er her head—
Clash'd swords, and tongues that seem'd **to vie**
With the rude riot of the sky.—
But, hark !—that war-whoop on the deck—
    That crash, as if each engine there,
Masts, sails, and all, were gone to wreck,
    'Mid yells and stampings of despair !
Merciful Heaven ! what *can* it be?
'Tis not the storm, though fearfully
The ship has shudder'd as she rode
O'er mountain-waves—"Forgive me, God !
Forgive me !" shrieked the maid, and knelt,
Trembling all over—for she felt
As if her judgment hour was near,
While crouching round, half dead with fear,
Her handmaids clung, nor breath'd, nor stir'd—
When, hark !—a second crash—a third—
And now, as if a bolt of thunder
Had riv'n the laboring planks asunder,
The deck falls in—what horrors then !
Blood, waves, and tackle, swords and men
Come mix'd together through the chasm,—
Some wretches in their dying spasm

Still fighting on—and some that call
"For God and Iran!" as they fall!

Whose was the hand that turn'd away
The perils of the infuriate fray,
And snatch'd her breathless from beneath
This wilderment of wreck and death?
She knew not—for a faintness came
Chill o'er her, and her sinking frame
Amid the ruins of that hour
Lay, like a pale and scorched flower,
Beneath the red volcano's shower.
But, oh! the sights and sounds of dread
That shock'd her ere her senses fled!
The yawning deck—the crowd that strov
Upon the tottering planks above—
The sail, whose fragments, shivering o'er
The strugglers' heads all dash'd with gore
Flutter'd like bloody flags—the clash
Of sabres, and the lightning's flash
Upon their blades, high toss'd about
Like meteor brands [276]—as if throughout
    The elements one fury ran,
One general rage, that left a doubt
    Which was the fiercer, Heaven or Man!

Once too—but no—it could not be—
'Twas fancy all—yet once she thought
While yet her fading eyes could see,
    High on the ruin'd deck she caught
A glimpse of that unearthly form,
    That glory of her soul,—e'en then,

Amid the whirl of wreck and storm,
  Shining above his fellow-men,
As, on some black and troubloug night,
The Star of EGYPT,[277] whose proud light
Never hath beam'd on those who rest
In the White Islands of the West,[278]
Burns though the storm with looks of flame
That put Heaven's cloudier eyes to shame.
But no—'twas but the minute's dream—
A fantasy—and ere the scream
Had half-way pass'd her pallid lips,
A death-like swoon, a chill eclipse
Of soul and sense its darkness spread
Around her, and she sunk, as dead.

How calm, how beautiful comes on
The stilly hour, when storms are gone;
When warring winds have died away,
And clouds, beneath the glancing ray,
Melt off, and leave the land and sea
Sleeping in bright tranquillity,—
Fresh as if Day again were born,
Again upon the lap of Morn!—
When the light blossoms, rudely torn
And scatter'd at the whirlwind's will,
Hang floating in the pure air still,
Filling it all with precious balm,
In gratitude for this sweet calm;—
And every drop the thunder-showers
Have left upon the grass and flowers
Sparkles, as 'twere that lightning-gem[278]
Whose liquid flame is born of them!

When, 'stead of one unchanging breeze,
  There blow a thousand gentle airs,
  And each a different perfume bears,—
As if the loveliest plants and trees
Had vassal breezes of their own
To watch and wait on them alone,
  And waft no other breath than theirs:
When the blue waters rise and fall,
In sleepy sunshine mantling all;
And e'en that swell the tempest leaves
Is like the full and silent heaves
Of lovers' hearts, when newly blest,
Too newly to be quite at rest.

Such was the golden hour that broke
Upon the world, when HINDA woke
From her long trance, and heard around
No motion but the water's sound
Rippling against the vessel's side,
As slow it mounted o'er the tide.—
But where is she?—her eyes are dark,
Are wilder'd still—is this the bark,
The same, that from HARMOZIA's bay
Bore her at morn—whose bloody way
The sea-dog track'd?—no—strange and new
Is all that meets her wondering view.
Upon a galliot's deck she lies,
  Beneath no rich pavilion's shade,—
No plumes to fan her sleeping eyes,
  Nor jasmine on her pillow laid.
But the rude litter, roughly spread
With war-cloaks, is her homely bed

And shawl and sash, on javelins hung,
For awning o'er her head are flung,
Shuddering she look'd around—there lay
   A group of warriors in the sun,
Resting their limbs, as for that day
   Their ministry of death were done.
Some gazing on the drowsy sea,
Lost in unconscious reverie ;
And some, who seem'd but ill to brook
That sluggish calm, with many a look
To the slack sail impatient cast,
As loose it flagg'd around the mast.

Blest ALLA ! who shall save her now ?
   There's not in all that warrior band
One Arab sword, one turban'd brow
   From her own Faithful Moslem land.
Their garb—the leathern belt [280] that wraps
   Each yellow vest [281]—that rebel hue—
The Tartar fleece upon their caps [282]
   Yes—yes—her fears are all too true,
And Heaven hath, in this dreadful hour,
Abandon'd her to HAFED's power ;—
HAFED, the Gheber !—at the thought
   Her very heart's blood chills within ;
He, whom her soul was hourly taught
To loathe, as some foul fiend of sin,
Some minister, whom Hell had sent
To spread its blast, where'er he went,
And fling, as o'er our earth he trod,
His shadow betwixt man and God !
And she is now his captive,—thrown
In his fierce hands, alive, alone ;

His the infuriate band she sees,
All infidels—all enemies !
What was the daring hope that then
Cross'd her like lightning, as again,
With boldness that despair had lent,
  She darted through that armed crowd
A look so searching, so intent,
  That e'en the sternest warrior bow'd
Abash'd, when he her glances caught,
As if he guess'd whose form they sought?
But no—she sees him not—'tis gone,
The vision that before her shone
Through all the maze of blood and storm,
Is fled—'twas but a phantom form—
One of those passing, rainbow dreams,
Half light, half shade, which Fancy's beams
Paint on the fleeting mists that roll
In trance or slumber round the soul.

But now the bark, with livelier bound,
  Scales the blue wave—the crew's in motion,
The oars are out, and with light sound
  Break the bright mirror of the ocean,
Scattering its brilliant fragments round.
And now she sees—with horror sees,
  Their course is tow'rd that mountain-
    hold,—
Those towers, that make her life-blood freeze,
Where MECCA's godless enemies
  Lie, like beleaguer'd scorpions, roll'd
  In their last deadly, venomous fold !
Amid the illumin'd land and flood
Sunless that mighty mountain stood ;

Save where, above its awful head,
There shone a flaming cloud, blood-red,
As 'twere the flag of destiny
Hung out to mark where death would be!

Had her bewilder'd mind the power
Of thought, in this terrific hour,
She well might marvel where or how
Man's foot could scale that mountain's brow,
Since ne'er had Arab heard or known
Of path but through the glen alone.—
But every thought was lost in fear,
When, as their bounding bark drew near
The craggy base, she felt the waves
Hurry them tow'rd those dismal caves,
That from the Deep in windings pass
Beneath that Mount's volcanic mass;—
And loud a voice on deck commands
To lower the mast and light the brands!—
Instantly o'er the dashing tide
Within a cavern's mouth they glide,
Gloomy as that eternal Porch
  Through which departed spirits go :—
Not e'en the flare of brand and torch
  Its flickering light could further throw
  Than the thick flood that boil'd below.
Silent they floated—as if each
Sat breathless, and too aw'd for speech
In that dark chasm, where even sound
Seem'd dark,—so sullenly around
The goblin echoes of the cave
Mutter'd it o'er the long black wave,
As 'twere some secret of the grave!

But soft—they pause—the current turns
   Beneath them from its onward track :—
Some mighty, unseen barrier spurns
   The vexed tide, all foaming, back,
And scarce the oars' redoubled force
Can stem the eddy's whirling force ;
When, hark !—some desperate foot has sprung
Among the rocks—the chain is flung—
The oars are up—the grapple clings,
And the toss'd bark in moorings swings.
Just then, a day-beam through the shade
Broke tremulous—but, ere the maid
Can see from whence the brightness steals,
Upon her brow she shuddering feels
A viewless hand, that promptly ties
A bandage round her burning eyes ;
While the rude litter where she lies,
Uplifted by the warrior throng,
O'er the steep rocks is borne along.

Blest power of sunshine !—genial Day,
What balm, what life is in thy ray !
To feel thee is such real bliss,
That had the world no joy but this,
To sit in sunshine calm and sweet,—
It were a world too exquisite
For man to leave it for the gloom,
The deep, cold shadow of the tomb.
E'en Hinda, though she saw not where
   Or whither wound the perilous road,
Yet knew by that awakening air,
   Which suddenly around her glow'd,

That they had risen from darkness then,
And breath'd the sunny world again !
But soon this balmy freshness fled—
For now the steepy labyrinth led
Through damp and gloom—'mid crash of
    boughs,
And fall of loosen'd crags that rouse
The leopard from his hungry sleep,
  Who, starting, thinks each crag a prey,
And long is heard, from steep to steep,
  Chasing them down their thundering way !
The jackal's cry—the distant moan
Of the hyæna, fierce and lone—
And that eternal saddening sound
  Of torrents in the glen beneath,
As 'twere the ever-dark Profound
  That rolls beneath the Bridge of Death !
All, all is fearful—e'en to see,
  To gaze on those terrific things
She now but blindly hears, would be
  Relief to her imaginings ;
Since never yet was shape so dread,
  But Fancy, thus in darkness thrown
And by such sounds of horror fed,
  Could frame more dreadful of her own.

But does she dream ? has Fear again
Perplex'd the workings of her brain,
Or did a voice, all music, then
Come from the gloom, low whispering near—
"Tremble not, love, thy Gheber's here !"
She *does* not dream—all sense, all ear,
She drinks the words, "Thy Gheber's here."

'Twas his own voice—she could not err—
   Throughout the breathing world's extent
There was but *one* such voice for her,
   So kind, so soft, so eloquent!
Oh, sooner shall the rose of May
   Mistake her own sweet nightingale,
And to some meaner minstrel's lay
   Open her bosom's glowing veil,
Than Love shall ever doubt a tone,
A breath of the beloved one!

Though blest, 'mid all her ills, to think
   She has that one beloved near,
Whose smile, though met on ruin's brink,
   Hath power to make e'en ruin dear,—
Yet soon this gleam of rapture, crost
By fears for him, is chill'd and lost.
How shall the ruthless HAFED brook
That one of Gheber blood should look,
With aught but curses in his eye,
On her—a maid of ARABY—
A Moslem maid—the child of him,
   Whose bloody banner's dire success
Hath left their altars cold and dim,
   And their fair land a wilderness!
And, worse than all, that night of blood
   Which comes so fast—oh! who shall stay
The sword, that once hath tasted food
Of Persian hearts, or turn its way?
What arm shall then the victim cover,
Or from her father shield her lover?
"Save him, my God!" she inly cries—
"Save him this night—and if thine eyes

Have ever welcom'd with delight
The sinner's tears, the sacrifice
Of sinner's hearts—guard him this night,
And here, before Thy throne, I swear
From my heart's inmost core to tear
　　Love, hope, remembrance, though they be
Linked with each quivering life-string there,
　　And give it bleeding all to Thee !
Let him but live,—the burning tear,
The sighs, so sinful, yet so dear,
Which have been all too much his own,
Shall from this hour be Heaven's alone.
Youth pass'd in penitence, and age
In long and painful pilgrimage,
Shall leave no traces of the flame
That wastes me now—nor shall his name
E'er bless my lips, but when I pray
For his dear spirit, that away
Casting from its angelic ray
The eclipse of earth, he, too, may shine
Redeem'd all glorious and all Thine !
Think—think what victory to win
One radiant soul like his from sin.—
One wandering star of virtue back
To its own native, heavenward track !
Let him but live, and both are Thine,
　　Together Thine—for, blest or crost,
Living or dead, his doom is mine,
　　And, if *he* perish, both are lost ! "

THE next evening, LALLA ROOKH was en-
treated by her Ladies to continue the relation

of her wonderful dream ; but the fearful **interest**
that hung round the fate of HINDA and her lover
had completely removed every trace of it from
her mind ;—much to the disappointment of a
fair seer or two in her train, who prided themselves on their skill in interpreting visions, and
who had already remarked, as an unlucky
omen, that the Princess, on the very morning
after the dream, had worn a silk dyed with the
blossoms of the sorrowful tree, Nilica.[284]

FADLADEEN, whose indignation had more than
once broken out during the recital of some
parts of this heterodox poem, seemed at length
to have made up his mind to the infliction ;
and took his seat this evening with all the patience of a martyr, while the Poet resumed **his**
profane and seditious story as follows :—

To tearless eyes and hearts at ease
The leafy shores and sun-bright seas,
That lay beneath that mountain's **height,**
Had been a fair enchanting sight.
'Twas one of those ambrosial eves
A day of storm so often leaves
At its calm setting—when the West
Opens her golden bowers of rest,
And a moist radiance from the skies
Shoots trembling down, as from the **eyes**
Of some meek penitent, whose last
Bright hours atone for dark ones **past,**

And whose sweet tears, o er wrong forgiven,
Shine, as they fall, with light from heaven!

'Twas stillness all—the winds that late
   Had rush'd through KERMAN's almond groves
And shaken from her bowers of date
   That cooling feast the traveller loves,[285]
Now, lull'd to languor, scarcely curl
   The Green Sea wave, whose waters gleam
Limpid, as if her mines of pearl
   Were melted all to form the stream:
And her fair islets, small and bright,
   With their green shores reflected there,
Look like those PERI isles of light,
   That hang by spell-work in the air.

But vainly did those glories burst
On HINDA's dazzled eyes, when first
The bandage from her brow was taken,
And, pale and awed as those who waken
In their dark tombs—when, scowling near,
The Searchers of the Grave [286] appear,—
She shuddering turn'd to read her fate
   In the fierce eyes that flash'd around;
And saw those towers all desolate,
   That o'er her head terrific frown'd,
As if defying e'en the smile
Of that soft heaven to gild their pile.
In vain, with mingled hope and fear,
She looks for him, whose voice so dear
Had come, like music, to her ear—
Strange, mocking dream! again 'tis fled
And oh, the shoots, the pangs of dread

That through her inmost bosom run,
    When voices from without proclaim
" HAFED, the Chief "—and, one by one,
    The warriors shout that fearful name!
He comes—the rock resounds his tread—
How shall she dare to lift her head,
Or meet those eyes whose scorching glare
Not YEMEN's boldest sons can bear?
In whose red beam, the Moslem tells,
Such rank and deadly lustre dwells,
As in those hellish fires that light
The mandrake's charnel leaves at night.[237]
How shall she bear that voice's tone,
At whose loud battle-cry alone
Whole squadrons oft in panic ran,
Scatter'd like some vast caravan,
When, stretch'd at evening round the well,
They hear the thirsting tiger's yell!
Breathless she stands, with eyes cast down
Shrinking beneath the fiery frown
Which, fancy tells her, from that brow
Is flashing o'er her fiercely now :
And shuddering as she hears the tread
    Of his retiring warrior band.
Never was pause so full of dread ;
    Till HAFED with a trembling hand
Took hers, and, leaning o'er her, said,
" HINDA ; "—that word was all he spoke,
And 'twas enough—the shriek that broke
    From her full bosom told the rest.—
Panting with terror, joy, surprise,
The maid but lifts her wondering eyes,
    To hide them on her Gheber's breast!

'Tis he, 'tis he—the man of blood,
The fellest of the Fire-fiend's brood,
HAFED, the demon of the fight,
Whose voice unnerves, whose glances blight,—
Is her own loved Gheber, mild
And glorious as when first he smil'd
In her lone tower, and left such beams
Of his pure eye to light her dreams,
That she believ'd her bower had given
Rest to some wanderer from heaven.

Moments there are, and this was one,
Snatch'd like a minute's gleam of sun
Amid the black Simoom's eclipse—
    Or, like those verdant spots that bloom
Around the crater's burning lips,
    Sweetening the very edge of doom !
The past—the future—all that Fate
Can bring of dark or desperate
Around such hours, but makes them cast
Intenser radiance while they last !

Even he, this youth—though dimm'd and gone
Each star of Hope that cheer'd him on—
His glories lost—his cause betray'd—
IRAN, his dear-lov'd country, made
A land of carcasses and slaves,
One dreary waste of chains and graves !—
Himself but lingering, dead at heart,
    To see the last, long struggling breath
Of Liberty's great soul depart,
    Then lay him down and share her death—

Even he, so sunk in wretchedness,
    With doom still darker gathering o'er him,
Yet, in this moment's pure caress,
    In the mild eyes that shone before him,
Beaming that blest assurance, worth
All other transports known on earth,
That he was lov'd—well, warmly lov'd—
Oh! in this precious hour he prov'd
How deep, how thorough-felt the glow
Of rapture, kindling out of woe ; —
How exquisite one single drop
Of bliss, thus sparkling to the top
Of misery's cup—how keenly quaff'd,
Though death must follow on the draught.

She, too, while gazing on those eyes
    That sink into her soul so deep,
Forgets all fears, all miseries,
    Or feels them like the wretch in sleep,
Whom fancy cheats into a smile,
Who dreams of joy, and sobs the while!
The mighty Ruins where they stood,
    Upon the mount's high, rocky verge,
Lay open tow'rds the ocean flood,
    Where lightly o'er the illumin'd surge
Many a fair bark that, all the day,
Had lurk'd in sheltering creek or bay,
Now bounded on, and gave their sails,
Yet dripping, to the evening gales ;
Like eagles, when the storm is done,
Spreading their wet wings in the sun.
The beauteous clouds, though daylight's Star
Had sunk behind the hills of LAR,

Were still with lingering glories bright,—
As if, to grace the gorgeous West,
  The Spirit of departing Light
That eve had left his sunny vest
  Behind him, ere he wing'd his flight.
Never was scene so form'd for love!
Beneath them waves of crystal move
In silent swell—Heaven glows above,
And their pure hearts, to transport given,
Swell like the wave, and glow like Heaven.

But, ah! too soon that dream is past—
  Again, again her fear returns;—
Night, dreadful night. is gathering fast,
  More faintly the horizon burns,
And every rosy tint that lay
On the smooth sea hath died away.
Hastily to the darkening skies
A glance she casts—then wildly cries:
" *At night*, he said—and look, 'tis near—
  Fly, fly—if yet thou lov'st me, fly—
Soon will his murderous band be here,
  And I shall see thee bleed and die.—
Hush! heard'st thou not the tramp of men
Sounding 'rom yonder fearful glen?—
Perhaps e'en now they climb the wood—
  Fly, fly—though still the West is bright,
He'll come—oh! yes—he wants thy blood
  I know him—he'll not wait for night!"
In terrors e'en to agony
  She clings around the wondering Chief;—
" Alas, poor wilder'd maid! to me
  Thou ow'st this raving trance of grief.

Lost as I am, nought ever grew
Beneath my shade but perish'd too—
My doom is like the Dead Sea air,
And nothing lives that enters there !
Why were our barks together driven
Beneath this morning's furious heaven ?
Why when I saw the prize that chance
  Had thrown into my desperate arms,—
When, casting but a single glance
  Upon thy pale and prostrate charms,
I vow'd (though watching viewless o'er
  Thy safety through that hour's alarms)
To meet the unmanning sight no more—
Why have I broke that heart-wrung vow ?
Why weakly, madly met thee now ?—
Start not—that noise is but the shock
  Of torrents through yon valley hurl'd—
Dread nothing here—upon this rock
  We stand above the jarring world,
Alike beyond its hope—its dread—
In gloomy safety, like the Dead !
Or, could e'en earth and hell unite
In league to storm this Sacred Height,
Fear nothing thou—myself, to-night,
And each o'erlooking star that dwells
Near God, will be thy sentinels ;—
And ere to-morrow's dawn shall glow,
Back to thy sire—"

                " To-morrow !—no "—
The maiden scream'd—"thou'lt never see
To-morrow's sun—death, death will be
The night-cry through each reeking tower,
Unless we fly, ay, fly this hour !

Thou art betray'd—some wretch who knew
That dreadful glen's mysterious clew—
Nay, doubt not—by yon stars, 'tis true—
Hath sold thee to my vengeful sire;
This morning, with that smile so dire
He wears in joy, he told me all,
And stamp'd in triumph through our hall,
As though thy heart already beat
Its last life-throb beneath his feet!
Good Heaven, how little dream'd I then
  His victim was my own lov'd youth !—
Fly—send—let some one watch the glen—
  By all my hopes of heaven 'tis truth!"

Oh! colder than the wind that freezes
  Founts, that but now in sunshine play'd,
Is that congealing pang which seizes
  The trusting bosom, when betray'd.
He felt it—deeply felt—and stood,
As if the tale had frozen his blood,
  So maz'd and motionless was he ;—
Like one whom sudden spells enchant,
Or some mute, marble habitant
  Of the still Halls of ISHMONIE ! 288

But soon the painful chill was o'er,
And his great soul, herself once more,
Look'd from his brow in all the rays
Of her best, happiest, grandest days.
Never, in moment most elate,
  Did that high spirit loftier rise ;—
While bright, serene, determinate,
  His looks are lifted to the skies.

As if the signal lights of Fate
   Were shining in those awful eyes!
'Tis come—his hour of martyrdom
In Iran's sacred cause is come ;
And, though his life hath pass'd away
Like lightning on a stormy day,
Yet shall his death-hour leave a track
   Of glory, permanent and bright,
To which the brave of after-times,
The suffering brave, shall long look back
   With proud regret,—and by its light
   Watch through the hours of slavery's night
For vengeance on the oppressor's crimes.
This rock, his monument aloft,
   Shall speak the tale to many an age ;
And hither bards and heroes oft
   Shall come in secret pilgrimage,
And bring their warrior sons, and tell
The wondering boys where Hafed fell ;
And swear them on those lone remains
Of their lost country's ancient fanes,
Never—while breath of life shall live
Within them—never to forgive
The accursed race, whose ruthless chain
Hath left on Iran's neck a stain.
Blood, blood alone can cleanse again !
Such are the swelling thoughts that now
Enthrone themselves on Hafed's brow ;
And ne'er did saint of Issa [289] gaze
   On the red wreath, for martyrs twin'd,
More proudly than the youth surveys
   That pile, which through the gloom behind,

Half lighted by the altar's fire,
Glimmers—his destin'd funeral **pyre** !
Heap'd by his own, his comrades' **hands,**
    Of every wood of odorous breath,
There, by the Fire-God's shrine it **stands,**
    Ready to fold in radiant death
The few, still left of those who swore
To perish there, when hope was o'er—
The few, to whom that couch of flame,
Which rescues them from bonds and **shame,**
Is sweet and welcome as the bed
From their own infant Prophet spread,
When pitying Heaven to roses turn'd
The death-flames that beneath him **burn'd** ! **200**

With **watchfulness** the maid attends
His **rapid** glance, where'er it bends—
Why **shoot** his eyes such awful beams ?
What plans he now ? what thinks or **dreams?**
Alas ! why stands he musing here,
When every moment teems with fear ?
" HAFED, my own beloved Lord,"
She kneeling cries—" first, last ador'd !
If in that soul thou'st ever felt
    Half what thy lips impassion'd **swore,**
Here, on my knees that never knelt
    To any but their God before,
I pray thee, as thou lov'st me, fly—
Now, now—ere yet their blades are **nigh.**
Oh haste—the bark that brought me **hither**
    Can waft us o'er you darkening sea
East—west—alas, I care not whither,
    So thou art safe, and I with **thee** !

Go where we will, this hand in thine,
　　Those eyes before me smiling thus,
Through good and ill, through storm and shine,
　　The world's a world of love for us !
On some calm, blessed shore we'll dwell,
Where 'tis no crime to love too well ;—
Where thus to worship tenderly
An erring child of light like thee
Will not be sin—or, if it be,
Where we may weep our faults away,
Together kneeling, night and day,
Thou, for *my* sake, at ALLA's shrine,
And I—at *any* God's for thine ! "

Wildly these passionate words she spoke—
　　Then hung her head, and wept for shame
Sobbing as if a heart-string broke
　　With every deep-heav'd sob that came.
While he,　young, warm—oh ! wonder not
　　If, for a moment, pride and fame,
　　His oath—his cause—that shrine of flame,
And IRAN's self are all forgot
For her whom at his feet he sees
Kneeling in speechless agonies.
No, blame him not, if Hope awhile
Dawn'd in his soul, and threw her smile
O'er hours to come—o'er days and nights,
Wing'd with those precious, pure delights
Which she, who bends all beauteous there,
Was born to kindle and to share.
A tear or two, which, as he bow'd
　　To raise the suppliant, trembling stole,
First warn'd him of this dangerous cloud

Of softness passing o'er his soul.
Starting, he brush'd the drops away,
Unworthy o'er that cheek to stray ;—
Like one who, on the morn of fight,
Shakes from his sword the dews of night,
That had but dimm'd, not stain'd its light.
Yet, though subdued the unnerving thrill,
Its warmth, its weakness linger'd still,
   So touching in each look and tone
That the fond, fearing, hoping maid
Half counted on the flight she pray'd,
   Half thought the hero's soul was grown
   As soft, as yielding as her own,
And smil'd and bless'd him, while he said,—
" Yes—if there be some happier sphere,
Where fadeless truth like ours is dear,—
If there be any land of rest
   For those who love and ne'er forget,
Oh ! comfort thee—for safe and blest
   We'll meet in that calm region yet ! "

Scarce had she time to ask her heart
If good or ill these words impart,
When the rous'd youth impatient flew
To the tower-wall, where, high in view,
A ponderous sea-horn [291] hung, and blew
A signal, deep and dread as those
The storm-fiend at his rising blows.—
Full well his Chieftains, sworn and true
Through life and death, that signal knew ;
For 'twas the appointed warning-blast,
The alarm, to tell when hope was past,
And the tremendous death-die cast !

And there, upon the mouldering tower,
Hath hung this sea-horn many an hour,
Ready to sound o'er land and sea
That dirge-note of the brave and free.
They came—his Chieftains at the call
Came slowly round, and with them all—
Alas, how few !—the worn remains
Of those who late o'er KERMAN'S plains
Went gayly prancing to the clash
    Of Moorish zel and tymbalon,
Catching new hope from every flash
    Of their long lances in the sun,
And, as their coursers charg'd the wind,
And the white ox-tails stream'd behind, ⁰
Looking as if the steeds they rode
Were wing'd, and every Chief a God !
How fallen, how alter'd now ! how wan
Each scarr'd and faded visage shone,
As round the burning shrine they came !—
    How deadly was the glare it cast,
As mute they paus'd before the flame
    To light their torches as they pass'd !
'Twas silence all—the youth had plann'd
The duties of his soldier-band ;
And each determin'd brow declares
His faithful Chieftains well know theirs,
But minutes speed—night gems the skies—
And oh, how soon, ye blessed eyes,
That look from heaven, ye may behold
Sights that will turn your star-fires cold !
    reathless with awe, impatience, hope,
The maiden sees the veteran group
Her litter silently prepare,

And lay it at her trembling feet ;—
And now the youth, with gentle care,
    Hath placed her in the shelter'd seat,
And press'd her hand—that lingering press
    Of hands, that for the last time sever ;
Of hearts, whose pulse of happiness,
    When that hold breaks, is dead forever.
And yet to *her* this sad caress
    Gives hope—so fondly hope can err !
'Twas joy, she thought, joy's mute excess—
    Their happy flight's dear harbinger ;
'Twas warmth—assurance—tenderness—
    'Twas anything but leaving her.

" Haste, haste ! " she cried, " the clouds grow
        dark,
But still, ere night, we'll reach the bark ;
    And by to-morrow's dawn—oh bliss !
    With thee upon the sun-bright deep,
Far off, I'll but remember this,
    As some dark vanish'd dream of sleep ;
And thou——" but ah !—he answers not—
    Good Heaven !—and does she go alone ?
She now has reach'd that dismal spot,
    Where, some hours since, his voice's tone
Had come to soothe her fears and ills,
Sweet as the angel ISRAFIL'S, [293]
When every leaf on Eden's tree
    Is trembling to his minstrelsy—
Yet now—oh, now, he is not nigh.—
    " HAFED ! my HAFED !—if it be
Thy will, thy doom this night to die,
    Let me but stay to die with thee,

And I will bless thy loved name,
Till the last life-breath leave this frame.
Oh ! let our lips, our cheeks be laid
But near each other while they fade ;
Let us but mix our parting breaths,
And I can die ten thousand deaths !
You too, who hurry me away
So cruelly, one moment stay—

    Oh ! stay—one moment is not much—
He yet may come—for *him* I pray—
HAFED ! dear HAFED !—" all the way
    In wild lamentings, that would touch
A heart of stone, she shriek'd his name
To the dark woods—no HAFED came :—
No—hapless pair—you've look'd your last :—
    Your hearts should both have broken then.
The dream is o'er—your doom is cast—
    You'll never meet on earth again !

Alas for him, who hears her cries !
    Still half-way down the steep he stands
Watching with fix'd and feverish eyes
    The glimmer of those burning brands,
That down the rocks, with mournful ray,
Light all he loves on earth away !
Hopeless as they who, far at sea,
    By the cold moon have just consign'd
The corse of one, lov'd tenderly,
    To the bleak flood they leave behind ;
And on the deck still lingering stay,
And long look back, with sad delay,
To watch the moonlight on the wave,
That ripples o'er that cheerless grave.

But see—he starts—what heard he then?
That dreadful shout!—across the glen
From the land-side it comes, and loud
Rings through the chasm; as if the crowd
Of fearful things, that haunt that dell,
Its Gholes and Dives and shapes of hell,
Had all in one dread howl broke out,
So loud, so terrible that shout!
"They come—the Moslems come!" he cries.
His proud soul mounting to his eyes,—
"Now, Spirits of the Brave, who roam
Enfranchis'd through yon starry dome,
Rejoice—for souls of kindred fire
Are on the wing to join your choir!"
He said—and, light as bridegrooms bound
  To their young loves, reclimb'd the steep
And gain'd the Shrine—his Chiefs stood round—
  Their swords, as with instinctive leap,
Together, at that cry accurst,
Had from their sheaths, like sunbeams, burst.
And hark!—again—again it rings;
Near and more near its echoings
Peal through the chasm—oh! who that then
Had seen those listening warrior-men,
With their swords grasp'd, their eyes of flame
Turn'd on their Chief—could doubt the shame,
The indignant shame with which they thrill
To hear those shouts and yet stand still?

He read their thoughts—they were his own—
  "What! while our arms can wield these
      blades,
Shall we die tamely? die alone?

Without one victim to our shades,
One Moslem heart, where, buried deep,
The sabre from its toil may sleep ?
No—God of IRAN's burning skies !
Thou scorn'st the inglorious sacrifice.
No—though of all earth's hope bereft,
Life, swords, and vengeance still are left.
We'll make yon valley's reeking caves
   Live in the awe-struck minds of men,
Till tyrants shudder, when their slaves
   Tell of the Gheber's bloody glen.
Follow, brave hearts !—this pile remains
Our refuge still from life and chains ;
But his the best, the holiest bed,
Who sinks entomb'd in Moslem dead ! "
Down the precipitous rocks they sprung,
While vigor, more than human, strung
Each arm and heart.—The exulting foe
Still through the dark defiles below,
Track'd by his torches' lurid fire, ²⁹⁴
   Wound slow, as through GOLCONDA's vale ²⁹⁴
The mighty serpent, in his ire,
   Glides on with glittering, deadly trail.
No torch the Ghebers need—so well
They know each mystery of the dell,
So oft have, in their wanderings,
Cross'd the wild race that round them dwell,
   The very tigers from their delves
Look out and let them pass, as things
   Untam'd and fearless like themselves !

There was a deep ravine, that lay
Yet darkling in the Moslem's way ;

Fit spot to make invaders rue
The many fallen before the few.
The torrents from that morning's sky
Had fill'd the narrow chasm breast high,
And, on each side, aloft and wild,
Huge cliffs and toppling crags were pil'd,
The guards with which young Freedom lines
The pathways to her mountain-shrines.
Here, at this pass, the scanty band
Of IRAN's last avengers stand ;
Here wait, in silence like the dead,
And listen for the Moslem's tread
So anxiously, the carrion-bird
Above them flaps his wing unheard !

They come—that plunge into the water
Gives signal for the work of slaughter.
Now, Ghebers, now—if e'er your blades
    Had point or prowess, prove them now—
Woe to the file that foremost wades !
    They come—a falchion greets each brow
And, as they tumble, trunk on trunk,
Beneath the gory waters sunk,
Still o'er their drowning bodies press
New victims quick and numberless ;
Till scarce an arm in HAFED's band,
    So fierce their toil, hath power to stir,
But listless from each crimson hand
    The sword hangs, clogg'd with massacre.
Never was horde of tyrants met
With bloodier welcome—never yet
To patriot vengeance hath the sword
More terrible libations pour'd.

All up the dreary, long ravine,
By the red, murky glimmer seen
Of half-quench'd brands that o'er the flood
Lie scatter'd round and burn in blood,
What ruin glares! what carnage swims!
Heads, blazing turbans, quivering limbs,
Lost swords that, dropp'd from many a hand,
In that thick pool of slaughter stand ;—
Wretches who wading, half on fire
   From the toss'd brands that round them
     fly,
'Twixt flood and flame in shrieks expire ;
   And some who, grasp'd by those that die,
Sink woundless with them, smother'd o'er
In their dead brethren's gushing gore !

But vainly hundreds, thousands bleed,
Still hundreds, thousands more succeed ;
Countless as tow'rds some flame at night
The North's dark insects wing their flight,
And quench or perish in its light,
To this terrific spot they pour—
Till, bridg'd with Moslem bodies o'er,
It bears aloft their slippery tread,
And o'er the dying and the dead,
Tremendous causeway! on they pass.
Then, hapless Ghebers, then, alas !
What hope was left for you? for you,
Whose yet warm pile of sacrifice
Is smoking in their vengeful eyes?
Whose swords how keen, how fierce they
     knew,
And burn with shame to find how few ?

Crush'd down by that vast multitude,
Some found their graves where first **they**
    stood ;
While some with hardier struggle died,
And still fought on by HAFED's side,
Who, fronting to the foe, trod back
Tow'rds the high towers his gory track ;
And, as a lion swept away
    By sudden swell of JORDAN's pride
From the wild covert where he lay, 205
    Long battles with the o'erwhelming tide,
So fought he back with fierce delay,
And kept both foes and fate at bay.

But whither now ? their track is lost,
    Their prey escap'd—guide, torches gone—
By torrent-beds and labyrinths crost,
    The scatter'd crowd rush blindly on—
"Curse on those tardy lights that wind"
They panting cry, "so far behind ;
Oh for a bloodhound's precious scent,
To track the way the Gheber went !"
Vain wish—confusedly along
They rush, more desperate as more wrong :
Till, wilder'd by the far-off lights,
Yet glittering up those gloomy heights,
Their footing, maz'd and lost, they miss,
And down the darkling precipice
Are dash'd into the deep abyss ;
Or midway hang, impal'd on rocks,
A banquet, yet alive, for flocks
Of ravening vultures,—while the dell
Re-echoes with each horrible yell.

Those sounds—the last, to vengeance dear,
That e'er shall ring in HAFED's ear,—
Now reach'd him, as aloft, alone,
Upon the steep way breathless thrown,
He lay beside his reeking blade,
   Resign'd, as if life's task were o'er,
Its last blood-offering amply paid,
   And IRAN's self could claim no more.
One only thought, one lingering beam
Now broke across his dizzy dream
Of pain and weariness—'twas she,
   His heart's pure planet, shining yet
Above the waste of memory,
   When all life's other lights were set.
And never to his mind before
Her image such enchantment wore.
It seem'd as if each thought that stain'd,
   Each fear that chill'd their loves, was past,
And not one cloud of earth remain'd
   Between him and her radiance cast ;—
As if to charms, before so bright,
   New grace from other worlds was given
And his soul saw her by the light
Now breaking o'er itself from heaven !
A voice spoke near him—'twas the tone
Of a lov'd friend, the only one
Of all his warriors, left with life
From that short night's tremendous strife.—
"And must we then, my Chief, die here?
Foes round us, and the Shrine so near !"
These words have rous'd the last remains
   Of life within him—"What ! not yet
Beyond the reach of Moslem chains !"

The thought could make e'en Death forget
His icy bondage—with a bound
He springs, all bleeding, from the ground,
And grasps his comrade's arm, now grown
E'en feebler, heavier than his own,
And up the painful pathway leads,
Death gaining on each step he treads.
Speed them, thou God, who heard'st their vow!
They mount—they bleed—oh, save them now!
The crags are red they've clamber'd o'er,
The rock-weed's dripping with their gore ;—
Thy blade too, HAFED, false at length,
Now breaks beneath thy tottering strength!
Haste, haste—the voices of the Foe
Come near and nearer from below—
One effort more—thank Heaven! 'tis past,
They've gain'd the topmost steep at last,
And now they touch the temple's walls,
    Now HAFED sees the Fire divine—
When, lo!—his weak, worn comrade falls
    Dead on the threshold of the Shrine.
" Alas, brave soul, too quickly fled!
    And must I leave thee withering here,
The sport of every ruffian's tread,
    The mark for every coward's spear?
No, by yon altar's sacred beams!"
He cries, and, with a strength that seems
Not of this world, uplifts the frame
Of the fallen Chief, and tow'rds the flame
Bears him along ;—with death-damp hand
    The corpse upon the pyre he lays,
Then lights the consecrated brand,
    And fires the pile, whose sudden blaze

Like lightning bursts o'er OMAN'S Sea.—
"Now, Freedom's God!   I come to Thee,"
The youth exclaims, and with a smile
Of triumph vaulting on the pile
In that last effort, ere the fires
Have harm'd one glorious limb, expires!

What shriek was that on OMAN'S tide?
   It came from yonder drifting bark,
That just hath caught upon her side
   The death-light—and again is dark.
It is the boat—ah, why delay'd?—
That bears the wretched Moslem maid;
Confided to the watchful care
   Of a small veteran band, with whom
Their generous Chieftain would not share
   The secret of his final doom,
But hop'd when HINDA, safe and free,
   Was render'd to her father's eyes,
Their pardon, full and prompt, would be
   The ransom of so dear a prize.—
Unconscious, thus, of HAFED'S fate,
And proud to guard their beauteous freight,
Scarce had they clear'd the surfy waves
That foam around those frightful caves,
When the curst war-whoops, known so well,
Came echoing from the distant dell—
Sudden each oar, upheld and still,
   Hung dripping o'er the vessel's side,
And, driving at the current's will,
   They rock'd along the whispering tide;
While every eye, in mute dismay,
   Was tow'rd that fatal mountain turn'd,

Where the dim altar's quivering ray
   As yet all lone and tranquil burn'd.

Oh ! 'tis not, HINDA, in the power
   Of Fancy's most terrific touch
To paint thy pangs in that dread hour—
   Thy silent agony—'twas such
As those who feel could paint too well,
But none e'er felt and lived to tell !
'Twas not alone the dreary state
Of a lorn spirit crush'd by fate,
When, though no more remains to dread,
   The panic chill will not depart ;—
When, though the inmate Hope be dead,
   Her ghost still haunts the mouldering heart
No—pleasures, hope, affections gone,
The wretch may bear, and yet live on,
Like things, within the cold rock found
Alive, when all's congeal'd around.
But there's a blank repose in this,
A calm stagnation, that were bliss
To the keen, burning, harrowing pain,
Now felt through all thy breast and brain ;—
That spasm of terror, mute, intense,
That breathless, agoniz'd suspense,
From whose hot throb, whose deadly aching,
The heart hath no relief but breaking !

Calm is the wave—heaven's brilliant lights
   Reflected dance beneath the prow ;—
Time was when, on such lovely nights,
   She who is there, so desolate now,
Could sit all cheerful, though alone,

And ask no happier joy than seeing
That starlight o'er the waters thrown—
No joy but that, to make her blest,
And the fresh, buoyant sense of being,
Which bounds in youth's yet careless breast,
Itself a star, not borrowing light,
But in its own glad essence bright.
How different now !—but, hark, again
The yell of havoc rings !—brave men,
In vain, with beating hearts, ye stand
On the bark's edge—in vain each hand
Half draws the falchion from its sheath ;
    All's o'er—in rust your blades may lie :—
He, at whose word they've scatter'd death,
    E'en now, this night, himself must die !
Well may ye look to yon dim tower,
    And ask, and wondering guess what means
The battle-cry at this dead hour—
    Ah ! she could tell you—she, who leans
Unheeded there, pale, sunk, aghast,
With brow against the dew-cold mast ;
    Too well she knows—her more than life,
Her soul's first idol and its last,
    Lies bleeding in that murderous strife.

But see—what moves upon the height ?
Some signal !—'tis a torch's light.
    What bodes its solitary glare ?
In gasping silence tow'rd the Shrine
All eyes are turn'd—thine, HINDA, thine
    Fix their last fading life-beams there.
'T was but a moment—fierce and high
The death-pile blaz'd into the sky,

And far away, o'er rock and flood,
  Its melancholy radiance sent ;
While HAFED, like a vision, stood
Reveal'd before the burning pyre,
Tall, shadowy, like a Spirit of Fire
  Shrin'd in its own grand element !
" 'T is he ! "—the shuddering maid exclaims,—
  But, while she speaks, he's seen no more ;
High burst in air the funeral flames,
  And IRAN's hopes and hers are o'er !
One wild, heart-broken shriek she gave ;
  Then sprung, as if to reach that blaze,
  Where still she fix'd her dying gaze,
And, gazing, sunk into the wave,—
Deep, deep,—where never care or pain
Shall reach her innocent heart again !

Farewell—farewell to thee, ARABY's daughter !
  (Thus warbled a PERI beneath the dark sea,)
No pearl ever lay, under OMAN's green water,
  More pure in its shell than thy spirit in thee.

Oh! fair as the sea-flower close to thee growing,
  How light was thy heart till Love's witchery
    came,
Like the wind of the south [296] o'er a summer
    lute blowing,
  And hush'd all its music, and wither'd its
    frame !

But long, upon ARABY's green sunny highlands,
  Shall maids and their lovers remember the
    doom

Of her, who lies sleeping among the Pearl
    Islands,
  With nought but the sea-star [297] to light up
    her tomb.

And still, when the merry date-season is burn-
    ing, [298]
  And calls to the palm-groves the young and
    the old,
The happiest there, from their pastime return-
    ing
  At sunset, will weep when the story is told,

The young village-maid, when with flowers she
    dresses
  Her dark flowing hair for some festival day,
Will think of thy fate till, neglecting her tresses,
  She mournfully turns from the mirror away.

Nor shall IRAN, belov'd of her Hero! forget
    thee—
  Though tyrants watch over her tears as they
    start.
Close, close by the side of that Hero she'll set
    thee,
  Embalm'd in the innermost shrine of her heart.

Farewell—be it ours to embellish thy pillow
  With everything beauteous that grows in the
    deep;
Each flower of the rock and each gem of the
    billow
  Shall sweeten thy bed and illumine thy sleep.

Around thee shall glisten the loveliest amber
   That ever the sorrowing sea-bird has wept ;[299]
With many a shell, in whose hollow-wreath'd
     chamber
   We, Peris of Ocean, by moonlight have slept.

We'll dive where the gardens of coral lie dark-
     ling,
   And plant all the rosiest stems at thy head :
We'll seek where the sands of the Caspian [800]
     are sparkling,
   And gather their gold to strew over thy bed.

Farewell—farewell—until Pity's sweet fountain
   Is lost in the hearts of the fair and the brave,
They'll weep for the Chieftain who died on that
     mountain,
   They'll weep for the Maiden who sleeps in
   this wave.

THE singular placidity with which FADLADEEN
had listened, during the latter part of this ob-
noxious story, surprised the Princess and FERA-
MORZ exceedingly ; and even inclined towards
him the hearts of these unsuspicious young persons, who little knew the source of a compla-
cency so marvellous. The truth was, he had
been organizing, for the last few days, a most
notable plan of persecution against the Poet, in
consequence of some passages that had fallen
from him on the second evening of recital,—
which appeared to this worthy Chamberlain to

contain language and principles, **for which nothing** short of the summary criticism of the Chabuk [301] would be advisable. It was his intention, therefore, immediately on their arrival at Cashmere, to give information to the King of Bucharia of the very dangerous sentiments of of his minstrel; and if, unfortunately, that monarch did not act with suitable vigor on the occasion, (that is, if he did not give the Chabuk to FERAMORZ, and a place to FADLADEEN,) there would be an end, he feared, of all legitimate government in Bucharia. He could not help, however, auguring better both for himself and the cause of potentates in general; and it was the pleasure arising from these mingled anticipations that diffused such unusual satisfaction through his features, and made his eyes shine out, like poppies of the desert, over the wide and lifeless wilderness of that countenance.

Having decided upon the Poet's chastisement in this manner, he thought it but humanity to spare him the minor tortures of criticism. Accordingly, when they assembled the following evening in the pavilion, and LALLA ROOKH was expecting to see all the beauties of her bard melt away, one by one, in the acidity of criticism, like pearls in the cup of the Egyptian queen,—he agreeably disappointed her, by merely saying, with an ironical smile. that the merits of such a poem deserved to be tried at a much higher tribunal; and then suddenly passed off into a panegyric upon all Mussulman

sovereigns, more particularly his august and
Imperial master, Aurungzebe,—the wisest and
best of the descendants of Timur,—who, among
other great things he had done for mankind,
had given to him, FADLADEEN, the very profit-
able posts of Betel-carrier and Taster of Sherbets to the Emperor, Chief Holder of the Girdle
of Beautiful Forms,[302] and Grand Nazir, or
Chamberlain of the Haram.

They were now not far from that Forbidden
River,[303] beyond which no pure Hindoo can
pass; and were reposing for a time in the rich
valley of Hussun Abdaul, which had always
been a favorite resting-place of the Emperors
in their annual migrations to Cashmere. Here
often had the Light of the Faith, Jehan-Guire,
been known to wander with his beloved and
beautiful Nourmahal; and here would LALLA
ROOKH have been happy to remain forever, giving up the throne of Bucharia and the world for
FERAMORZ and love in this sweet, lonely valley.
But the time was now fast approaching when
she must see him no longer,—or, what was still
worse, behold him with eyes whose every look
belonged to another; and there was a melancholy preciousness in these last moments, which
made her heart cling to them as it would to life.
During the latter part of the journey, indeed,
she had sunk into a deep sadness, from which
nothing but the presence of the young minstrel
could awake her. Like those lamps in tombs,
which only light up when the air is admitted,

it was only at his approach that her eyes became smiling and animated.   But here, in this
dear valley, every moment appeared an age of
pleasure ; she saw him all day, and was, therefore, all day happy,—resembling, she often
thought, that people of Zinge, who attribute
the unfading cheerfulness they enjoy to one
genial star that rises nightly over their heads.[304]

The whole party, indeed, seemed in their
liveliest mood during the few days they passed
in this delightful solitude.   The young attendants of the Princess, who were here allowed a
much freer range than they could safely be indulged with in a less sequestered place, ran wild
among the gardens and bounded through the
meadows, lightly as young roes over the aromatic plains of Tibet.   While FADLADEEN, in
addition to the spiritual comfort derived by him
from a pilgrimage to the tomb of the Saint from
whom the valley is named, had also opportunities of indulging, in a small way, his taste
for victims, by putting to death some hundreds
of those unfortunate little lizards[305] which all
pious Mussulmans make it a point to kill ;—
taking for granted, that the manner in which
the creature hangs its head is meant as a mimicry of the attitude in which the Faithful say
their prayers.

About two miles from Hussun Abdaul were
those Royal Gardens[306] which had grown
beautiful under the care of so many lovely

eyes, and were beautiful still, though those eyes could see them no longer. This place. with its flowers and its holy silence, interrupted only by the dipping of the wings of birds in its marble basins filled with the pure water of those hills, was to LALLA ROOKH all that her heart could fancy of fragrance, coolness, and almost heavenly tranquillity. As the Prophet said of Damascus, "It was too delicious;" [307] and here, in listening to the sweet voice of FERA-MORZ, or reading in his eyes what yet he never dared to tell her, the most exquisite moments of her whole life were passed. One evening, when they had been talking of the Sultana Nourmahal, the Light of the Haram, [308] who had so often wandered among these flowers, and fed with her own hands, in those marble basins, the small shining fishes of which she was so fond,[309]—the youth, in order to delay the moment of separation, proposed to recite a short story, or rather rhapsody, of which this adored Sultana was the heroine. It related, he said, to the reconcilement of a sort of lovers' quarrel which took place between her and the Emperor during a Feast of Roses at Cashmere ; and would remind the Princess of that differ-ence between Haroun-al-Raschid and his fair mistress Marida [310] which was so happily made up by the soft strains of the musician Moussali. As the story was chiefly to be told in song, and FERAMORZ had unluckily forgotten his own lute in the valley, he borrowed the vina of LALLA ROOKH's little Persian slave, and thus began :

THE LIGHT OF THE HARAM.

WHO has not heard of the vale of CASHMERE,
    With its roses the brightest that earth ever
      gave,[311]
Its temples, and grottos, and fountains as clear
    As the love-lighted eyes that hang over their
      wave?

Oh! to see it at sunset,—when warm o'er the
      Lake
    Its splendor at parting a summer eve throws,
Like a bride, full of blushes, when ling'ring to
      take
    A last look of her mirror at night ere she
      goes!—
When the shrines through the foliage are gleam-
      ing half shown,
And each hallows the hour by some rites of its
      own.
Here the music of pray'r from a minaret swells,
    Here the Magian his urn, full of perfume, is
      swinging,
And here, at the altar, a zone of sweet bells
    Round the waist of some fair Indian dancer
      is ringing.[312]
Or to see it by moonlight.—when mellowly
      shines
The light o'er its palaces, gardens, and shrines;

When the water-falls gleam, like a quick fall of
    stars,
And the nightingale's hymn from the Isle of
    Chenars
Is broken by laughs and light echoes of feet
From the cool, shining walks where the young
    people meet, —
Or at morn, when the magic of daylight awakes
A new wonder each minute, as slowly it breaks,
Hills, cupolas, fountains, call'd forth every one
Out of darkness, as if but just born of the Sun.
When the Spirit of Fragrance is up with the
    day,
From his Haram of night-flowers stealing
    away ;
And the wind, full of wantonness, woos like a
    lover
The young aspen-trees,[318] till they tremble all
    over.
When the East is as warm as the light of first
    hopes,
    And Day, with his banner of radiance
      unfurl'd,
Shines in through the mountainous portal [314]
    that opes,
    Sublime, from that Valley of Bliss to the
      world !

But never yet, by night or day,
In dew of spring or summer's ray,
Did the sweet Valley shine so gay
As now it shines—all love and light,
Visions by day and feasts by night!
  13

A happier smile illumes each brow,
  With quicker spread each heart encloses,
And all is ecstasy—for now
  The Valley holds its Feast of Roses ; 315
The joyous Time, when pleasures pour
Profusely round, and, in their shower,
Hearts open, like the Season's Rose,—
  The Flow'ret of a hundred leaves, 316
Expanding while the dew-fall flows,
  And every leaf its balm receives.

'Twas when the hour of evening came
  Upon the Lake, serene and cool,
When Day had hid his sultry flame
  Behind the palms of BARAMOULE, 317
When maids began to lift their heads,
Refresh'd from their embroider'd beds,
Where they had slept the sun away,
And wak'd to moonlight and to play.
All were abroad—the busiest hive
On BELA's 318 hills is less alive,
When saffron-beds are full in flower,
Than look'd the Valley in that hour.
A thousand restless torches play'd
Through every grove and island shade ;
A thousand sparkling lamps were set
On every dome and minaret ;
And fields and pathways, far and near,
Were lighted by a blaze so clear,
That you could see, in wandering round,
The smallest rose-leaf on the ground.
Yet did the maids and matrons leave
Their veils at home, that brilliant eve ;

And there were glancing eyes about,
And cheeks, that would not dare shine out
In open day, but thought they might
Look lovely then, because 'twas night.
And all were free, and wandering,
  And all exclaim'd to all they met,
That never did the summer bring
  So gay a Feast of Roses yet;—
The moon had never shed a light
  So clear as that which bless'd them there;
The roses ne'er shone half so bright,
  Nor they themselves look'd half so fair.
And what a wilderness of flowers !
It seem'd as though from all the bowers
And fairest fields of all the year,
The mingled spoil were scatter'd here.
The Lake, too, like a garden breathes,
  With the rich buds that o'er it lie,—
As if a shower of fairy wreaths
  Had fall'n upon it from the sky !
And then the sounds of joy,—the beat
Of tabors and of dancing feet;—
The minaret-crier's chant of glee
Sung from his lighted gallery, [819]
And answer'd by a ziraleet
From neighboring Haram, wild and sweet;—
The merry laughter, echoing
From gardens, where the silken swing [820]
Wafts some delighted girl above
The top leaves of the orange grove;
Or, from those infant groups at play
Among the tents [821] that line the way.

Flinging, unaw'd by slave or mother,
Handfuls of roses at each other. —
Then, the sounds from the Lake, the low
    whispering in boats,
  As they shoot through the moonlight ;—the
    dipping of oars,
And the wild, airy warbling that everywhere
    floats
  Through the groves, round the islands, as if
    all the shores,
Like those of KATHAY, utter'd music, and gave
An answer in song to the kiss of each wave. [322]
But the gentlest of all are those sounds, full of
    feeling,
That soft from the lute of some lover are
    stealing, —
Some lover, who knows all the heart-touching
    power
Of a lute and a sigh in this magical hour.
Oh ! best of delights as it everywhere is
To be near the lov'd *One*, —what a rapture is
    his
Who in moonlight and music thus sweetly may
    glide
O'er the Lake of CASHMERE, with that *One* by
    his side !
If woman can make the worst wilderness
    dear,
Think, think what a Heaven she must make of
    CASHMERE !
So felt the magnificent Son of ACBAR, [323]
When from power and pomp and the trophies
    of war

He flew to that Valley, forgetting them all
With the Light of the Haram, his young Nour-
    MAHAL.
When free and uncrown'd as the Conqueror
    rov'd
By the banks of that Lake, with his only belov'd,
He saw, in the wreaths she would playfully
    snatch
From the hedges, a glory his crown could not
    match,
And preferr'd in his heart the least ringlet that
    curl'd
Down her exquisite neck to the throne of the
    world.

There's a beauty, forever unchangingly bright,
Like the long, sunny lapse of a summer-day's
    light,
Shining on, shining on, by no shadow made
    tender,
Till Love falls asleep in its sameness of
    splendor.
This *was* not the beauty—oh, nothing like this,
That to young NOURMAHAL gave such magic of
    bliss !
But that loveliness, ever in motion, which
    plays
Like the light upon autumn's soft shadowy
    days,
Now here and now there, giving warmth as it
    flies
From the lip to the cheek, from the cheek to
    the eyes ;

Now melting in mist and now breaking in
    gleams,
Like the glimpses a saint hath of Heav'n in his
    dreams.
When pensive, it seem'd as if that very grace,
That charm of all others, was born with her
    face !
And when angry,—for e'en in the tranquillest
    climes
Light breezes will ruffle the blossoms some-
    times—
The short, passing anger but seem'd to
    awaken
New beauty, like flowers that are sweetest
    when shaken.
If tenderness touch'd her, the dark of her
    eye
At once took a darker, a heavenlier dye,
From the depth of whose shadow, like holy
    revealings
From innermost shrines, came the light of her
    feelings.
Then her mirth—oh ! 'twas sportive as ever
    took wing
From the heart with a burst, like the wild-bird
    in spring ;
Illum'd by a wit that would fascinate sages,
Yet playful as Peris just loos'd from their
    cages. [324]
While her laugh, full of life, without any
    control
But the sweet one of gracefulness, rung from
    her soul ;

And where it most sparkled no glance could discover,

In lip, cheek or eyes, for she brighten'd all over, —

Like any fair lake that the breeze is upon,

When it breaks into dimples and laughs in the sun.

Such, such were the peerless enchantments that gave

NOURMAHAL the proud Lord of the East for her slave:

And though bright was his Haram, — a living parterre

Of the flowers [325] of this planet — though treasures were there,

For which SOLIMAN's self might have giv'n all the store

That the navy from OPHIR e'er wing'd to his shore,

Yet dim before *her* were the smiles of them all,

And the Light of his Haram was young NOUR-MAHAL!

But where is she now, this night of joy,

When bliss is every heart's employ? —

   When all around her is so bright,

So like the visions of a trance,

That one might think, who came by chance

   Into the Vale this happy night,

   He saw that City of Delight [326]

In Fairy-land whose streets and towers

Are made of gems and light and flowers! —

Where is the lov'd Sultana? where,
When mirth brings out the young and fair,
Does sne, the fairest, hide her brow,
In melancholy stillness now?
Alas!—how light a cause may move
Dissension between hearts that love!
Hearts that the world in vain had tried,
And sorrow but more closely tied;
That stood the storm, when waves were
　　rough,
Yet in a sunny hour fall off,
Like ships that have gone down at sea,
When heaven was all tranquillity!
A something, light as air—a look,
　A word unkind or wrongly taken—
Oh! love, that tempests never shook,
　A breath, a touch like this hath shaken.
And ruder words will soon rush in
To spread the breach that words begin;
And eyes forget the gentle ray
They wore in courtship's smiling day;
And voices lose the tone that shed
A tenderness round all they said;
Till fast declining, one by one,
The sweetnesses of love are gone,
And hearts, so lately mingled, seem
Like broken clouds,—or like the stream,
That smiling left the mountain's brow
　As though its waters ne'er could sever,
Yet, ere it reach the plain below,
　Breaks into floods, that part forever.
Oh, you, that have the charge of Love,
　Keep him in rosy bondage bound,

As in the Fields of Bliss above
   He sits, with flow'rets fetter'd round;[327]
Loose not a tie that round him clings,
Nor ever let him use his wings;
For e'en an hour, a minute's flight
Will rob the plumes of half their light:
Like that celestial bird,—whose nest
   Is found beneath far Eastern skies,—
Whose wings, though radiant when at rest,
   Lose all their glory when he flies![328]
Some difference, of this dangerous kind,—
By which, though light, the links that bind
The fondest hearts may soon be riven;
Some shadow in Love's summer heaven,
Which, though a fleecy speck at first,
May yet in awful thunder burst;—
Such cloud it is that now hangs over
The heart of the Imperial Lover,
And far hath banish'd from his sight
His Nourmahal, his Haram's Light!
Hence is it, on this happy night,
When Pleasure through the fields and groves
Has let loose all her world of loves,
And every heart has found it own,
He wanders, joyless and alone,
And weary as that bird of Thrace
Whose pinion knows no resting-place.[329]
In vain the loveliest cheeks and eyes
This Eden of the Earth supplies
   Come crowding round—the cheeks are pale,
The eyes are dim:—though rich the spot
With every flow'r this earth has got,
   What is it to the nightingale,

If there his darling rose is not ? [380]
In vain the Valley's smiling throng
Worship him, as he moves along ;
He heeds them not—one smile of hers
Is worth a world of worshippers.
They but the Star's adorers are,
She is the Heav'n that lights the Star !

Hence is it, too, that NOURMAHAL,
　Amid the luxuries of this hour,
Far from the joyous festival,
　Sits in her own sequester'd bower,
With no one near, to soothe or aid,
But that inspir'd and wondrous maid,
NAMOUNA, the Enchantress ;—one,
O'er whom his race the golden sun
For unremember'd years has run,
Yet never saw her blooming brow
Younger or fairer than 'tis now.
Nay, rather,—as the west wind's sigh
Freshens the flower it passes by,—
Time's wing but seem'd, in stealing o'er,
To leave her lovelier than before.
Yet on her smiles a sadness hung,
And when, as oft, she spoke or sung
Of other worlds, there came a light
From her dark eyes so strangely bright,
That all believ'd nor man nor earth
Were conscious of NAMOUNA's birth !
All spells and talismans she knew,
　From the great Mantra, [381] which around
The Air's sublimer Spirits drew,
　To the gold gems [382] of AFRIC, bound

Upon the wandering Arab's arm,
To keep him from the Siltim's [333] harm.
And she had pledg'd her powerful art,—
Pledg'd it with all the zeal and heart
Of one who knew, though high her sphere,
What 'twas to lose a love so dear,—
To find some spell that should recall
Her Selim's [334] smile to NOURMAHAL!

'Twas midnight—through the lattice, wreath'd
With woodbine, many a perfume breath'd
From plants that wake when others sleep
From timid jasmine buds, that keep
Their odour to themselves all day.
But, when the sunlight dies away,
Let the delicious secret out
To every breeze that roams about;—
When thus NAMOUNA:—"'Tis the hour
That scatters spells on herb and flower,
And garlands might be gather'd now,
That, twin'd around the sleeper's brow,
Would make him dream of such delights,
Such miracles and dazzling sights,
As Genii of the Sun behold,
At evening, from their tents of gold,
Upon the horizon—where they play
Till twilight comes, and, ray by ray,
Their sunny mansions melt away.
Now, too, a chaplet might be wreath'd
Of buds o'er which the moon has breath'd,
Which worn by her, whose love has stray'd,
    Might bring some Peri from the skies,
Some sprite, whose very soul is made

Of flow'rets' breaths and lovers' sighs.
And who might tell——"

                              "For me, for me,"
Cried NOURMAHAL impatiently,—
"Oh! twine that wreath for me to-night."
Then, rapidly, with foot as light
As the young musk-roe's, out she flew,
To cull each shining leaf that grew
Beneath the moonlight's hallowing beams,
For this enchanted Wreath of Dreams.
Anemones and Seas of Gold, [335]
   And new-blown lilies of the river,
And those sweet flow'rets that unfold
   Their buds on CAMADEVA's quiver; [336]
The tuberose, with her silvery light,
   That in the Gardens of Malay
Is call'd the Mistress of the Night, [337]
So like a bride, scented and bright,
   She comes out when the sun's away;—
Amaranths, such as crown the maids
That wander through ZAMARA's shades; [338]
And the white moon-flower, as it shows,
On SERENDIB's high crags, to those
Who near the isle at evening sail,
Scenting her clove-trees in the gale;
In short, all flow'rets and all plants,
   From the divine Amrita tree, [339]
That blesses heaven's inhabitants
   With fruits of immortality,
Down to the basil tuft, [340] that waves
Its fragrant blossom over graves,
   And to the humble rosemary,

Whose sweets so thanklessly are shed
To scent the desert [341] and the dead :—
All in that garden bloom, and all
Are gather'd by young NOURMAHAL,
Who heaps her baskets with the flowers
  And leaves, till they can hold no more
Then to NAMOUNA flies, and showers
  Upon her lap the shining store.

With what delight the Enchantress views
So many buds, bath'd with the dews
And beams of that bless'd hour !— her glance
  Spoke something, past all mortal pleasures,
As, in a kind of holy trance,
  She hung above those fragrant treasures,
Bending to drink their balmy airs,
As if she mix'd her soul with theirs.
And 'twas, indeed, the perfume shed
From flow'rs and scented flame, that fed
Her charmed life—for none had e'er
Beheld her taste of mortal fare,
Nor ever in aught earthly dip,
But the morn's dew, her roseate lip.
Fill'd with the cool, inspiring smell,
The Enchantress now begins her spell,
Thus singing as she winds and weaves
In mystic form the glittering leaves :—

———

I know where the wing'd visions dwell
  That around the night-bed play ;
I know each herb and flow'ret's bell,
  Where they hide their wings by day.

Then hasten we, maid,
To twine our braid,
To-morrow the dreams and flowers **will fade.**

The image of love, that nightly flies
To visit the bashful maid,
Steals from the jasmine flower, that sighs
Its soul, like her, in the shade.
The dream of a future, happier hour,
That alights on misery's brow,
Springs out of the silvery almond-flower,
That blooms on a leafless bough. [342]
Then hasten we, maid,
To twine our braid,
To-morrow the dreams and flowers will fade.

The visions, that oft to worldly eyes
The glitter of mines unfold,
Inhabit the mountain-herb, [343] that dyes
The tooth of the fawn like gold.
The phantom shapes—oh touch not them !—
That appal the murderer's sight,
Lurk in the fleshly mandrake's stem,
That shrieks, when pluck'd at night !
Then hasten we, maid,
To twine our braid,
To-morrow the dreams and flowers **will fade.**

The dream of the injur'd, patient mind,
That smiles at the wrongs of men,
Is found in the bruis'd and wounded rind
Of the cinnamon, sweetest then.
Then hasten we, maid,
To twine our braid,
To-morrow the dreams and flowers **will fade.**

No sooner was the flowery crown
Plac'd on her head, than sleep came down,
Gently as nights of summer fall,
Upon the lids of NOURMAHAL ; —
And, suddenly, a tuneful breeze,
As full of small, rich harmonies
As ever wind, that o'er the tents
Of AZAB [344] blew, was full of scents,
Steals on her ear, and floats and swells,
  Like the first air of morning creeping
Into those wreathy, Red-Sea shells,
    Where Love himself, of old, lay sleeping ;[345]
And now a Spirit form'd, 'twould seem,
  Of music and of light,—so fair,
So brilliantly his features beam,
    And such a sound is in the air
Of sweetness when he waves his wings,
Hovers around her, and thus sings :—

From CHINDARA's [346] warbling fount I come,
  Call'd by that moonlight garland's spell ;
From CHINDARA's fount, my fairy home,
  Where in music, morn and night, I dwell :
Where lutes in the air are heard about,
  And voices are singing the whole day long,
And every sigh the heart breathes out
  Is turn'd, as it leaves the lips, to song !
      Hither I come
      From my fairy home ;
And if there's a magic in Music's strain,
      I swear by the breath
      Of that moonlight wreath,
Thy Lover shall sigh at thy feet again.

For mine is the lay that lightly floats,
And mine are the murmuring, dying notes,
That fall as soft as snow on the sea,
And melt in the heart as instantly :—
And the passionate strain that, deeply going,
    Refines the bosom it trembles through,
As the musk-wind, over the water blowing,
    Ruffles the wave, but sweetens it too.

Mine is the charm, whose mystic sway
The Spirits of past Delight obey ;
Let but the tuneful talisman sound,
And they come, like Genii, hovering round.
And mine is the gentle song that bears
    From soul to soul, the wishes of love,
As a bird, that wafts through genial airs
    The cinnamon-seed from grove to grove.³⁴⁷

'Tis I that mingle in one sweet measure
The past, the present, and future of pleasure ;³⁴⁸
When Memory links the tone that is gone
    With the blissful tone that's still in the ear ;
And Hope from a heavenly note flies on
    To a note more heavenly still that is near.
The warrior's heart, when touch'd by me,
Can as downy soft and as yielding be
As his own white plume, that high amid death
Through the field has shone—yet moves with
        a breath !
And oh ! how the eyes of Beauty glisten,
    When Music has reach'd her inward soul,
Like the silent stars, that wink and listen
    While Heaven's eternal melodies roll.

So, hither I come
From my fairy home ;
And if there's a magic in Music's strain,
I swear by the breath
Of that moonlight wreath,
Thy Lover shall sigh at thy feet again.

'Tis dawn—at least that earlier dawn,
Whose glimpses are again withdrawn, 340
As if the morn had wak'd, and then
Shut close her lids of light again.
And NOURMAHAL is up and trying
    The wonders of her lute, whose strings—
Oh, bliss !—now murmur like the sighing
    From that ambrosial Spirit's wings.
And then, her voice—'tis more than human—
    Never, till now, had it been given
To lips of any mortal woman
    To utter notes so fresh from heaven ;
Sweet as the breath of angel sighs,
    When angel sighs are most divine.—
"Oh ! let it last till night," she cries,
    "And he is more than ever mine."
And hourly she renews the lay,
    So fearful lest its heavenly sweetness
Should, ere the evening, fade away,—
    For things so heavenly have such fleetness !
But, far from fading, it but grows
Richer, diviner as it flows ;
Till rapt she dwells on every string,
    And pours again each sound along,
Like echo, lost and languishing,
    In love with her own wondrous song.
  56

That evening, (trusting that his soul
   Might be from haunting love releas'd
By mirth, by music, and the bowl,)
   The Imperial SELIM held a feast
In his magnificent Shalimar : [350]—
In whose Saloons, when the first star
Of evening o'er the waters trembled,
The Valley's loveliest all assembled ;
All the bright creatures that, like dreams
Glide though its foliage, and drink beams
Of beauty from its founts and streams ; [351]
And all those wandering minstrel-maids,
Who leave—how *can* they leave?—the shades
Of that dear Valley, and are found
   Singing in Gardens of the South [352]
Those songs, that ne'er so sweetly sound
   As from a young Cashmerian's mouth.
There, too, the Haram's inmates smile ;—
   Maids from the West, with sun-bright hair,
And from the Garden of the NILE,
Delicate as the roses there ; [353]—
Daughter of Love from CYPRUS' rocks,
With Paphian diamonds in their locks ; [354]—
Light PERI forms, such as there are
On the gold meads of CANDAHAR ; [355]
And they, before whose sleepy eyes,
   In their own bright Kathaian bowers,
Sparkle such rainbow butterflies,
   That they might fancy the rich flowers,
That round them in the sun lay sighing,
Had been by magic all set flying. [356]

———

Everything young, everything fair

From East and West is blushing there,
Except—except—oh,—NOURMAHAL!
Thou loveliest, dearest of them all,
The one whose smile shone out alone,
Amidst a world the only one;
Whose light, among so many lights,
Was like that star on starry nights,
The seaman singles from the sky,
To steer his bark forever by!
Thou wert not there—so SELIM thought,
    And everything seem'd drear without thee;
But ah! thou wert, thou wert,—and brought
    Thy charm of song all fresh about thee.
Mingling unnoticed with a band
Of lutanists from many a land,
And veil'd by such a mask as shades
The features of young Arab maids, [857]—
A mask that leaves but one eye free,
To do its best in witchery,—
She rov'd, with beating heart, around,
    And waited, trembling, for the minute,
When she might try if still the sound
    Of her lov'd lute had magic in it.

The board was spread with fruits and wine;
With grapes of gold, like those that shine
On CASBIN'S hills, [858]—pomegranates full
    Of melting sweetness, and the pears,
And sunniest apples [859] that CAUBUL
    In all its thousand gardens [860] bears:—
Plantains, the golden and the green,
MALAYA'S nectar'd mangusteen! [861]

Prunes of BOKARA, and sweet nuts
　　From the far groves of SAMARCAND,
And BASRA dates and apricots,
　　Seed of the Sun,[362] from IRAN's land ;—
With rich conserve of VISNA cherries, [363]
Of orange flowers, and of those berries
That, wild and fresh, the young gazelles
Feed on in ERAC's rocky dells.[364]
All these in richest vases smile,
　　In baskets of pure sandal-wood,
And urns of porcelain from that isle [365]
　　Sunk underneath the Indian flood,
Whence oft the lucky diver brings
Vases to grace the halls of kings.
Wines, too, of every clime and hue,
Around their liquid lustre threw ;
Amber Rosolli,[366]—the bright dew
From vineyards of the Green-Sea gushing ;[367]
And SHIRAZ wine, that richly ran
　　As if that jewel, large and rare,
The ruby for which KUBLAI-KHAN
Offer'd a city's wealth,[368] was blushing
　　Melted within the goblets there !

And amply SELIM quaffs of each,
And seems resolv'd the flood shall reach
His inward heart,—shedding around
　　A genial deluge, as they run,
That soon shall leave no spot undrown'd,
　　For Love to rest his wings upon.
He little knew how well the boy
　　Can float upon a goblet's streams,

Lighting them with his smile of joy ;—
  As bards have seen him in their dreams,
Down the blue GANGES laughing glide
  Upon a rosy lotus wreath, [369]
Catching new lustre from the tide
  That with his image shone beneath.

But what are cups, without the aid
  Of song to speed them as they flow?
And see—a lovely Georgian maid,
  With all the bloom, the freshen'd glow
Of her own country maidens' looks,
When warm they rise from TEFLIS' brooks ; [370]
And with an eye, whose restless ray,
  Full, floating, dark—oh, he, who knows
His heart is weak, of Heaven should pray
  To guard him from such eyes as those!—
With a voluptuous wildness flings
Her snowy hand across the strings
Of a syrinda, [371] and thus sings :—

Come hither, come hither—by night and by
        day,
  We linger in pleasures that never are gone ;
Like the waves of the summer, as one dies
        away,
  Another as sweet and as shining comes on.
And the love that is o'er, in expiring, gives
        birth
    To a new one as warm, as unequall'd in
        bliss ;
And, oh ! if there be an Elysium on earth,
            It is this, it is this. [372]

Here maidens are sighing, and fragrant **their**
       sigh
As the flower of the Amra just op'd by a bee ; ³⁷³
And precious their tears as that rain from the
       sky. ³⁷⁴
     Which turns into pearls as it falls in the sea.
Oh ! think what the kiss and the smile must be
       worth
     When the sigh and the tear are so perfect in
       bliss,
And own if there be an Elysium on earth,
            It is this, it is this.

Here sparkles the nectar, that, hallow'd by love,
     Could draw down those angels of old from
       their sphere,
Who for wine of this earth ³⁷⁵ left the fountains
       above,
     And forgot heaven's stars for the eyes we have
       here.
And, bless'd with odor our goblet gives forth,
     What Spirit the sweets of his Eden would
       miss ?
For, oh ! if there be an Elysium on earth,
            It is this, it is this.

The Georgian's song was scarcely mute,
     When the same measure, sound for sound,
Was caught up by another lute,
     And so divinely breathed around,
That all stood hush'd and wondering,
     And turn'd and look'd into the air,
As if they thought to see the wing
     Of Israfil, ³⁷⁶ the Angel, there ;

So powerfully on every soul
That new, enchanted measure stole.
While now a voice, sweet as the note
Of the charm'd lute, was heard to float
Along its chords, and so entwine
    Its sounds with theirs, that none knew
        whether
The voice or lute was most divine,
    So wondrously they went together :—

            ———

There's a bliss beyond all that the minstrel has
    told,
    When two, that are link'd in one heavenly tie,
With heart never changing, and brow never
    cold,
    Love on through all ills, and love on till they
        die !
One hour of a passion so sacred is worth
    Whole ages of heartless and wandering bliss ;
And, oh ! if there *be* an Elysium on earth,
           It is this, it is this.

            ———

'Twas not the air, 'twas not the words,
But that deep magic in the chords
And in the lips, that gave such power
As Music knew not till that hour.
At once a hundred voices said,
" It is the mask'd Arabian maid ! "
While Selim, who had felt the strain
Deepest of any, and had lain
Some minutes rapt, as in a trance,
    After the fairy sounds were o'er,
Too inly touch'd for utterance,
    Now motion'd with his hand for more ;—

Fly to the desert, fly with me,
Our Arab tents are rude for thee ;
But, oh ! the choice what heart can doubt
Of tents with love, or thrones without?

Our rocks are rough, but smiling there
The acacia waves her yellow hair,
Lonely and sweet, nor lov'd the less
For flowering in a wilderness.

Our sands are bare, but down their slope
The silvery-footed antelope
As gracefully and gayly springs
As o'er the marble courts of kings.

Then come—thy Arab maid will be
The lov'd and lone acacia-tree,
The antelope, whose feet shall bless
With their light sound thy loneliness.

Oh ! there are looks and tones that dart
An instant sunshine through the heart,—
As if the soul that minute caught
Some treasure it through life had sought ;

As if the very lips and eyes,
Predestin'd to have all our sighs,
And never be forgot again,
Sparkled and spoke before us then !

So came thy every glance and tone,
When first on me they breathed and shone;
Now, as if brought from other spheres,
Yet welcome as if loved for years.

Then fly with me,—if thou hast known
No other flame, nor falsely thrown
A gem away, that thou hadst sworn
Should ever in thy heart be worn.

Come, if the love thou hast for me
Is pure and fresh as mine for thee,—
Fresh as the fountain under ground,
When first 'tis by the lapwing found.[275]

But if for me thou dost forsake
Some other maid, and rudely break
Her worshipp'd image from its base,
To give to me the ruin'd place ;—

Then, fare thee well—I'd rather make
My bower upon some icy lake
When thawing suns begin to shine,
Than trust to love so false as thine !

———

There was a pathos in this lay,
    That, e'en without enchantment's art,
Would instantly have found its way
    Deep into SELIM's burning heart ;
But, breathing, as it did, a tone
To earthly lutes and lips unknown,
With every chord fresh from the touch
Of Music's Spirit,—'twas too much !
Starting, he dash'd away the cup,—
    Which, all the time of this sweet air,
His hand had held, untasted, up,
    As if 'twere fix'd by magic there,—
And naming her, so long unnam'd,
So long unseen, wildly exclaim'd,

"O Nourmahal! O Nourmahal!
   Hadst thou but sung this witching strain,
I could forget—forgive thee all,
   And never leave those eyes again."
The mask is off—the charm is wrought—
And Selim to his heart has caught,
In blushes, more than ever bright,
His Nourmahal, his Haram's Light!
And well do vanish'd frowns enhance
The charm of every brighten'd glance;
And dearer seems each dawning smile
For having lost its light awhile:
And, happier now for all her sighs,
   As on his arm her head reposes,
She whispers him with laughing eyes,
   "Remember, love, the Feast of Roses!"

Fadladeen, at the conclusion of this light rhapsody, took occasion to sum up his opinion of the young Cashmerian's poetry,—of which, he trusted, they had that evening heard the last. Having recapitulated the epithets " frivolous "—"inharmonious "—"nonsensical," he proceeded to say that, viewing it in the most favorable light, it resembled one of those Maldivian boats to which the Princess had alluded in the relation of her dream,[878]—a slight, gilded thing, sent adrift without rudder or ballast, and with nothing but vapid sweets and faded flowers on board. The profusion, indeed, of flowers and birds which this poet had ready on all occasions,—not to mention dews, gems, etc.,—was a most oppressive kind of opulence to his hearers ; and had the unlucky effect of giving to his style all the glitter of the flower-garden without its method, and all the flutter of the aviary without its song.   In addition to this, he chose his subjects badly, and was always most inspired by the worst parts of them. The charms of paganism, the merits of rebellion, these were the themes honored with his particular enthusiasm ; and, in the poem just recited, one of his most palatable passages was in praise of that beverage of the Unfaithful, wine ;—"being perhaps," said he, relaxing into a smile, as conscious of his own character in the Haram on this point, "one of those bards whose fancy owes all its illumination to the grape, like that painted porcelain,[879] so curious and so rare, whose images are only visible when liquor is poured into it."   Upon the whole it was his opinion, from the specimens which they had heard, and which, he begged to say, were the most tiresome part of the journey, that— whatever other merits this well-dressed young gentleman might possess—poetry was by no means his proper avocation : "and indeed," continued the critic, "from his fondness for flowers and for birds, I would venture to suggest that a florist or a bird-catcher is a much more suitable calling for him than a poet."

They had now begun to ascend those barren mountains which separate Cashmere from the rest of India ; and as the heats were intolerable, and the time of their encampment limited

to the few hours necessary for refreshment **and**
repose, there was an end to all their delightful
evenings, and LALLA ROOKH saw no more of
FERAMORZ.   She now felt that her short dream
of happiness was over, and that she had
nothing but the recollection of its few blissful
hours, like the one draught of sweet water that
serves the camel across the wilderness, to be
her heart's refreshment during the dreary waste
of life that was before her.   The blight that had
fallen upon her spirits soon found its way to
her cheek, and her ladies saw with regret—
though not without some suspicion of the cause
—that the beauty of their mistress, of which
they were almost as proud of as their own, was
fast vanishing away at the very moment of all
when she had most need of it.   What must the
King of Bucharia feel, when, instead of the
lively and beautiful LALLA ROOKH, whom the
poets of Delhi had described as more perfect
than the divinest images in the house of AZOR, [880]
he should receive a pale and inanimate victim,
upon whose cheek neither health nor pleasure
bloomed, and from whose eyes Love had fled,—
to hide himself in her heart?

If anything could have charmed away the
melancholy of her spirits, it would have been
the fresh airs and enchanting scenery of that
Valley which the Persians so justly called the
Unequalled. [881]   But neither the coolness of its
atmosphere, so luxurious after toiling up those
bare and burning mountains,—neither the
splendor of the minarets and pagodas that

shone out from the depth of its woods, nor the
grottos, hermitages, and miraculous fountains[382]
which make every spot of that region holy
ground,—neither the countless waterfalls that
rush into the Valley, from all those high and
romantic mountains that encircle it, nor the fair
city on the Lake, whose houses, roofed with
flowers,[383] appeared at a distance like one vast
and variegated parterre;—not all these wonders
and glories of the most lovely country under
the sun could steel her heart for a minute from
those sad thoughts, which but darkened and
grew bitterer every step she advanced.

The gay pomps and processions that met
her upon her entrance into the Valley, and the
magnificence with which the roads all along
were decorated, did honor to the taste and gal-
lantry of the young King. It was night when
they approached the city, and, for the last two
miles, they had passed under arches, thrown
from hedge to hedge, festooned with only those
rarest roses from which the Attar Gul, more
precious than gold, is distilled, and illuminated
in rich and fanciful forms with lanterns of the
triple-colored tortois-shell of Pegu.[384] Sometimes, from a dark wood by the side of the
road, a display of fireworks would break out,
so sudden and so brilliant, that a Brahmin
might fancy he beheld that grove in whose
purple shades the God of Battles was born,
bursting into a flame at the moment of his
birth ;—while, at other times, a quick and play-
ul irradiation continued to brighten all the

fields and gardens by which they passed, forming a line of dancing lights along the horizon; like the meteors [385] the north, as they are seen by those hunters of who pursue the white and blue foxes on the confines of the Icy Sea.

These arches and fireworks delighted the Ladies of the Princess exceedingly; and with their usual good logic, they deduced from his taste for illuminations, that the King of Bucharia would make the most exemplary husband imaginable. Nor, indeed, could LALLA ROOKH herself help feeling the kindness and splendor with which the young bridegroom welcomed her; but she also felt how painful is the gratitude which kindness from those we cannot love excites; and that their best blandishments come over the heart with all that chilling and deadly sweetness which we can fancy in the cold, odoriferous wind [386] that is to blow over this earth in the last days.

The marriage was fixed for the morning after her arrival, when she was, for the first time, to be presented to the monarch in that Imperial Palace beyond the lake called the Shalimar. Though never before had a night of more wakeful and anxious thought been passed in th' Happy Valley, yet, when she rose in the morning, and her Ladies came around her, to assist in the adjustment of the bridal ornaments, the thought they had never seen her look half s' beautiful. What she had lost of the bloo' and radiancy of her charms was more tha' made up by that intellectual expression, th' soul beaming forth from the eyes, which is worth all the rest of loveliness. When they had tinged her fingers with the Henna leaf, and placed upon her brow a small coronet of jewels, of the shape worn by the ancient Queens of Bucharia they flung over her head the rose-colored bridal veil, and she proceeded to the barge that was to convey her across the Lake ; —first kissing, with a mournful look, the little amulet of cornelian which her father at parting had hung about her neck.

The morning was as fresh and fair as the maid on whose nuptials it rose, and the shining Lake, all covered with boats, the minstrels playing upon the shores of the islands, and the crowded summer-houses on the green hills around, with shawls and banners waving from their roofs, presented such a picture of animated rejoicing, as only she, who was the object of it all, did not feel with transport. To LALLA ROOKH alone it was a melancholy pageant ; nor could she have even borne to look upon the scene, were it not for a hope that, among the crowds around, she might once more perhaps catch a glimpse of FERAMORZ. So much was her imagination haunted by this thought, that there was scarcely an islet or boat she passed on the way at which her heart did not flutter with the momentary fancy that he was there. Happy, in her eyes, the humblest slave upon whom the light of his dear looks fell !—in the barge immediately after the Princess sat FADLADEEN, with his silken curtains thrown widely apart,

that all might have the benefit of his august
presence, and with his head full of the speech
he was to deliver to the King, "concerning
FERAMORZ, and literature, and the Chabuk, as
connected therewith."

They now had entered the canal which leads
from the Lake to the splendid domes and saloons of the Shalimar, and went gliding on
through the gardens that ascended from each
bank, full of flowering shrubs that made the
air all perfume ; while from the middle of the
canal rose jets of water, smooth and unbroken,
to such a dazzling height, that they stood like
tall pillars of diamond in the sunshine. After
sailing under the arches of various saloons,
they at length arrived at the last and most
magnificent, where the monarch awaited the
coming of his bride ; and such was the agita-
tion of her heart and frame that it was with
difficulty she could walk up the marble steps,
which were covered with cloth of gold for her
ascent from the barge. At the end of the hall
stood two thrones, as precious as the Cerulean
Throne of Coolburga, [387] on one of which sat
ALIRIS the youthful King of Bucharia, and on
the other was, in a few minutes, to be placed
the most beautiful Princess in the world. Immediately upon the entrance of LALLA ROOKH
into the saloon, the monarch descended from
his throne to meet her ; but scarcely had he
time to take her hand in his, when she screamed
with surprise, and fainted at his feet. It was
FERAMORZ himself that stood before her ! FER-

ABORZ was, himself, the Sovereign of Bucharia, who in this disguise had accompanied his young bride from Delhi, and, having won her love as an humble minstrel, now amply deserved to enjoy it as a King.

The consternation of FADLADEEN at this discovery was, for the moment, almost pitiable. But change of opinion is a resource too convenient in courts for this experienced courtier not to have learned to avail himself of it. His criticisms were all, of course, recanted instantly: he was seized with an admiration of the King's verses, as unbounded as, he begged him to believe, it was disinterested; and the following week saw him in possession of an additional place, swearing by all the Saints of Islam that never had there existed so great a poet as the Monarch ALIRIS, and, moreover, ready to prescribe his favorite regimen of the Chabuk for every man, woman, and child that dared to think otherwise.

Of the happiness of the King and Queen of Bucharia, after such a beginning, there can be but little doubt; and, among the lesser symptoms, it is recorded of LALLA ROOKH, that, to the day of her death, in memory of their delightful journey, she never called the King by any other name than FERAMORZ.

17

NOTES.

NOTE 1, p. 23.—*He embarked for Arabia.*—These particulars of the visit of the King of Bucharia to Aurungzebe are found in Dow's *History of Hindostan,* vol. iii. p. 392.

Note 2, p. 23.—LALLA ROOKH.—Tulip cheek.

Note 3, p. 23.—*Leila.*—The mistress of Mejnoun, upon whose story so many romances in all the languages of the East are founded.

Note 4, p. 23.—*Shirine.*—For the loves of this celebrated beauty with Khosrou and with Ferhad, see D'Herbelot, Gibbon, *Oriental Collections, etc.*

Note 5, p. 23.—*Dewildé.*—"The history of the loves of Dewildé and Chizer, the son of the Emperor Alla, is written in an elegant poem, by the noble Chusero." —*Ferishta.*

Note 6, p. 24.—*Scattering of the Roses.*—Gul Reazee.

Note 7, p. 24.—*Emperor's favor.*—"One mark of honor or knighthood bestowed by the Emperor is the permission to wear a small kettledrum at the bows of their saddles, which at first was invented for the training of hawks, and to call them to the lure, and is worn in the field by all sportsmen to that end."—*Fryer's Travels.*

"Those on whom the King has conferred the privilege must wear an ornament of jewels on the right side of the turban, surmounted by a high plume of the feathers of a kind of egret. This bird is found only in

Cashmere, and the feathers are carefully collected for
the King, who bestows them on his nobles."—*Elphinstone's Account of Caubul.*

Note 8, p. 24.—*Keder Khan.*—"Khedar Khan, the
Khakan, or King of Turquestan beyond the Gihon (at
the end of the eleventh century), whenever he appeared abroad, was preceded by seven hundred horse-
men with silver battle-axes, and was followed by an
equal number bearing maces of gold. He was a great
patron of poetry, and it was he who used to preside at
public exercises of genius, with four basins of gold
and silver by him to distribute among the poets who
excelled."—*Richardson's Dissertation* prefixed to his
Dictionary.

Note 9, p. 24.—*Gilt pine-apples.*—"The kubdeh, a
large golden knob, generally in the shape of a pine-
apple, on the top of the canopy over the litter or pal-
anquin."—*Scott's Notes on the Bahardanush.*

Note 10, p. 25.—*Sumptuous litter.*—In the Poem of
Zohair, in the Moallakat, there is the following lively
description of "a company of maidens seated on
camels."

"They are mounted in carriages covered with costly
awnings, and with rose-colored veils, the linings of
which have the hue of crimson Andem-wood.

"When they ascend from the bosom of the vale,
they sit forward on the saddle-cloth, with every mark
of a voluptuous gayety.

"Now, when they have reached the brink of yon
blue-gushing rivulet, they fix the poles of their tents
like the Arab with a settled mansion."

Note 11, p. 25.—*Argus pheasant's wing.*—See Bernier's description of the attendants on Raucha-nara-
Begum, in her progress to Cashmere.

Note 12, p. 25.—*Munificent protector.*—This hypo-
critical Emperor would have made a worthy associate
of certain Holy Leagues.—"He held the cloak of religion," says Dow, "between his actions and the vul-

gar ; and impiously thanked the Divinity for a success which he owed to his own wickedness.   When he
was murdering and persecuting his brothers and their
families, he was building a magnificent mosque at
Delhi, as an offering to God for his assistance to him
in the civil wars.   He acted as high priest at the con-
secration of this temple ; and made a practice of attending divine service there, in the humble dress of a
Fakeer.   But when he lifted one hand to the Divinity,
he, with the other, signed warrants for the assassin-
ation of his relations."—*History of Hindostan*, vol.
iii. p. 335.   See also the curious letter of Aurungzebe,
given in the *Oriental Collections*, vol. i. p. 320.

Note 13, p. 25.—*The Idol of Jaghernaut.*—"The idol
at Jaghernat has two fine diamonds for eyes.   No
goldsmith is suffered to enter the Pagoda, one having
stolen one of these eyes, being locked up all night with
the Idol."—*Tavernier*.

Note 14, p. 26.—*Royal Gardens of Delhi.*—See a
description of these Royal Gardens in "An Account of
the present State of Delhi," by Lieut. W. Franklin;
Asiat. Research, vol. iv. p. 417.

Note 15, p. 26.—*Lake of Pearl.*—"In the neighborhood is Notte Gill, or the Lake of Pearl, which receives this name from its pellucid water."—*Pennant's
Hindostan*.

"Nasir Jung encamped in the vicinity of the Lake
of Tonoor, amused himself with sailing on that clear
and beautiful water, and gave it the fanciful name of
Motee Talah, 'the Lake of Pearls,' which it still re-
tains."—*Wilks's South of India*.

Note 16, p. 26.—*Isles of the West.*—Sir Thomas Roe,
Ambassador from James I. to Jehan-Guire.

Note 17, p. 26.—*Ezra.*—"The romance Wemak-
weazra, written in Persian verse, which contains the
loves of Wamak and Ezra, two celebrated lovers who
lived before the time of Mahomet."—*Note on the Oriental Tales*.

Note 18, p. 26.—*Rodahver.*—Their amour is recounted in the Shah-Nameh of Ferdousi ; and there is much beauty in the passage which describes the slaves of Rodahver sitting on the bank of the river, and throwing flowers into the stream, in order to draw the attention of the young Hero who is encamped on the opposite side. (See Champion's translation.)

Note 19, p. 26.—*White Demon.*—Rustam is the Hercules of the Persians. For the particulars of his victory over the Sepeed Deeve, or White Demon, see *Oriental Collections,* vol. ii. p. 45.—" Near the city of Shirauz is an immense quadrangular monument, in commemoration of this combat, called the Kelaat-i-Deev Sepeed, or castle of the White Giant, which Father Angelo, in his *Gazophilacium Persicum,* p. 127, declares to have been the most memorable monument of antiquity which he had seen in Persia." (See Ouseley's *Persian Miscellanies.*)

Note 20, p. 27.—*Golden anklets.*—" The women of the Idol, or dancing girls of the Pagoda, have little golden bells fastened to their feet, the soft harmonious tinkling of which vibrates in unison with the exquisite melody of their voices."—*Maurice's Indian Antiquities.*

" The Arabian courtesans, like the Indian women, have little golden bells fastened round their legs, neck, and elbows, to the sound of which they dance before the King. The Arabian princesses wear golden rings on their fingers, to which little bells are suspended, as well as in the flowing tresses of their hair, that their superior rank may be known, and they themselves receive in passing the homage due to them." (See Calmet's *Dictionary,* art. Bells.)

Note 21, p. 17.—*Delicious opium.*—"Abou-Tige, ville de la Thebaide, ou il croit beaucoup de pavot noir, dont se fait le meilleur opinion."—*D'Herbelot.*

Note 22, p. 28.—*Crishna.*—The Indian Apollo.—" He and the three Ramas are described as youths of perfect beauty; and the princesses of Hindustan, were

all passionately in love with Chrishna, **who continues
to** this hour the darling God of the Indian women."
—*Sir W. Jones, on the Gods of Greece, Italy, and
India.*

Note 23, p. 28.—*Shawl-goats of Tibet.*—See Turner's
Embassy for a description of this animal, "the most
beautiful among the whole tribe of goats." The
material for the shawls (which is carried to Cashmere)
is found next the skin.

Note 24, p. 28.—*Veiled Prophet of Khorassan.*—For
the real history of this Impostor, whose original name
was Hakem ben Haschem, and who was called
Mokanna from the veil of silver gauze (or, as others
say, golden) which he always wore, see D'Herbelot.

Note 25, p. 29.—*Khorassan.*—Khorassan signifies.
in the old Persian language, Province or Region of
the Sun.—*Sir W. Jones.*

Note 26, p. 29.—*Flow'rets and fruits blush over every
stream.*
' The fruits of Meru are finer than those of any
other place ; and one cannot see in any other city
such palaces with groves, and streams, and gardens."
—*Ebu Haukal's Geography.*

Note 27, p. 29.—*Among* MEROU'S *bright palaces and
groves.*
One of the royal cities of Khorassan.

Note 28, p. 29.—MOUSSA'S.—Moses.

Note 29, p. 29.—*O'er* MOUSSA'S *cheek when down
the Mount he trod.*
"Ses disciples assuroient qu'il se couvroit le visage,
pour ne pas eblouir ceux qui l'approchoient par l'eclat
de son visage comme Moyse."—*D'Herbelot.*

Note 30, p. 30.—*In hatred to the Caliph's hue of
night.*
Black was the color adopted by the Caliphs of the
House of Abbas, in their garments, turbans, and
standards.—" Il faut remarquer ici touchant les habits

blancs des disciples de Hakem, que la couleur des habits, des coiffures et des etendards des Khalifes Abassides etant la noire, ce chef de Rebelles ne pouvoit pas choisir une qui lui fut plus opposee."— *D'Herbelot.*

Note 31, p. 30.—*With javelins of the light Kathaian reed.*

" Our dark javelins, exquisitely wrought of Khathaian reeds, slender and delicate."—*Poem of Amru.*

Note 32, p. 30.—*Fill'd with the stems.*
Pichula, used anciently for arrows by the Persians.

Note 33, p. 30.—*That bloom on IRAN's rivers.*

The Persians call this plant Gaz. The celebrated shaft of Isfendiar, one of their ancient heroes, was made of it.—" Nothing can be more beautiful than the appearance of this plant in flower during the rains on the banks of rivers, where it is usually interwoven with a lovely twining asclepias."—*Sir W. Jones, Botanical Observations on Select Indian Plants.*

Note 34, p. 30.—*Like a chenar-tree grove, when Winter throws.*

The Oriental plane. "The chenar is a delightful tree; its bole is of a fine white and smooth bark; and its foliage, which grows in a tuft at the summit, is of a bright green."—*Morier's Travels.*

Note 35, p. 31.—*From those who kneel at BRAHMA's burning founts.*

The burning fountains of Brahma near Chittagong, esteemed as holy.—*Turner.*

Note 36, p. 31.—*To the small, half-shut glances of* KATHAY.—China.

Note 37, p. 31.—*Like tulip beds of different shape and dyes.*

" The name of tulip is said to be of Turkish extraction, and given to the flower on account of its resemblance to a turban."—*Beckmann's History of Inventions.*

Note 38, p. 31.—*And fur-bound bonnet of Bucharian shape.*

"The inhabitants of Bucharia wear a round cloth bonnet, shaped much after the Polish fashion, having a large fur border. They tie their kaftans about the middle with a girdle of a kind of silk crape, several times round the body."—*Account of Independent Tartary, in Pinkerion's Collection.*

Note 39, p. 32.—*O'erwhelm'd in fight and captive to the Greek.*

In the war of the Caliph Mahadi against the Empress Irene, for an account of which *vide* Gibbon, vol. x.

Note 40, p. 33.—*The flying throne of star-taught* SOLIMAN.

This wonderful throne was called The Star of the Genii. For a full description of it, see the Fragment, translated by Captain Franklin, from a Persian MS. entitled, "The History of Jerusalem," *Oriental Collections,* vol i. p. 235.—When Soliman travelled, the Eastern writers say, "He had a carpet of green silk on which his throne was laced, being of a prodigious length and breadth, and sufficient for all his forces to stand upon, the men placing themselves on his right hand, and the spirits on his left; and that when all were in order, the wind, at his command, took up the carpet, and transported it, with all that were upon it, wherever he pleased: the army of birds at the same time flying over their heads, and forming a kind of canopy to shade them from the sun."—*Sale's Koran,* vol. ii. p. 214, note.

Note 41, p. 33.—*For many an age, in every chance and change.*

The transmigration of souls was one of his doctrines. (*Vide* D'Herbelot.)

Note 42, p. 33.—*To which all Heaven, except the Proud One, knelt.*

"And when we said unto the angels, Worship Adam, they all worshipped except Eblis (Lucifer), who refused."—*The Koran,* chap. ii.

Note 43, p. 34.—*In* Moussa's *frame,—and, thence de-scending, flow'd.*—Moses.

Note 44, p. 34—*Through many a Prophet's breast.*

This is according to D'Herbelot's account of the doctrines of Mokanna :—"Sa doctrine etoit, que Dieu avoit pris une forme et figure humaine, depuis qu'il eut commande aux Anges d'adorer Adam, le premier des hommes. Qu'apres la mort d'Adam, Dieu etoit apparu sous la figure de plusieurs Prophetes, et autres grands hommes qu'il avoit choisis, jusqu'a ce qu'il prit celle d'Abu Moslem, Prince de Khorassan, lequel professoit l'erreur de la Tenassukhiah ou Metempsychose ; et qu'apres la mort de ce Prince, la Divinite etoit passee et descendue en sa personne."

Note 45, p. 34.—*In* Issa *shone.*—Jesus.

Note 46, p. 37.—*Born by that ancient flood, which from its spring.*

The Amoo, which rises in the Belur Tag, or Dark Mountains, and, running nearly from east to west, splits into two branches ; one of which falls into the Caspian Sea, and the other into Aral Nahr, or the Lake of Eagles.

Note 47, p. 33.—*The bulbul utters, ere her soul depart.*—The nightingale.

Note 48, p. 45.—*In holy* Koom, *or* Mecca's *dim arcades.*

The Cities of Com (or Koom) and Cashan are full of mosques, mausoleums, and sepulchres of the descendants of Ali, the Saints of Persia.—*Chardin.*

Note 49, p. 46.—*Stood vases, fill'd with* Kishmee's *golden wine.*

An island in the Persian Gulf, celebrated for its white wine.

Note 50, p. 46.—*Like* Zemzem's *Spring of Holiness, had power.*

The miraculous well at Mecca ; so called, says Sale, from the murmuring of its waters.

Note 51, p. 46.—*Whom* INDIA *serves, the monkey deity.*

The God Hannaman.—"Apes are in many parts of India highly venerated, out of respect to the God Hannaman, a deity partaking of the form of that race."—*Pennant's Hindostan.*

See a curious account, in Stephen's *Persia,* of a solemn embassy from some part of the Indies to Goa, when the Portuguese were there, offering vast treasures for the recovery of a monkey's tooth, which they held in great veneration, and which had been taken away upon the conquest of the kingdom of Jafanapatan.

Note 52, p. 46.—*To bend in worship,* LUCIFER *was right.*

The resolution of Eblis not to acknowledge the new creature, man, was, according to Mahometan tradition, thus adopted:—"The earth (which God had selected for the materials of His work) was carried into Arabia to a place between Mecca and Tayef, where, being first kneaded by the angels, it was afterwards fashioned by God Himself into a human form, and left to dry for the space of forty days, or, as others say, as many years; the angels, in the meantime, often visiting it, and Eblis (then one of the angels nearest to God's presence, afterwards the devil) among the rest; but he, not contented with looking at it, kicked it with his foot till it rung; and knowing God designed that creature to be his superior, took a secret resolution never to acknowledge him as such."—*Sale on the Koran.*

Note 53, p. 47.—*From dead men's marrow guides them best at night.*

A kind of lantern formerly used by robbers, called the Hand of Glory, the candle for which was made of the fat of a dead malefactor. This, however, was rather a Western than an Eastern superstition.

Note 54, p. 47.—*In that best marble of which Gods are made.*

The material of which images of Gaudma (the Birman Deity) are made, is held sacred. "Birmans may not purchase the marble in mass, but are suffered, and indeed encouraged, to buy figures of the Deity ready made."—*Symes's Ava*, vol. ii. p. 376.

Note 55, p. 51.—*Of Kerzrah flowers, came fill'd with pestilence.*

"It is commonly said in Persia that if a man breathe in the hot south wind, which in June or July passes over that flower (the Kerzereh), it will kill him."—*Thevenot.*

Note 56, p. 53.—*Within the crocodile's stretch'd jaws to come.*

The humming-bird is said to run this risk for the purpose of picking the crocodile's teeth. The same circumstance is related of the lapwing, as a fact to which he was witness, by Paul Lucas, *Voyage fait en 1714.*

The ancient story concerning the Trochilus, or humming-bird, entering with impunity into the mouth of the crocodile, is firmly believed at Java.—*Barrow's Cochin China.*

Note 57, p. 55.—*That rank and venomous food on which she lives.*

"Circum easdem ripas (Nili, viz.) ales est Ibis. Ea serpentium populatur ova, gratissimamque ex his escam nidis suis refert."—*Solinus.*

Note 58, p. 56.—*Yamtcheou.*—"The Feast of Lanters is celebrated at Yamtcheou with more magnificence than anywhere else: and the report goes that the illuminations there are so splendid that the Emperor once, not daring openly to leave his Court to go thither, committed himself with the Queen and several Princesses of his family into the hands of a magician, who promised to transport them thither in a trice. He made them in the night to ascend magnificent thrones that were borne up by swans, which in a moment arrived at Yamtcheou. The Emperor saw at his leisure all the solemnity, being carried upon a cloud that hovered over the city and descended by degrees; and came back again with the same speed and equipage, nobody at court perceiving his absence,"—*The Present State of China*, p. 156.

Note 59, p. 56.—*Sceneries of bamboo-work.*—See a description of the nuptials of Vizier Alee in the *Asiatic Annual Register* for 1804.

Note 60, p. 56.—*Chinese illuminations.*—"The vulgar ascribe it to an accident that happened in the family of a famous mandarin, whose daughter, walking one evening upon the shore of a lake, fell in and was drowned; the afflicted father, with his family, ran thither, and, the better to find her, he caused a great company of lanterns to be lighted. All the inhabitants of the place thronged after him with torches. The year ensuing they made fires upon the shores the same day: they continued the ceremony every year; every one lighted his lantern, and by degrees it grew into a custom."—*Present State of China.*

Note 61, p. 58.—*Like* SEBA'S *Queen could vanquish with that one.*
"Thou hast ravished my heart with one of thine eyes."—*Sol. Song.*

Note 62, p. 58.—*The fingers' ends with a bright roseate hue.*
"They tinged the ends of their fingers scarlet with henna, so that they resembled branches of coral."—*Story of Prince Futtun in Bahardanush.*

Note 63, p. 58.—*To give that long, dark languish to the eye.*
"The women blacken the inside of their eyelids with a powder named the black kohol."—*Russel.*
"None of these ladies," says Shaw, "take themselves to be completely dressed, till they have tinged the hair and edges of their eyelids with the powder of lead ore. Now, as this operation is performed by dipping first into the powder a small wooden bodkin of the thickness of a quill, and then drawing it atten-

wards through the eyelids over the ball of the eye, we
shall have a lively image of what the Prophet (Jer. iv.
30) may be supposed to mean by *rending the eyes
with painting.* This practice is no doubt of great
antiquity; for besides the instance already taken
notice of, we find that where Jezebel is said (2 Kings
ix. 30) *to have painted her fair face,* the original
words are, *she adjusted her eyes with the powder of
lead ore."* *Shaw's Travels.*

Note 64, p. 58.—*In her full lap the Champac's leaves
of gold.*
The appearance of the blossoms of the gold-colored
Champac on the black hair of the Indian women has
supplied the Sanscrit poets with many elegant allusions
(See *Asiatic Researches,* vol. iv.)

Note 65, p. 58.—*The sweet Elcaya, and that courteous
tree.*
A tree famous for its perfume, and common on the
hills of Yemen.—*Niebuhr.*

Note 66, p. 58.—*Which bows to all who seek its
canopy.*
Of the genus mimosa, "which droops its branches
whenever any person approaches it, seeming as if it
saluted those who retire under its shade."—*Ibid.*

Note 67, p. 59.—*The bowers of* TIBET, *send forth
odorous light.*
"Cloves are a principal ingredient in the composition of the perfumed rods, which men of rank keep
constantly burning in their presence."—*Turner's Tibet.*

Note 68, p. 60.—*With odoriferous woods of* COMORIN.
"C'est p' ou vient le bois d'aloës que les Arabes appellent Oud Comari, et celui du sandal, qui s'y trouve en
grande quantite."—*D'Herbelot.*

Note 69, p. 60.—*The crimson blossoms of the coral
tree.*
"Thousands of variegated lories visit the coral
trees."—*Barrow.*

Note 70, p. 60.—*Mecca's blue sacred pigeon.*

" In Mecca there are quanities of blue pigeons, which none will affright or abuse, much less kill."—*Pitt's account of the Mahometans.*

Note 71, p. 60.—*The thrush of Hindostan.*

"The Pagoda Thrush is esteemed among the first choristers of India. It sits perched on the sacred pagodas, and from thence delivers its melodious song."—*Pennant's Hindostan.*

Note 72, p. 60.—*About the gardens, drunk with that sweet food.*

Tavernier adds, that while the birds of Paradise lie in this intoxicated state, the emmets come and eat off their legs ; and that hence it is they are said to have no feet.

Note 73, p. 60.—*Whose scent hath lur'd them o'er the summer flood.*

Birds of Paradise, which, at the nutmeg season, come in flights from the southern isles to India ; and "the strength of the nutmeg," says Tavernier, " so intoxicates them, that they fall dead drunk to the earth."

Note 74, p. 60.—*Build their high nests of budding cinnamon.*

" That bird which liveth in Arabia, and buildeth its nest with cinnamon."—*Browne's Vulgar Errors.*

Note 75, p. 60.—*Sleeping in light, like the green birds that dwell.*

" The spirits of the martyrs will be lodged in the crops of green birds."—*Gibbon*, vol. ix. p. 421.

Note 76, p. 60.—*More like the luxuries of that impious King.*

Shedad, who made the delicious gardens of Irim, in imitation of Paradise, and was destroyed by lightning the first time he attempted to enter them.

Note 77, p. 62.—*In its blue blossoms hum themselves to sl*

" My Pandits assure me that the plant before us

(the Nilica) is their Sephalica, thus named because the bees are supposed to sleep on its blossoms."—*Sir W. Jones.*

Note 78, p. 63.—*As they were captives to the King of Flowers.*

"They deferred it till the King of Flowers should ascend his throne of enamelled foliage."—*The Bahardanush.*

Note 79, p. 64.—*But a light golden chain-work round her hair.*

"One of the head-dresses of the Persian women is composed of a light golden chain-work, set with small pearls, with a thin gold plate pendant, about the bigness of a crown-piece, on which is impressed an Arabian prayer, and which hangs upon the cheek below the ear."—*Hanway's Travels.*

Note 80, p. 64.—*Such as the maids of* YEZD *and* SHIRAS *wear.*

"Certainly the women of Yezd are the handsomest women in Persia. The proverb is, that to live happy a man must have a wife of Yezd, eat the bread of Yezdecas, and drink the wine of Shiraz."—*Tavernier.*

Note 81, p. 65.—*Upon a musnud's edge.*

Musnuds are cushioned seats, usually reserved for persons of distinction.

Note 82, p. 65.—*In the pathetic mode of* ISFAHAN.

The Persians, like the ancient Greeks, call their musical modes or Perdas by the names of different countries or cities, as the mode of Isfahan, the mode of Irak, etc.

Note 83, p. 65.—*There's a bower of roses by* BENDE-MEER'S *stream.*

A river which flows near the ruins of Chilminar

Note 84, p. 67.—*The hills of crystal on the Caspian shore.*

"To the north of us (on the coast of the Caspian, near Badku) was a mountain, which sparkled like diamonds, arising from the sea-glass and crystals with which it abounds."—*Journey of the Russian Ambassador to Persia, 1746.*

Note 85, p. 67.—*Of* EDEN, *shake in the eternal breeze.*

"To which will be added the sound of bells, hanging on the trees, which will be put in motion by the wind proceeding from the throne of God, as often as the blessed wish for music."—*Sale.*

Note 86, p. 68.—*And his floating eyes—oh! they resemble.*

"Whose wanton eyes resemble blue water-lilies. agitated by the breeze."—*Jayadeva.*

Note 88, p. 68.—*Blue water-lilies.*

The blue lotus, which grows in Cashmere and in Persia.

Note 88, p. 69.—*To muse upon the pictures that hung round.*

It has been generally supposed that the Mahometans prohibit all pictures of animals ; but Toderini shows that, though the practice is forbidden by the Koran, they are not more averse to painted figures and images than other people. From Mr. Murphy's work, too, we find that the Arabs of Spain had no objection to the introduction of figures into painting.

Note 89, p. 69.—*Whose orb when half retir'd looks loveliest.*

This is not quite astronomically true. " Dr. Hadley (says Keil) has shown that Venus is brightest when she is about forty degrees removed from the sun ; and that then but *only a fourth part* of her lucid disk is to be seen from the earth."

Note 90, p. 69.—*He read that to be blest is to be wise.*

For the loves of King Solomon (who was supposed to preside over the whole race of Genii) with Balkis, the Queen of Sheba or Saba, see D'Herbelot, and the *Notes on the Koran*, chap. ii.

" In the palace which Solomon ordered to be built

18

against the arrival of the Queen of Saba. the floor of pavement was of transparent glass, laid over running water, in which fish were swimming." This led the Queen into a very natural mistake, which the Koran has not thought beneath its dignity to commemorate. "It was said unto her, 'Enter the palace.' And when she saw it she imagined it to be a great water; and she discovered her legs, by lifting up her robe to pass through it. Whereupon Solomon said to her, 'Verily, this is the place evenly floored with glass.'"— Chap. xxvii.

Note 91, p. 69.—*Here fond* ZULEIKA *woos with open arms.*

The wife of Potiphar, thus named by the Orientals.

"The passion which this frail beauty of antiquity conceived for her young Hebrew slave has given rise to a much-esteemed poem in the Persian language, entitled *Yusef vau Zelikha*, by Noureddin Jami; the manuscript copy of which, in the Bodleian Library at Oxford, is supposed to be the finest in the whole world."—*Note upon Nott's Translation of Hafez.*

Note 92, p. 69.—*With a new text to consecrate their love.*

The particulars of Mahomet's amour with Mary, the Coptic girl, in justification of which he added a new chapter to the Koran, may be found in Gagnier's *Notes upon Abulfeda*, p. 151.

Note 93, p. 71.—*But in that deep-blue, melancholy dress.*

"Deep blue is their mourning color."—*Hanway.*

Note 94, p. 72.—*Sat in her sorrow like the sweet night-flower.*

The sorrowful nyctanthes, which begins to spread its rich odor after sunset.

Note 95, p. 73.—*As the viper weaves its wily covering.*

"Concerning the vipers, which Pliny says were frequent among the balsam-trees, I made very particular inquiry; several were brought me alive both to Yambo and Juuda."—*Bruce.*

Note 96, p. 79.—*The sunny apples of Istkahar.*—"In the territory of Istkahar there is a kind of apple, half of which is sweet and half sour."—*Ebn Haukal.*

Note 97, p.79.—*They saw a young Hindoo girl upon the bank.*—For an account of this ceremony, see Grandpre's *Voyage in the Indian Ocean.*

Note 98, p. 79.—*The Oton-tala, or Sea of Stars.*—"The place where the Whangho, a river of Tibet, rises, and where there are more than a hundred springs, which sparkle like stars ; whence it is called Hotun-nor, that is, the Sea of Stars."—*Pinkerton's Description of Tibet.*

Note 99, p. 80.—*Hath sprung up here.*
"The Lescar or Imperial Camp is divided, like a regular town, into squares, alleys, and streets, and from a rising ground furnishes one of the most agreeable prospects in the world. Starting up in a few hours in an uninhabited plain, it raises the idea of a city built by enchantment. Even those who leave their houses in cities to follow the prince in his progress are frequently so charmed by the Lescar, when situated in a beautiful and convenient place, that they cannot prevail with themselves to remove. To prevent this inconvenience to the court, the Emperor, after sufficient time is allowed to the tradesmen to follow, orders them to be burnt out of their tents."—*Dow's Hindostan.*

Colonel Wilks gives a lively picture of an Eastern encampment : "His camp, like that of most Indian armies, exhibited a motley collection of covers from the scorching sun and dews of the night, variegated according to the taste or means of each individual, by extensive enclosures of colored calico surrounding superb suites of tents ; by ragged cloths or blankets stretched over sticks or branches: palm-leaves hastily spread over similar supports ; handsome tents and splendid canopies ; horses, oxen, elephants, and camels ; all intermixed without any exterior mark of order or design, except the flags of the chiefs, which

usually mark the centres of a congeries of these
masses ; the only regular part of the encampment being the streets of shops, each of which is constructed
nearly in the manner of a booth at an English fair."
—*Historical Sketches of the South of India.*

Note 100, p. 80.—*Built the high pillar'd halls of*
CHILMINAR.

The edifices of Chilminar and Balbec are supposed
to have been built by the Genii, acting under the
orders of Jan ben Jan, who governed the world long
before the time of Adam.

Note 101, p. 81.—*And camels, tufted o'er with*
Yemen's shells.

"A superb camel, ornamented with strings and
tufts of small shells."—*Ali Bey.*

Note 102, p. 81.—*But the far torrent, or the locust*
bird.

A native of Khorassan, and allured southward by
means of the water of a fountain between Shiraz and
Ispahan, called the Fountain of Birds, of which it
is so fond that it will follow wherever that water is
carried.

Note 103, p. 81.—*Of laden camels and their drivers'*
songs.

"Some of the camels have bells about their necks,
and some about their legs, like those which our
carriers put about their fore-horses' necks, which,
together with the servants (who belong to the camels,
and travel on foot), singing all night, make a pleasant
noise, and the journey passes away delightfully."—
Pitt's Account of the Mahometans.

"The camel-driver follows the camels, singing, and
sometimes playing upon his pipe ; the louder he sings
and pipes, the faster the camels go. Nay, they will
stand still when he gives over his music."—*Taver-*
nier.

Note 104, p. 81.—*Of the Abyssinian trumpet, swell*
and float.

"This trumpet is often called, in Abyssinia, *nesser*

ganno, which signifies the Note of the Eagle."—*Note of Bruce's Editor.*

Note 105, p. 81.—*The Night and Shadow, over yonder tent.*
The two black standards borne before the Caliphs of the House of Abbas were called, allegorically, The Night and the Shadow. (See Gibbon.)

Note 106, p. 81.—*Defiance fierce at Islam.*—The Mahometan religion.

Note 107, p. 81.—*But, having sworn upon the Holy Grave.*
"The Persians swear by the tomb of Shah Besade, who is buried at Casbin ; and when one desires another to asseverate a matter, he will ask him if he dare swear by the Holy Grave."—*Struy.*

Note 108, p. 82.—*Were spoil'd to feed the Pilgrim's luxury.*
Mahadi, in a single pilgrimage to Mecca, expended six millions of dinars of gold.

Note 109, p. 82.—*Of* MECCA's *sun, with urns of Persian snow.*
"Nivem Meccam apportavit, rem ibi aut nunquam aut raro visam."—*Abulfeda.*

Note 110, p. 82.—*First, in the van, the People of the Rock.*
The inhabitants of Hejaz or Arabia Petræa, called by an Eastern writer "the People of the Rock." (See Ebn Haukal.)

Note 111, p. 82.—*On their light mountain steeds, of royal stock.*
"Those horses, called by the Arabians Kochlani, of whom a written genealogy has been kept for 2,000 years. They are said to derive their origin from King Solomon's steeds."—*Niebuhr.*

Note 112, p. 82.—*The flashing of their swords' rich marquetry.*
"Many of the figures on the blades of their swords

are wrought in gold or silver, or in marquetry with small gems."—*Asiat. Misc.* v. 1.

Note 113, p. 82.—*With dusky legions from the land of Myrrh.*

Azab or Saba.

Note 114, p. 83.—*Waving their heron crests with martial grace.*

"The chiefs of the Uzbek Tartars wear a plume of white heron's feathers in their turbans."—*Account of Independent Tartary.*

Note 115, p. 83.—*Wild warriors of the turquoise hills.*

"In the mountains of Nishapour and Tous (in Khorassan) they find turquoises."—*Ebn Haukal.*

Note 116, p. 83.—*Of* HINDOO KOSH, *in stormy freedom bred.*

For a description of these stupendous ranges of mountains, see Elphinstone's *Caubul.*

Note 117, p. 83.—*Her Worshippers of Fire.*

The Ghebers or Guebres, those original natives of Persia who adhered to their ancient faith, the religion of Zoroaster, and who, after the conquest of their country by the Arabs, were either persecuted at home, or forced to become wanderers abroad.

Note 118, p. 83.—*From* YEZD'S *Eternal Mansion of the Fire.*

"Yezd, the chief residence of those ancient natives who worship the Sun and the Fire, which latter they have carefully kept lighted, without being once extinguished for a moment, about 3,000 years, on a mountain near Yezd, called Ater Quedah, signifying the House or Mansion of the Fire. He is reckoned very unfortunate who dies off that mountain."—*Stephen's Persia.*

Note 119, p. 83.—*That burn into the* CASPIAN, *fierce they came.*

"When the weather is hazy, the springs of naphtha (on an island near Baku) boil up the higher, and the naphtha often takes fire on the surface of the earth, and runs in a flame into the sea to a distance almost incredible."—*Hanway on the Everlasting Fire at Baku.*

Note 120, p. 84.—*By which the prostrate Caravan is aw'd.*

Savary says of the south wind, which blows in Egypt from February to May, "Sometimes it appears only in the shape of an impetuous whirlwind, which passes rapidly, and is fatal to the traveller surprised in the middle of the deserts. Torrents of burning sand roll before it, the firmament is enveloped in a thick veil, and the sun appears of the color of blood. Sometimes whole caravans are buried in it."

Note 121, p. 84.—*The Champions of the Faith through* BEDER's *vale.*

In the great victory gained by Mahomed at Beder, he was assisted, say the Mussulmans, by three thousand angels, led by Gabriel, mounted on his horse Hiazum. (See *The Koran and its Commentators.*)

Note 122, p. 86.—*" Alla Akbar!"*

The Tecbir, or cry of the Arabs. " Alla Acbar!" says Ockley, means " God is most mighty."

Note 123, p. 86.—*And light your shrines and chant your ziraleets.*

The ziraleet is a kind of chorus, which the women of the East sing upon joyful occasions.—*Russel.*

Note 124, p. 86.—*Or warm or brighten,—like that Syrian Lake.*

The Dead Sea, which contains neither animal nor vegetable life.

Note 125, p. 88.—*O'er his lost throne—then pass'd the* JIHON's *flood.*

The ancient Oxus.

Note 126, p. 88.—*Rais'd the white banner within* NEKSHEB's *gates.*

A city of Transoxiana.

Note 127, p. 88.—*To-day's young flower is springing in its stead.*

" You never can cast your eyes on this tree, but you meet there either blossoms or fruit; and as the blossoms drop underneath on the ground (which is frequently covered with these purple-colored flowers), others come forth in their stead," etc., etc.—*Nieuhoff.*

Note 128, p. 89.—*With which the Dives have gifted him.*

The Demons of the Persian mythology.

Note 129, p. 89.—*That spangle* INDIA's *fields on showery nights.*

Carreri mentions the fire-flies in India during the rainy seasons. (See his Travels.)

Note 130, p. 89.—*Who brush'd the thousands of the Assyrian King.*

Sennacherib, called by the Orientals King of Moussal.—*D'Herbelot.*

Note 131, p. 90.—*Of* PARVIZ.
Chosroes. For the description of his Throne or Palace, see Gibbon and D'Herbelot.

There were said to be under this Throne or Palace of Khosrou Parviz a hundred vaults filled with " treasures so immense that some Mahometan writers tell us, their Prophet, to encourage his disciples, carried them to a rock which, at his command, opened, and gave them a prospect through it of the treasures of Khosrou."—*Universal History.*

Note 132, p. 90.—*And the heron crest that shone.*

" The crown of Gerashid is cloudy and tarnished before the heron tuft of thy turban."—From one of the elegies or songs in praise of Ali, written in characters of gold round the gallery of Abbas's tomb. (See Chardin.)

Note 133, p. 90.—*Magnificent, o'er* ALI's *beauteous eyes.*

The beauty of Ali's eyes was so remarkable that

whenever the Persians would describe anything as very lovely, they say it is Ayn Hali, or the Eyes of Ali.—*Chardin.*

Note 134, p. 90.—*Rise from the Holy Well, and cast its light.*
We are not told more of this trick of the Impostor than that it was "une machine qu'il disoit etre la Lune." According to Richardson, the miracle is perpetuated in Nekscheb.—"Nakshab, the name of a city in Transoxiana, where they say there is a well, in which the appearance of the moon is to be seen night and day."

Note 135, p. 90.—*Round the rich city and the plain for miles.*
"Il amusa pendant deux mois le peuple de la ville de Nekscheb, en faisant sortir toutes les nuits du fond d'un puits un corps lumineux semblable a la Lune, qui portoit sa lumiere jusqu'a la distance de plusieurs milles."—*D'Herbelot.* Hence he was called Sazendehmah, or the Moon-maker.

Note 136, p. 90.—*Had rested on the Ark.*
The Shechinah, called Sakînat in the Koran. (See Sale's Note, chap. ii.)

Note 137, p. 91.—*Of the small drum with which they count the night.*
The parts of the night are made known as well by instruments of music, as by the rounds of the watchmen with cries and small drums. (See Burder's *Oriental Customs,* vol. i. p. 119.)

Note 138, p. 91.—*On for the lamps, that light yon lofty screen.*
The Serrapurda, high screens of red cloth, stiffened with cane, used to enclose a considerable space round the royal tents.—*Notes on the Bahardanush.*
The tents of Princes were generally illuminated. Norden tells us that the tent of the Bey of Girge was

distinguished from the other tents by forty lanterns being suspended before it. (See Harmer's *Observations on Job*.)

Note 139, p. 91.—*Pour to the spot, like bees of* KAUZEROON.

"From the groves of orange-trees at Kauzeroon the bees cull a celebrated honey."—*Morier's Travels*.

Note 140, p. 93.—*Of nuptial pomp, she sinks into his tide.*

"A custom still subsisting at this day seems to me to prove that the Egyptians formerly sacrificed a young virgin to the God of the Nile; for they now make a statue of earth in shape of a girl, to which they give the name of the Betrothed Bride, and throw it into the river."—*Savary*.

Note 141, p. 94.—*Engines of havoc in, unknown before.*

That they knew the secret of the Greek fire among the Mussulmans early in the eleventh century, appears from Dow's *Account of Mamood I.* "When he arrived at Moultan, finding that the country of the Jits was defended by great rivers, he ordered fifteen hundred boats to be built, each of which he armed with six iron spikes, projecting from their prows and sides, to prevent their being boarded by the enemy, who were very expert in that kind of war. When he had launched this fleet, he ordered twenty archers into each boat, and five others with fire-balls, to burn the craft of the Jits, and naphtha to set the whole river on fire."

The *agnee aster*, too, in Indian poems the Instrument of Fire, whose flame cannot be extinguished, is supposed to signify the Greek fire. (See Wilks's *South of India*, vol. i. p. 471.) And in the curious Javan Poem, the *Brata Yudha*, given by Sir Stamford Raffles in his *History of Java*, we find, "He aimed at the heart of Soeta with the sharp-pointed Weapon of Fire."

The mention of gunpowder as in use among the Arabians, long before its supposed discovery in Europe, is introduced by Ebn Fadhl, the Egyptian geographer, who lived in the thirteenth century. Bodies, he says, "in the form of scorpions, bound round and filled with nitrous powder, glide along, making a gentle noise; then, exploding, they lighten, as it were, and burn. But there are others which, cast into the air, stretch along like a cloud, roaring horribly, as thunder roars, and on all sides vomiting out flames, burst, burn, and reduce to cinders whatever comes in their way." The historian Ben Abdalla, in speaking of the sieges of Abulualid in the year of the Hegira 712, says, "A fiery globe, by means of combustible matter, with a mighty noise suddenly emitted, strikes with the force of lightning, and shakes the citadel." (See the extracts from Casiri's *Biblioth. Arab. Hispan.* in the Appendix to Berington's *Literary History of the Middle Ages.*)

Note 142, p. 94.—*And horrible as new;—javelins that fly.*

The Greek fire, that was occasionally lent by the emperors to their allies. "It was," says Gibbon, either launched in red-hot balls of stone and iron, or darted in arrows or javelins, twisted round with flax and tow, which had deeply imbibed the inflammable oil."

Note 143, p. 94.—*Discharge, as from a kindled Naphtha fount.*

See Hanway's *Account of the Springs of Naphtha at Baku* (which is called by Lieutenant Pottinger "Joala Mokee," or the Flaming Mouth) taking fire and running into the sea. Dr. Cooke, in his Journal, mentions some wells in Circassia, strongly impregnated with this inflammable oil, from which issue boiling water. "Though the weather," he adds, "was now very cold, the warmth of these wells of hot water produced near them the verdure and flowers of spring."

Major Scott Waring says, that naphtha is used by the Persians, as we are told it was in hell, for lamps.

> ". . . . . . . many a row
> Of starry lamps and blazing cressets, fed
> With naphtha and asphaltus, yielding light
> As from a sky."

Note 144, p. 94.—*Like those wild birds that by the Magians oft.*

"At the great festival of fire, called the Sheb Sezè, they used to set fire to large branches of dry combustibles, fastened round wild beasts and birds, which being then let loose, the air and earth appeared one great illumination; and as these terrified creatures naturally fled to the woods for shelter, it is easy to conceive the conflagrations they produced."—*Richardson's Dissertation.*

Note 145, p. 95.—*Keep, seal'd with precious musk, for those they love.*

"The righteous shall be given to drink of pure wine, sealed; the seal whereof shall be musk."—*Koran,* chap. lxxxiii.

Note 146, p. 98.—*On its own brood ;—no Demon of the Waste.*

"The Afghauns believe each of the numerous solitudes and deserts of their country to be inhabited by a lonely demon, whom they call the Ghoolee Beeabau, or Spirit of the Waste. They often illustrate the wildness of any sequestered tribe, by saying, They are wild as the Demon of the Waste."—*Elphinstone's Caubul.*

Note 147, p. 99.—*With burning drugs, for this last hour distill'd.*

"Il donna du poison dans le vin à tous ses gens, et se jeta lui même ensuite dans une cuve pleine de drogues brûlantes et consumantes, afin qu'il ne restât rien de tous les membres de son corps, et que ceux qui restoient de sa secte pussent croire qu'il étoit monté au ciel, ce qui ne manqua pas d'arriver."—*D'Herbelot.*

Note 148, p. 100.—*In the lone Cities of the Silent dwell.*

"They have all a great reverence for burial-grounds, which they sometimes call by the poetical name of Cities of the Silent, and which they people with the ghosts of the departed, who sit each at the head of his own grave, invisible to mortal eyes."—*Elphinstone.*

Note 149, p. 105.—*And to eat any mangoes but those of Mazagong was, of course, impossible.*—"The celebrity of Mazagong is owing to its mangoes, which are certainly the best fruit I ever tasted. The parent tree, from which all those of this species have been grafted, is honored during the fruit-season by a guard of sepoys ; and, in the reign of Shah Jehan, couriers were stationed between Delhi and the Mahratta coast to secure an abundant and fresh supply of mangoes for the royal table."—*Mrs. Graham's Journal of a Residence in India.*

Note 150, p. 105.—*Laden with his fine antique porcelain.*—This old porcelain is found in digging, and "if it is esteemed, it is not because it has acquired any new degree of beauty in the earth, but because it has retained its ancient beauty ; and this alone is of great importance in China, where they give large sums for the smallest vessels which were used under the Emperors Yan and Chun, who reigned many ages before the dynasty of Tang, at which time porcelain began to be used by the Emperors" (about the year 442).—*Dunn's Collection of curious Observations,* etc. ;—a bad translation of some parts of the *Lettres édifiantes et curieuses* of the Missionary Jesuits.

Note 151, p. 107.—*And if Nasser, the Arabian merchant, told no better.*—"La lecture de ces Fables plaisoit si fort aux Arabes, que, quand Mahomet les entretenoit de l'Histoire de l'Ancien Testament, ils la méprisoient, lui disant que celles que Nasser leur racontoit étoient beaucoup plus belles. Cette préférence

attira à Nasser la malédiction de Mahomet et de tous
ses disciples."—*D'Herbelot.*

Note 152, p. 107.—*Like the blacksmith's apron converted into a banner.*—The blacksmith Gao, who successfully resisted the tyrant Zohak, and whose apron
became the Royal Standard of Persia.

Note 153, p. 109.—*That sublime bird, which flies
always in the air, and never touches the earth.*—"The
Huma, a bird peculiar to the East. It is supposed to
fly constantly in the air, and never touch the ground :
it is looked upon as a bird of happy omen ; and that
every head it overshades will in time wear a crown."
—*Richardson.*

In the terms of alliance made by Fuzzel Oola Khan
with Hyder in 1760, one of the stipulations was, "that
he should have the distinction of two honorary attendants standing behind him, holding fans composed of
the feathers of the Huma, according to the practice
of his family."—*Wilks's South of India.* He adds in
a note :—"The Huma is a fabulous bird. The head
over which its shadow once passes will assuredly be
circled with a crown. The splendid little bird suspended over the throne of Tippoo Sultaun, found at
Seringapatam in 1799, was intended to represent this
poetical fancy."

Note 154, p. 109.—*Like those on the Written Mountain, last forever.*—"To the pilgrims of Mount Sinai
we must attribute the inscriptions, figures, etc., on
those rocks, which have from thence acquired the
name of the Written Mountain."—*Volney.* M. Gebe-
lin and others have been at much pains to attach
some mysterious and important meaning to these inscriptions ; but Niebuhr, as well as Volney, thinks
that they must have been executed at idle hours by
the travellers to Mount Sinai, "who were satisfied
with cutting the unpolished rock with any pointed
instrument ; adding to their names and the date of
their journeys some rude figures, which bespeak the

hand of a people but little skilled in the arts."—
Niebuhr.

Note 155, p. 109.—*Like the Old Man of the Sea, upon
his back.*—The Story of Sinbad.

Note 156, p. 110.—*To which Hafez compares his
mistress's hair.*—See Nott's Hafez, Ode v.

Note 157, p. 110.—*To the Camalata, by whose rosy
blossoms the heaven of Indra is scented.*—"The Camalata (called by Linnæus, Ipomæa) is the most beautiful of its order, both in the color and form of its
leaves and flowers ; its elegant blossoms are 'celestial
rosy red, Love's proper hue,' and have justly procured it the name of Camalata, or Love's Creeper."—
Sir W. Jones.

"Camalata may also mean a mythological plant by
which all desires are granted to such as inhabit the
heaven of Indra ; and if ever flower was worthy of
Paradise, it is our charming Ipomæa."—*Sir W. Jones.*

Note 158, p. 110.—*That flower-loving nymph whom
they worship in the temples of Kathay.*—"According
to Father Premare, in his tract on Chinese Mythology,
the mother of Fo-hi was the daughter of heaven, sur-
named Flower-loving ; and as the nymph was walking alone on the bank of a river, she found herself
encircled by a rainbow, after which she became pregnant, and, at the end of twelve years, was delivered
of a son radiant as herself."—*Asiatic Researches.*

Note 159, p. 111.—*With its plane-tree Isle reflected
clear.*

"Numerous small islands emerge from the Lake of
Cashmere. One is called Char Chenaur, from the
plane-trees upon it."—*Foster.*

Note 160, p. 111.—*And the golden floods that thitherward stray.*

"The Altan Kol or Golden River of Tibet, which
runs into the Lakes of Sing-su-hay, has abundance of
gold in its sands, which employs the inhabitants all

the summer in gathering it."—*Pinkerton's Description of Tibet.*

Note 161, p. 112.—*Blooms nowhere but in Paradise.*
"The Brahmins of this province insist that the blue campac flowers only in Paradise."—*Sir W. Jones.*
It appears, however, from a curious letter of the Sultan of Menangcabow, given by Marsden, that one place on earth may lay claim to the possession of it. "This is the Sultan, who keeps the flower champaka that is blue, and to be found in no other country but his, being yellow elsewhere."—*Marsden's Sumatra.*

Note 162, p. 112.—*Flung at nigh from angel hands.*
"The Mahometans suppose that falling stars are the firebrands wherewith the good angels drive away the bad, when they approach too near the empyrean or verge of the heavens."—*Frier.*

Note 163, p. 113.—*Beneath the pillars of* CHILMINAR.
The Forty Pillars ; so the Persians call the ruins of Persepolis. It is imagined by them that this palace and the edifices at Balbec were built by Genii, for the purpose of hiding in their subterraneous caverns immense treasures, which still remain there. (See D'Herbelot and Volney.)

Note 164, p. 113.—*To the south of sun-bright Araby.*
The Isles of Panchaia.
Diodorus mentions the Isle of Panchaia, to the south of Arabia Felix, where there was a temple of Jupiter. This island, or rather cluster of isles, has disappeared, "sunk (says Grandpre) in the abyss made by the fire beneath their foundations."—*Voyage to the Indian Ocean.*

Note 165, p. 113.—*The jewell'd cup of their King* JAMSHID.
"The cup of Jamshid, discovered, they say, when digging for the foundations of Persepolis."—*Richardson.*

Note 166, p. 113.—*O'er coral rocks, and amber beds.*

"It is not like the Sea of India, whose bottom is rich with pearls and ambergris, whose mountains of the coast are stored with gold and precious stones, whose gulfs breed creatures that yield ivory, and among the plants of whose shores are ebony, red wood, and the wood of Hairzan, aloes, camphor, cloves, sandal-wood, and all other spices and aromatics : where parrots and peacocks are birds of the forest, and musk and civet are collected upon the lands.' —*Travels of Two Mohammedans.*

Note 167, p. 114.—*Thy Pagods and thy pillar'd shades.*

"............ in the ground
The bended twigs take root, and daughters grow
About the mother-tree, *a pillar'd shade,*
High over-arch'd, and echoing walks between."
—MILTON.

For a particular description and plate of the Banyan-tree, see Cordiner's *Ceylon.*

Note 168, p. 114.—*Thy Monarchs and their Thousand Thrones.*

"With this immense treasure Mamood returned to Ghizni, and in the year 400 prepared a magnificent festival, where he displayed to the people his wealth in golden throne~ and in other ornaments, in a great plain without the city of Ghizni."—*Ferishta.*

Note 169, p. 114.—'*Tis he of Gazna—fierce in wrath*
"Mahmood of Gazna, or Ghizni, who conquered India in the beginning of the eleventh century." (See his history in Dow and Sir J. Malcolm.)

Note 170, p. 114.—*Of many a young and lov'd Sultana.*
"It is reported that the hunting equipage of the Sultan Mahmood was so magnificent that he kept 400 greyhounds and bloodhounds, each of which wore a collar set with jewels, and a covering edged with gold and pearls."—*Universal History,* vol. iii.

19

Note 171, p. 122.—*For Liberty shed, so holy, is.*

Objections may be made to my use of the word Liberty in this, and more especially in the story that follows it, as totally inapplicable to any state of things that has ever existed in the East ; but though I cannot, of course, mean to employ it in that enlarged and noble sense which is so well understood at the present day, and, I grieve to say, so little acted upon, yet it is no disparagement to the word to apply it to that national independence, that freedom from the interference and dictation of foreigners, without which, indeed, no liberty of any kind can exist ; and for which both Hindoos and Persians fought against their Mussulman invaders with, in many cases, a bravery that deserved much better success.

Note 172, p. 123.—*Now among* AFRIC's *lunar Mountains.*

"The Mountains of the Moon, or the Montes Lunæ of antiquity, at the foot of which the Nile is supposed to rise."—*Bruce.*

"Sometimes called," says Jackson, "Jibbel Kumrie, or the white or lunar-colored mountains ; so a white horse is called by the Arabians a moon-colored horse."

Note 173, p. 123.—*And hail the new-born Giant's smile.*

"The Nile, which the Abyssinians know by the names of Abey and Alawy, or the Giant."—*Asiatic Researches*, vol. i. p. 387.

Note 174, p. 123.—*Her grots, and sepulchres of Kinas.*

See Perry's *View of the Levant* for an account of the sepulchres in Upper Thebes, and the numberless grots, covered all over with hieroglyphics, in the mountains of Upper Egypt.

Note 175, p. 123.—*In warm* ROSETTA's *vale—now loves.*

"The orchards of Rosetta are filled with turtledoves."—*Sonnini.*

Note 176, p. 123.—*The azure calm of* MŒRIS' *Lake.*
Savary mentions the pelicans upon Lake Mœris.

Note 177, p. 123.—*Warns them to their silken beds.*
"The superb date-tree, whose head languidly reclines, like that of a handsome woman overcome with
sleep."—*Dafard el Hadad.*

Note 178, p. 124.—*Some purple-wing'd Sultana sitting.*
"That beautiful bird, with plumage of the finest
shining blue, with purple beak and legs, the natural
and living ornament of the temples and palaces of the
Greeks and Romans, which, from the stateliness of its
port, as well as the brilliancy of its colors, has obtained
the title of Sultana."—*Sonnini.*

Note 179, p. 124.—*Only the fierce hyæna stalks.*
Jackson, speaking of the plague that occured in
West Barbary, when he was there, says, "The birds of
the air fled away from the abodes of men. The
hyænas, on the contrary, visited the cemeteries," etc.

Note 180, p. 124.—*Throughout the city's desolate
walks.*
"Gondar was full of hyænas from the time it turned
dark till the dawn of day, seeking the different pieces
of slaughtered carcasses which this cruel and unclean
people expose in the streets without burial, and who
firmly believe that these animals are Falashta from
the neighboring mountains, transformed by magic,
and come down to eat human flesh in the dark in
safety."—*Bruce.*

Note 181. p. 124.—*The glaring of those large blue
eyes.*—*Bruce.*

Note 182, p. 126.—*But see—who yonder comes by
stealth.*
This circumstance has been often introduced into
poetry,—by Vincentius Fabricius, by Darwin, and
lately, with very powerful effect, by Mr. Wilson.

Note 183, p. 128.—*Who sings at the last his own
death-lay.*

"In the East, they suppose the Phœnix to have
fifty orifices in his bill, which are continued to his tail;
and that, after living one thousand years, he builds
himself a funeral pile, sings a melodious air of different harmonies through his fifty organ pipes, flaps his
wings with a velocity which sets fire to the wood, and
consumes himself."—*Richardson.*

Note 184, p. 129.—*The first sweet draught of glory
take.*

"On the shores of a quadrangular lake stand a
thousand goblets, made of stars, out of which souls
predestined to enjoy felicity drink the crystal wave."
—From Chateaubriand's Description of the Mahometan Paradise in his *Beauties of Christianity.*

Note 185, p. 129.—*Now, upon* SYRIA'S *land of roses.*
Richardson thinks that Syria had its name from
Suri, a beautiful and delicate species of rose, for
which that country has been always famous ;—hence,
Suristan, the Land of Roses.

Note 186, p. 130.—*Gay lizards, glittering on the walls.*
"The number of lizards I saw one day in the great
court of the Temple of the Sun at Balbec amounted
to many thousands ; the ground, the walls, and stones
of the ruined building were covered with them."—
Bruce.

Note 187. p. 130.—*Of shepherd's ancient reed.*
"The Syrinx, or Pan's pipe, is still a pastoral instrument in Syria."—*Russel.*

Note 188, p. 130.—*Of the wild bees of* PALESTINE.
"Wild bees, frequent in Palestine, in hollow trunks
or branches of trees, and the clefts of rocks. Thus it
is said (Psa. lxxxi.), '*honey out of the stony rock.*'"
—*Burder's Oriental Customs.*

Note 189, p. 130.—*And woods, so full of nightingales.*

"The river Jordan is on both sides beset with little, thick. and pleasant woods, among which thousands of nightingales warble all together."—*Thevenot.*

Note 190, p. 130.—*On that great Temple, once his own.*
The Temple of the Sun at Balbec.

Note 191, p. 131.—*The beautiful blue damsel flies*
" You behold there a considerable number of a re- narkable species of beautiful insects, the elegance of whose appearance and their attire procured for them the name of Damsels."—*Sonnini.*

Note 192. p. 131.—*Of a small imaret's rustic fount.*
Imaret, " hospice ou on loge et nourrit, gratis, les pelerins pendant trois jours."—*Toderini, translated by the Abbe de Cournand.* (See also Castellan's *Mœurs des Othomans,* tom. v. p. 145.)

Note 193, p. 132.—*Kneels, with his forehead to the south.*
" Such Turks as at the common hours of prayer are on the road, or so employed as not to find convenience to attend the mosques, are still obliged to execute that duty : nor are they ever known to fail, whateve busi- ness they are then about, but pray immediately when the hour alarms them, whatever they are about, in that very place they chance to stand on ; insomuch that when a janissary, whom you have to guard you up and down the city, hears the notice which is given him from the steeples, he will turn about, stand still, and beckon with his hand, to tell his charge he must have patience for a while : when, taking out his hand- kerchief, he spreads it on the ground, sits cross-legged thereupon. and says his prayers, though in the open market, which having ended, he leaps briskly up, salutes the person whom he undertook to convey, and renews his journey with the mild expression of *Ghell ghonnum ghel,* or, Come, dear, follow me."—*Aaron Hill's Travels.*

Note 194, v. 133.—*Upon* EGYPT'S *land, of so healing a power.*

The Nucta, or Miraculous Drop, which falls in Egypt precisely on St. John's Day, in June, and is supposed to have the effect of stopping the plague.

Note 195, p. 134.—*Are the diamond turrets of* SHADUKIAM.

The Country of Delight—the name of a province in the kingdom of Jinnistan, or Fairy Land, the capital of which is called the City of Jewels. Amberabad is another of the cities of Jinnistan.

Note 196, p. 135.—*My feast is now of the Tooba Tree.*

The tree Tooba, that stands in Paradise, in the palace of Mahomet, See Sale's *Prelim. Disc.*—Tooba, says D'Herbelot, signifies beatitude, or eternal happiness.

Note 197, p. 135.—*To the lote-tree, springing by* ALLA'S *throne.*

Mahomet is described, in the 53d chapter of the Koran, as having seen the Angel Gabriel " by the lote-tree, beyond which there is no passing : near it is the Garden of Eternal Abode." This tree, say the commentators, stands in the seventh Heaven, on the right hand of the Throne of God.

Note 198, p. 135.—*As the hundred and twenty thousand streams of Basra.*—" It is said that the rivers or streams of Basra were reckoned in the time of Pelal ben Abi Bordeh, and amounted to the number of one hundred and twenty thousand streams."—*Ebn Haukal.*

Note 199, p. 136.—*Who, like them, flung the jereed carelessly.*—The name of the javelin with which the Easterns exercise. (See Castellan, *Mœurs des Othomans*, tom. iii. p. 161.)

Note 200, p. 137.—*The Banyan Hospital.*—" This account excited a desire of visiting the Banyan Hos-

pital, as I had heard much of their benevolence to all kinds of animals that were either sick, lame, or infirm, through age or accident. On my arrival, there were presented to my view many horses, cows, and oxen, in one apartment; in another, dogs, sheep, goats, and monkeys, with clean straw for them to repose on. Above stairs were depositories for seeds of many sorts, and flat, broad dishes for water, for the use of birds and insects."—*Parsons's Travels.*

It is said that all animals know the Banyans, that the most timid approach them, and that birds will fly nearer to them than to other people. (See *Grandpre.*)

Note 201, p. 137.—*Like that of the fragrant grass near the Ganges.*—"A very fragrant grass from the banks of the Ganges, near Heridwar, which in some places covers whole acres, and diffuses, when crushed, a strong odor."—*Sir W. Jones, on the Spikenard of the Ancients.*

Note 202, p. 137.—*No one had ever yet reached its summit.*—"Near this is a curious hill, called Koh Talism, the Mountain of the Talisman, because, according to the traditions of the country, no person ever succeeded in gaining its summit."—*Kinneir.*

Note 203, p. 139.—*Is warmed into life by the eyes alone.*—"The Arabians believe that the ostriches hatch their young by only looking at them." *P. Vanslebe, Relat. d'Egypte.*

Note 204, p. 139.—*And then lost them again forever.*—See *Sale's Koran,* note, vol. ii. p. 484.

Note 205, p. 139.—*While the artisans in chariots.*—*Oriental Tales.*

Note 206, p. 140.—*Who kept waving over their heads plates of gold and silver flowers.*—*Ferishta.* "Or rather," says Scott, upon the passage of Ferishta, from which this is taken, "small coins, stamped with the figure of a flower. They are still used in India to distribute in charity, and, on occasion, thrown by the purse-bearers of the great among the populace."

Note 207, p. 140.—*Alley of trees.*—The fine road made by the Emperor Jehan-Gune from Agra to Lahore, planted with trees on each side. This road is 250 leagues in length. It has "little pyramids or turrets," says Bernier, "erected every half league, to mark the ways, and frequent wells to afford drink to passengers, and to water the young trees."

Note 208, p. 142.—*That favorite tree of the luxurious bird that lights up the chambers of its nest with fireflies.*—The Baya, or Indian Grosbeak.—*Sir W. Jones.*

Note 209, p. 142.—*On the clear cold waters of which floated multitudes of the beautiful red lotus.*—"Here is a large pagoda by a tank, on the water of which float multitudes of the beautiful red lotus; the flower is larger than that of the white water-lily, and is the most lovely of the nymphæas I have seen."—*Mrs. Graham's Journal of a Residence in India.*

Note 210, p. 143.—*Had fled hither from their Arab conquerors.*—On les voit persecutes par les Khalif se retirer dans les montagnes du Kerman : plusieurs choisirent pour retraite la Tartarie et la Chine ; d'autres s'arreterent sur les bords du Gange, a l'est de Delhi."—*M. Anquetil, Memoires de l'Academie,* tom. xxxi. p. 346.

Note 211, p. 143.—*Like their own Fire in the Burning Field at* BAKOU.—The "Ager ardens" described by Kaempfer, *Amœnitat Exot.*

Note 212, p. 143.—*The prey of strangers.*—"Cashmere (says its historians) had its own princes 4,000 years before its conquest by Akbar in 1585. Akbar would have found some difficulty to reduce this paradise of the Indies, situated as it is within such a fortress of mountains, but its monarch Yusef-Khan was basely betrayed by his Omrahs."—*Pennant.*

Note 213, p. 144.—*Fire-worshippers.*—Voltaire tells us that in his tragedy, "Les Guebres," he was generally supposed to have alluded to the Jansenists. I should not be surprised if this story of the Fire-worshippers were found capable of a similar doubleness of application.

Note 214, p. 145.—*'Tis moonlight over* OMAN'S *Sea.* The Persian Gulf, sometimes so called, which separates the shores of Persia and Arabia.

Note 215, p. 145.—*'Tis moonlight in* HARMOZIA'S *walls.* The present Gombaroon, a town on the Persian side of the Gulf.

Note 216, p. 145.—*Of trumpet and the clash of zel.* A Moorish instrument of music.

Note 217, p. 145.—*The wind-tower on the* EMIR'S *dome.* "At Gombaroon and other places in Persia, they have towers for the purpose of catching the wind, and cooling the houses."—*Le Bruyn.*

Note 218, p. 146.—*His race hath brought on* IRAN'S *name.* "Iran is the true general name for the empire of Persia."—*Asiatic Researches*, Disc. 5.

Note 219, p. 146. *Engraven on his reeking sword.* "On the blades of their scimitars some verse from the Koran is usually inscribed."—*Russel.*

Note 220, p. 146.—*Draw venom forth that drives men mad.* "There is a kind of Rhododendron about Trebizond whose flowers the bee feeds upon, and the honey thence drives people mad."—*Tournefort.*

Note 221, p. 147.—*Upon the turban of a king.* "Their kings wear plumes of black herons' feathers upon the right side as a badge of sovereignty."—*Hanway.*

Note 222, p. 148.—*Springing in a desolate mountain.*

"The Fountain of Youth, by a Mahometan tradition, is situated in some dark region of the East."—*Richardson.*

Note 223, p. 148.—*On summer-eves, through* YEMEN'S *dales.*

Arabia Felix.

Note 224, p. 148.—*Who, lull'd in cool kiosk or bower.*

"In the midst of the garden is the chiosk, that is, a large room, commonly beautified with a fine fountain in the midst of it. It is raised nine or ten steps, and enclosed with gilded lattices, round which vines, jessamines, and honeysuckles make a sort of green wall; large trees are planted round this place, which is the scene of their greatest pleasures."—*Lady M. W. Montagu.*

Note 225, p. 148.—*Before their mirrors count the time.*

The women of the East are never without their looking-glasses. In "Barbary," says Shaw, "they are so fond of their looking-glasses, which they hang upon their breasts, that they will not lay them aside, even when, after the drudgery of the day, they are obliged to go two or three miles with a pitcher or a goat's skin to fetch water."—*Travels.*

In other parts of Asia they wear little looking-glasses on their thumbs. "Hence (and from the lotus being considered the emblem of beauty) is the meaning of the following mute intercourse of two lovers before their parents :—

> "'He, with salute of deference due
> A lotus to his forehead prest;
> She rais'd her mirror to his view,
> Then turn'd it inward to her breast.'"
> —*Asiatic Miscellany,* vol. ii.

Note 226, p. 149.—*Upon the emerald's virgin blaze.*

" They say that if a snake or serpent fix his eyes on the lustre of those stones (emeralds), he immediately becomes blind."—*Ahmed ben Abdalaziz, Treatise on Jewels.*

Note 227, p. 150.—*After the day-beam's withering fire.*

" At Gombaroon and the Isle of Ormus, it is sometimes so hot that the people are obliged to lie all day in the water."—*Marco Polo.*

Note 228, p. 150.—*Of* ARARAT'S *tremendous peak.*

This mountain is generally supposed to be inaccessible. Struy says, " I can well assure the reader that their opinion is not true, who suppose this mount to be inaccessible." He adds, that " the lower part of the mountain is cloudy, misty, and dark ; the middlemost part very cold, and like clouds of snow ; but the upper regions perfectly calm." It was on this mountain that the Ark was supposed to have rested after the Deluge, and part of it, they say, exists there still, which Struy thus gravely accounts for :— " Whereas none can remember that the air on the top of the hill did ever change or was subject either to wind or rain, which is presumed to be the reason that the Ark has endured so long without being rotten."—(See Carreri's *Travels*, where the Doctor laughs at this whole account of Mount Ararat.)

Note 229, p. 151.—*The bridegroom, with his locks of light.*

In one of the books of the *Shah Nameh*, when Zal (a celebrated hero of Persia, remarkable for his white hair) comes to the terrace of his mistress Rodahver at night, she lets down her long tresses to assist him in his ascent ;—he, however, manages it in a less romantic way, by fixing his crook in a projecting beam. (See Champion's *Ferdosi.*)

Note 230, p. 151.—*The rock-goats of* ARABIA *clamber.*

" On the lofty hills of Arabia Petræa are rock goats."—*Niebuhr.*

Note 231, p. 152.—*Some ditty to her soft Kanoon.*

"Canun, espece de psaltérion, avec des cordes de boyaux ; les dames en touchent dans le serail, avec des ecailles armees de pointes de cooc."—*Toderini, translated by De Cournand.*

Note 232, p. 156.—*The Gheber belt that round him clung.*

"They (the Ghebers) lay so much stress on their cushee or girdle, as not to dare to be an instant without it."—*Grose's Voyage.* "Le jeune homme nia d'abord la chose ; mais, ayant ete depouille de sa robe, et la large ceinture qu'il portoit comme Ghebr," etc., etc. —*D'Herbelot, art. Agduani.* "Pour se distinguer des Idolatres de l'Inde, les Guebres se ceignent tous d'un cordon de laine, ou de poil de chameau."—*Encyclopédie Francoise.*

D'Herbelot says this belt was generally of leather.

Note 233, p. 156.—*Among the living lights of heaven.*

"They suppose the Throne of the Almighty is seated in the sun, and hence their worship of that luminary."—*Hanway.* ' As to fire, the Ghebers place the spring-head of it in that globe of fire, the Sun, by them called Mythras, or Mihir, to which they pay the highest reverence, in gratitude for the manifold benefits flowing from its ministerial omniscience. But they are so far from confounding the subordination of the Servant with the majesty of its Creator, that they not only attribute no sort of sense or reasoning to the sun or fire, in any of its operations, but consider it as a purely passive blind instrument, directed and governed by the immediate impression on it of the will of God : but they do not even give that luminary, all-glorious as it is, more than the second rank amongst His works, reserving the first for that stupendous production of divine power, the mind of man."—*Grose.* The false charges brought against the religion of these people by their Mussulman tyrants is but one proof among many of the truth of this writer's remark, that, "calumny is often added to oppression, if but for the sake of justifying it."

Note 234, p. 158.—*And fiery darts, at intervals.*

"The Mameluks that were in the other boat, when it was dark, used to shoot up a sort of fiery arrows into the air, which in some measure resembled lightning or falling stars."—*Baumgarten.*

Note 235, p. 160.—*Which grows over the tomb of the musician, Tan-Sein.*—"Within the enclosure which surrounds this monument (at Gualior) is a small tomb to the memory of Tan-Sein, a musician of incomparable skill, who flourished at the court of Akbar. The tomb is overshadowed by a tree concerning which a superstitious notion prevails, that the chewing of its leaves will give an extraordinary melody to the voice."—*Narrative of a Journey from Agra to Ouzein, by W. Hunter, Esq.*

Note 236, p. 160.—*The awful signal of the bamboo staff.*—"It is usual to place a small white triangular flag, fixed to a bamboo staff of ten or twelve feet long, at the place where a tiger has destroyed a man. It is common for the passengers also to throw each a stone or brick ne᷄ the spot, so that in the course of a little time pile equal to a good wagon-load is collected. The sight of these flags and piles of stones imparts a certain melancholy, not perhaps altogether void of apprehension."— *Oriental Field Sports,* vol. ii.

Note 237, p. 160.—*Ornamented with the most beautiful porcelain.*—"The Ficus Indica is called the Pagod Tree and Tree of Councils ; the first, from the idols placed under its shade ; the second, because meetings were held under its cool branches. In some places it is believed to be th᷄ haunt of spectres, as the ancient spreading oaks ᷄f Wales have been of fairies ; in others are erected beneath the shade pillars of stone, or posts, elegantly carved, and ornamented with the most beautiful porcelain to supply the use of mirrors."
—*Pennant.*

Note 238, p. 160.—*And o'er the Green Sea palely shines.*
The Persian Gulf.—" To dive for pearls in the Green Sea, or Persian Gulf."—*Sir W. Jones.*

Note 239, p. 160.—*Revealing* BAHREIN'S *groves of palm,*
And lighting KISHMA'S *amber vines.*
Islands in the Gulf.

Note 240, p. 161.—*Blow round* SELAMA'S *sainted cape.*
Of Selemeh, the genuine name of the headland at the entrance of the Gulf, commonly called Cape Musseldom. " The Indians, when they pass the promontory, throw cocoanuts, fruits, or flowers, into the sea, to secure a propitious voyage."—*Morier.*

Note 241, p.161.—*The nightingale now bends her flight.*
" The nightingale sings from the pomegranate groves in the daytime, and from the loftiest trees at night."
—*Russel's Aleppo.*

Note 242, p. 161.—*The best and brightest scimitar.*
In speaking of the climate of Shiraz, Francklin says, " The dew is of such a pure nature, that if the brightest scimitar should be exposed to it all night, it would not receive the least rust."

Note 243, p. 162.—*Who, on* CADESSIA'S *bloody plains.*
The place where the Persians were finally defeated by the Arabs, and their ancient monarchy destroyed.

Note 244, p. 162.—*Beyond the Caspian's Iron Gates.*
Derbend.—" Les Turcs appellent cette ville Demir Capi, Porte de Fer : ce sont les Caspiæ Portæ des anciens."—*D'Herbelot.*

Note 245, p. 162.—*They burst, like* ZEILAN'S *giant palm.*
The Talpot or Talipot tree. "This beautiful palm

tree, which grows in the heart of the forests, may be classed among the loftiest trees, and becomes still higher when on the point of bursting forth from its leafy summit. The sheath which then envelops the flower is very large, and, when it bursts, makes an explosion like the report of a cannon."—*Thunberg.*

Note 246, p. 164.—*Before whose sabre's dazzling light.*

"When the bright scimitars make the eyes of our heroes wink."—*The Moallakat, Poem of Amru.*

Note 247, p. 165.—*Sprung from those old enchanted kings.*

Tahmuras, and other ancient kings of Persia; whose adventures in Fairy-land among the Peris and Dives may be found in Richardson's curious Dissertation. The griffin Simoorgh, they say, took some feathers from her breast for Tahmuras, with which he adorned his helmet, and transmitted them afterwards to his descendants.

Note 248, p. 165.—*Of sainted cedars on its banks.*

This rivulet, says Dandini, is called the Holy River, from the "cedar saints" among which it rises.

In the *Lettres Edifiantes,* there is a different cause assigned for its name of Holy. "In these are deep caverns, which formerly served as so many cells for a great number of recluses, who had chosen these retreats as the only witnesses upon earth of the severity of their penance. The tears of these pious penitents gave the river of which we have just treated the name of the Holy River."—*See Chateaubriand's Beauties of Christianity.*

Note 249, p. 166.—*Of* OMAN *beetling awfully.*

This mountain is my own creation, as the "stupendous chain," of which I suppose it a link, does not extend quite so far as the shores of the Persian Gulf. "This long and lofty range of mountains formerly divided Media from Assyria, and now forms the boundary of the Persian and Turkish empires. It runs parallel with the river Tigris and Persian Gulf, and, almost disappearing in the vicinity of Gomberoon (Harmozia), seems once more to rise in the southern districts of Kerman, and following an easterly course through the centre of Meckraun and Balouchistan, is entirely lost in the deserts of Sinde."—*Kinneir's Persian Empire.*

Note 250, p. 167.—*That oft the sleeping albatross.*
These birds sleep in the air. They are most common about the Cape of Good Hope.

Note 251, p. 167.—*Beneath the Gheber's lonely cliff.*
"There is an extraordinary hill in this neighborhood, called Kohé Gubr, or the Guebre's mountain. It rises in the form of a lofty cupola, and on the summit of it, they say, are the remains of an Atush Kudu, or Fire-Temple. It is superstitiously held to be the residence of Deeves or Sprites, and many marvellous stories are recounted of the injury and witchcraft suffered by those who essayed in former days to ascend or explore it."—*Pottinger's Beloochistan.*

Note 252, p. 168.—*Of that vast mountain stood on fire.*
The Ghebers generally built their temples over subterraneous fires.

Note 253, p. 168.—*Still did the mighty flame burn on.*
"At the city of Yezd, in Persia, which is distinguished by the appellation of the Darûb Abadut, or Seat of Religion, the Guebres are permitted to have an Atush Kudu, or Fire-Temple (which, they assert, has had the sacred fire in it since the days of Zoroaster), in their own compartment of the city; but for this indulgence they are indebted to the avarice, not the tolerance, of the Persian government, which taxes them at twenty-five rupees each man."—*Pottinger's Beloochistan.*

Note 254, p. 169.—*The blood of* ZAL *and* RUSTAM *rolls.*

Ancient heroes of Persia. "Among the Guebres there are some who boast their descent from Rustam." —*Stephen's Persia.*

Note 255, p. 170.—*Across the dark sea robber's way.*
See Russel's account of the panther's attacking travellers, in the night on the sea-shore about the roots of Lebanon.

Note 256, p. 170.—*The wandering Spirits of their Dead.*
"Among other ceremonies the Magi used to place upon the tops of high towers various kinds of rich viands, upon which it was supposed the Peris and the spirits of their departed heroes regaled themselves."— *Richardson.*

Note 257, p. 170.—*Nor charmed leaf of pure pome-granate.*
In the ceremonies of the Ghebers round their Fire, as described by Lord, "the Daroo," he says, "giveth them water to drink, and a pomegranate leaf to chew in the mouth, to cleanse them from inward unclean-ness."

Note 258, p. 170.—*Nor symbol of their worshipp'd planet.*
"Early in the morning, they (the Parsees or Ghebers at Oulam) go in crowds to pay their devotions to the Sun, to whom upon all the altars there are spheres consecrated, made by magic, resembling the circles of the sun, and when the sun rises these orbs seem to be inflamed, and to turn round with a great noise. They have every one a censer in their hands, and offer incense to the sun."—*Rabbi Benjamin.*

Note 259, p. 170.—*They swore the latest, holiest deed.*
"Nul d'entre eux oseroit se parjurer, quand il a pris a temoin cet element terrible et vengeur."—*En-cyclopedie Francoise.*

Note 260, p. 171.—*The Persian lily shines and towers.*

20

" A vivid verdure succeeds the autumnal rains, and the ploughed fields are covered with the Persian lily, of a resplendent yellow color."—*Russel's Aleppo.*

Note 261, p. 173.—*When toss'd at midnight furiously.*

" It is observed, with respect to the Sea of Herkend, that when it is tossed by tempestuous winds it sparkles like fire."—*Travels of Two Mohammedans.*

Note 262, p. 173.—*Up, daughter, up, — the* KERNA'S *breath.*

A kind of trumpet ;—it "was that used by Tamerlane, the sound of which is described as uncommonly dreadful, and so loud as to be heard at the distance of several miles."—*Richardson.*

Note 263, p. 174.—*Thou wor'st on* OHOD'S *field of death.*

" Mohammed had two helmets, an interior and exterior one ; the latter of which, called Al Mawashah, the fillet, wreath, or wreathed garland, he wore at the battle of Ohod."—*Universal History.*

Note 264, p. 176.—*But turn to ashes on the lips.*

They say that there are apple-trees upon the sides of this sea, which bear very lovely fruit, but within are all full of ashes.—*Thevenot.* The same is asserted of the oranges there ; *vide* Witman's *Travels in Asiatic Turkey.*

"The Asphalt Lake, known by the name of the Dead Sea, is very remarkable on account of the considerable proportion of salt which it contains. In this respect it surpasses every other known water on the surface of the earth. This great proportion of bitter-tasted salts is the reason why neither animal nor plant can live in this water."—*Klaproth's Chemical Analysis of the Water of the Dead Sea*, Annals of Philosophy, January, 1813. Hasselquist, however, doubts the truth of this last assertion, as there are shell-fish to be found in the lake.

Lord Byron has a similar allusion to the fruits of

the Dead Sea, in that wonderful display of genius, his third canto of *Childe Harold.*—magnificent beyond anything, perhaps, that even *he* has ever written.

Note 265, p. 176.—*While lakes, that shone in mockery nigh.*

"The Suhrab, or Water of the Desert, is said to be caused by the rarefaction of the atmosphere from extreme heat ; and, which augments the delusion, it is most frequent in hollows, where water might be expected to lodge. I have seen bushes and trees reflected in it with as much accuracy as though it had been the face of a clear and still lake."—*Pottinger.*

" As to the unbelievers, their works are like a vapor in a plain which the thirsty traveller thinketh to be water, until when he cometh thereto he findeth it to be nothing."—*Koran*, chap. xxiv.

Note 266. p. 176.—*The Bidmusk had just passed over.*
—" A wind which prevails in February, called Bidmusk, from a small and odoriferous flower of that name."—" The wind which blows these flowers commonly lasts till the end of the month."—*Le Bruyn.*

Note 267, p. 176.—*The sea-gipsies, who live forever on the water.*—" The Biajús are of two races: the one is settled on Borneo, and are a rude but warlike and industrious nation, who reckon themselves the original possessors of the Island of Borneo. The other is a species of sea-gipsies or itinerant fishermen, who live in small covered boats, and enjoy a perpetual summer on the Eastern Ocean, shifting to leeward from island to island, with the variations of the monsoon. In some of their customs, this singular race resemble the natives of the Maldivia islands. The Maldivians annually launch a small bark, loaded with perfumes, gums, flowers, and odoriferous wood, and turn it adrift at the mercy of winds and waves, as an offering to the *Spirit of the Winds ;* and sometimes similar offerings are made to the spirit whom they term the *King of the Sea.* In like manner the Biajús perform their c... ...ing to the God of Evil, launching a small bark, loa...d with all the sins and misfortunes of the nation, which are imagined to fall on the unhappy crew that may be so unlucky as first to meet with it."—*Dr. Leyden on the Languages and Literature of the Indo-Chinese Nations.*

Note 268, p. 177.—*The violet sherbets.*—"The sweet-scented violet is one of the plants most esteemed, particularly for its great use in Sorbet, which they make of violet sugar."—*Hasselquist.*

"The sherbet they most esteem, and which is drunk by the Grand Signor himself, is made of violets and sugar."—*Tavernier.*

Note 269, p. 177.—*The pathetic measure of Nava.*—"Last of all she took a guitar, and sung a pathetic air in the measure called Nava, which is always used to express the lamentations of absent lovers."—*Persian Tales.*

Note 270, p. 178.—*No music tim'd to their parting oar.*—"The Easterns used to set out on their longer voyages with music."—*Harmer.*

Note 271, p. 178.—*In silence through the Gate of Tears.*

"The Gate of Tears, the straits or passage into the Red Sea, commonly called Babelmandeb. It received this name from the old Arabians, on account of the danger of the navigation, and the number of shipwrecks by which it was distinguished; which induced them to consider as dead, and to wear mourning for, all who had the boldness to hazard the passage through it into the Ethiopic ocean."—*Richardson.*

Note 272, p. 179.—*In the still warm and living breath.*

"I have been told that whensoever an animal falls down dead, one or more vultures, unseen before, instantly appear."—*Pennant.*

Note 273, p. 179.—*As a young bird of* BABYLON.

"They fasten some writing to the wings of a Bagdat or Babylonian pigeon."—*Travels of Certain Englishmen.*

Note 274, p. 179.— *Shooting around their jasper fount.*

"The Empress of Jehan-Guire used to divert herself with feeding tame fish in her canals, some of which were many years afterwards known by fillets of gold, which she caused to be put round them."—*Harris.*

Note 275, p. 179.—*To tell her ruby rosary.*

"Le Tespih, qui est un chapelet composé de 99 petites boules d'agate, de jaspe, d'ambre, de corail, ou d'autre matiere precieuse. J'en ai vu un superbe au Seigneur Jerpos ; il étoit de belles et grosses perles parfaites et égales, estimé trente mille piastres."—*Toderini.*

Note 276, p. 182.—*Like meteor brands as if throughout.*

The meteors that Pliny calls "faces."

Note 277, p. 183.—*The Star of* EGYPT *whose proud light.*

"The brilliant Canopus, unseen in European climates."—*Brown.*

Note 278, p. 183.—*In the White Islands of the West.*

See Wilford's learned Essays on the Sacred Isles of the West.

Note 279, p. 183.—*Sparkles as 'twere that lightning gem.*

A precious stone of the Indies, called by the ancients Cerauneum, because it was supposed to be found in places where thunder had fallen. Tertullian says it has a glittering appearance, as if there had been fire in it ; and the author of the Dissertation in Harris's *Voyages* supposes it to be the opal.

Note 280, p. 185.—*Their garb—the leathern belt that wraps.*

D'Herbelot, art. *Agduani.*

Note 281, p. 185.—*Each yellow vest—that rebel hue.*
"The Guebres are known by a dark yellow color, which the men affect in their clothes."—*Thevenot.*

Note 282, p. 185.—*The Tartar fleece upon their caps.*
"The Kolah, or cap, worn by the Persians, is made of the skin of the sheep of Tartary."—*Waring.*

Note 283, p. 190.—*Open her bosom's glowing veil.*
A frequent image among the Oriental poets. "The nightingales warbled their enchanting notes, and rent the thin veils of the rosebud and the rose."—*Jami.*

Note 284, p. 192.—*The sorrowful tree, Nilica.*—
"Blossoms of the sorrowful Nyctanthes give a durable color to silk."—*Remarks on the Husbandry of Bengal*, p. 200. Nilica is one of the Indian names of this flower.—*Sir W. Jones.* The Persians call it Gul. —*Carreri.*

Note 285, p. 193.—*That cooling feast the traveller loves.*
"In parts of Kerman, whatever dates are shaken from the trees by the wind they do not touch, but leave them for those who have not any, or for travellers."—*Ebn Haukal.*

Note 286, p. 193.—*The Searchers of the Grave appear.*
The two terrible angels Monkir and Nakir, who are called "the Searchers of the Grave" in the "Creed of the orthodox Mahometans" given by Ockley, vol. ii.

Note 287, p. 194.—*The mandrake's charnel leaves at night.*
"The Arabians call the mandrake 'the Devil's candle,' on account of its shining appearance in the night."—*Richardson.*

Note 288, p. 199.—*Of the still Halls of* ISHMONIE.
For an account of Ishmonie, the petrified city in

Upper Egypt, where it is said there are many statues of men, women, etc., to be seen to this day, see Perry's *View of the Levant.*

Note 289, p. 200.—*And ne'er did saint of* ISSA *gaze.* —Jesus.

Note 290, p. 201.—*The death-flames that beneath him burn'd.*

The Ghebers say that when Abraham, their great Prophet, was thrown into the fire by order of Nimrod, the flame turned instantly into "a bed of roses, where the child sweetly reposed."—*Tavernier.*

Of their other Prophet, Zoroaster, there is a story told in Dion Prusæus, *Orat.* 36, that the love of wisdom and virtue leading him to a solitary life upon a mountain, he found it one day all in a flame, shining with celestial fire, out of which he came without any harm, and instituted certain sacrifices to God, who, he declared, then appeared to him. (See Patrick on Exodus iii. 2.)

Note 291, p. 203.—*A ponderous sea-horn hung, and blew.*

"The shell called Siiankos, common to India, Africa, and the Mediterranean, and still used in many parts as a trumpet for blowing alarms or giving signals: it sends forth a deep and hollow sound." —*Pennant.*

Note 292, p. 204.—*And the white ox-tails stream'd behind.*

"The finest ornament for the horses is made of six large flying tassels of long white hair, taken out of the tails of wild oxen, that are to be found in some places of the Indies."—*Thevenot.*

Note 293, p. 205.—*Sweet as the angel* ISRAFIL'S.

"The angel Israfil, who has the most melodious voice of all God's creatures."—*Sale.*

Note 294, p. 208.—*Wound slow, as through* GOLCONDA'S *vale.*

See Hoole upon the Story of Sinbad.

Note 295, p. 211.—*From the wild covert where he lay.*

"In this thicket upon the banks of the Jordan, several sorts of wild beasts are wont to harbor themselves, whose being washed out of the covert by the overflowings of the river gave occasion to that allusion of Jeremiah, *he shall come up like a lion from the swelling of Jordan.*"—*Maundrell's Aleppo.*

Note 296, p. 217.—*Like the wind of the south o'er a summer lute blowing,*

"This wind (the Samoor) so softens the strings of lutes that they can never be tuned while it lasts."—*Stephen's Persia.*

Note 297, p. 218.—*With nought but the sea-star to light up her tomb.*

"One of the greatest curiosities found in the Persian Gulf is a fish which the English call Star-fish. It is circular, and at night very luminous, resembling the full moon surrounded by rays."—*Mirza Abu Taleb.*

Note 298, p. 219.—*And still when the merry date-season is burning.*

For a description of the merriment of the date-time, of their work, their dances, and their return home from the palm-groves at the end of autumn with the fruits, see Kaempfer, *Amœnitat. Exot.*

Note 299, p. 219.—*That ever the sorrowing sea-bird has wept.*

Some naturalists have imagined that amber is a concretion of the tears of birds. (See *Trevoux Chambers.*

Note 300, p. 219.—*We'll seek where the sands of the Caspian are sparkling.*

"The bay Kieselarke, which is otherwise called the Golden Bay, the sand whereof shines as fire."—*Struy.*

Note 301, p. 220.—*The summary criticism of the Chabuk.*—"The application of whips or rods."—*Dubois.*

Note 302, p. 221.—*Chief Holder of the Girdle of Beautiful Forms.*—Kaempfer mentions such an officer among the attendants of the King of Persia, and calls him "formæ corporis æstimator." His business was, at stated periods, to measure the ladies of the Haram by a sort of regulation-girdle, whose limits it was not thought graceful to exceed. If any of them outgrew this standard of shape, they were reduced by abstinence till they came within proper bounds.

Note 303, p. 221.—*Forbidden River.*—The Attock. "Akbar on his way ordered a fort to be built upon the Nilab, which he called Attock, which means in the Indian language Forbidden ; for, by the superstition of the Hindoos, it was held unlawful to cross that river."—*Dow's Hindostan.*

Note 304, p. 222.—*One genial star that rises nightly over their heads.*—"The inhabitants of this country (Zinge) are never afflicted with sadness or melancholy ; on this subject the Sheikh Abu-al-Kheir-Azhari has the following distich :

"'Who is the man without care or sorrow, (tell) that I may rub my hand to him.

"'(Behold) the Zingians, without care or sorrow, frolicsome with tipsiness and mirth.'

"The philosophers have discovered that the cause of this cheerfulness proceeds from the influence of the star Soheil or Canopus, which rises over them every night."—*Extract from a Geographical Persian Manuscript called Heft Aklim, or the Seven Climates, translated by W. Ouseley, Esq.*

Note 305, p. 222.—*Lizards.*—"The lizard Stellio. The Arabs call it Hardun. The Turks kill it, for they imagine that by declining the head it mimics them when they say their prayers."—*Hasselquist.*

Note 306, p. 223.—*Royal Gardens.*—For these particulars respecting Hussun Abdaul, I am indebted to the very interesting Introduction of Mr. Elphinstone's work upon Caubul.

Note 307, p. 223.—*It was too delicious.*—"As you enter at that Bazar, without the gate of Damascus, you see the Green Mosque, so called because it hath a steeple faced with green glazed bricks, which render it very resplendent ; it is covered at top with a pavilion of the same stuff. The Turks say this mosque was made in that place, because Mahomet being come so far, would not enter the town, saying it was too delicious."—*Thevenot.* This reminds one of the following pretty passage in Isaac Walton :—" When I sat last on this primrose bank, and looked down these meadows, I thought of them as Charles the Emperor did of the city of Florence, 'that they were too pleasant to be looked on, but only on holidays.'"

Note 308, p. 223.—*The Sultana Nourmahal the Light of the Haram.*—Nourmahal signifies Light of the Haram. She was afterwards called Nourjehan, or the Light of the World.

Note 309, p. 223.—*The small shining fishes of which she was so fond.*—See note 274, p. 309.

Note 310, p. 223.—*Haroun-al-Raschid and his fair mistress Marida.*—" Haroun-al-Raschid, cinquieme Khalife des Abassides, s'étant un jour brouille avec une de ses maitresses nommee Maridah, qu'il aimoit cependant jusqu'a l'exces, et cette misintelligence ayant deja dure quelque tems, commenca a s'ennuyer. Giafar Barmaki, son favori, qui s'en apercut, commanda à Abbas-ben-Ahnaf, excellent poëte de ce temsla, de composer quelques vers sur le sujet de cette brouillerie. Ce poete executa l'ordre de Giafar, qui fit chanter ces vers par Moussali en presence du Khalife, et ce prince fut tellement touche de la tendresse des vers du poetre et de la douceur de la voix de musicien, qu'il alla aussit totrouver Maridah, et fit sa paix avec elle."—*D'Herbelot.*

Note 311, p. 224.—*With its roses the brightest that earth ever gave.*
" The rose of Kashmire, for its brilliancy and deli-

cacy of odor, has long been proverbial in the East."—
Forster.

Note 312, p. 224.—*Round the waist of some fair Indian dancer is ringing.*
"Tied round her waist the zone of bells, that sounded with ravishing melody."—*Song of Jayadeva.*

Note 313, p. 225.—*The young aspen-trees.*
"The little isles in the lake of Cachemire are set with arbors and large-leaved aspen-trees, slender and tall."—*Bernier.*

Note 314, p. 225.—*Shines in through the mountainous portal that opes.*
"The Tuckt Suliman, the name bestowed by the Mahometans on this hill, forms one side of a grand portal to the Lake."—*Forster.*

Note 315, p, 226.—*The Valley holds its Feast of Roses.*
"The Feast of Roses continues the whole time of their remaining in bloom." (See Pietro de la Valle.)

Note 316, p. 226.—*The Flow'ret of a hundred leaves.*
"Gul sad berk, the Rose of a hundred leaves. I believe a particular species."—*Ouseley.*

Note 317, p. 226.—*Behind the palms of BARAMOULE.*
—*Bernier.*

Note 318, p. 226.—*On BELA's hills is less alive.*
A place mentioned in the Toozck Jehangeery, or Memoirs of Jehan-Guire, where there is an account of the beds of saffron-flowers about Cashmere.

Note 319, p. 227.—*Sung from his lighted gallery.*
"It is the custom among the women to employ the Maazeen to chant from the gallery of the nearest minaret, which on that occasion is illuminated, and the women assembled at the house respond at intervals with a ziraleet or joyous chorus."—*Russel.*

Note 320, p. 227.—*From gardens, where the silken swing.*
"The swing is a favorite pastime in the East, as

promoting a circulation of air, extremely refreshing in those sultry climates."—*Richardson.*

"The swings are adorned with festoons. This pastime is accompanied with the music of voices and of instruments, hired by the masters of the swings."—*Thevenot.*

Note 321, p. 227.—*Among the tents that line the way.*

"At the keeping of the Feast of Roses we beheld an infinite number of tents pitched, with such a crowd of men, women, boys, and girls, with music, dances," etc., etc.—*Herbert.*

Note 322, p. 228.—*An answer in song to the kiss of each wave.*

"An old commentator of the Chou-King says, the ancients having remarked that a current of water made some of the stones near its banks send forth a sound, they detached some of them, and being charmed with the delightful sound they emitted, constructed King or musical instruments of them."—*Grosier.*

This miraculous quality has been attributed also to the shore of Attica. "Hujus littus, ait Capella, concentum musicum illisis terræ undis reddere, quod propter tantam eruditionis vim puto pictum."—*Ludov. Vives in Augustin de Civitat. Dei* lib. xviii. c. 8.

Note 323, p. 228.—*So felt the magnificent Son of Acbar.*

Jehan-Guire was the son of the Great Acbar.

Note 324, p. 230.—*Yet playful as Peris just loos'd from their cages.*

In the wars of the Dives with the Peris, whenever the former took the latter prisoners, "they shut them up in iron cages, and hung them on the highest trees. Here they were visited by their companions, who brought them the choicest odors."—*Richardson.*

Note 325, p. 231.—*Of the flowers of this planet—though treasures were there.*

In the Malay language the same word signifies women and flowers.

Note 326, p. 231.—*He saw that City of Delight.*
The capital of Shadukiam.   See note 195, p. 294.

Note 327, p. 233.—*He sits, with flow'rets fetter'd round.*
See the representation of the Eastern Cupid, pinioned closely round with wreaths of flowers, in Picart's *Ceremonies Religieuses.*

Note 328, p. 233.—*Lose all their glory when he flies.*
"Among the birds of Tonquin is a species of goldfinch, which sings so melodiously that it is called the Celestial Bird.   Its wings, when it is perched, appear variegated with beautiful colors, but when it flies they lose all their splendor.—*Grosier.*

Note 329, p. 233.—*Whose pinion knows no restingplace.*
"As these birds or the Bosphorus are never known to rest, they are called by the French 'les âmes damnees.' "—*Dalloway.*

Note 330, p. 234.—*If there his darling rose is not.*
"You may place a hundred handfuls of fragrant herbs and flowers before the nightingale, yet he wishes not, in his constant heart, for more than the sweet breath of his beloved rose."—*Jami.*

Note 331, p. 234.—*From the great Mantra, which around.*
"He is said to have found the great *Mantra,* spell or talisman, through which he ruled over the elements and spirits of all denominations."—*Wilford.*

Note 332, p. 234.—*To the gold gems of* AFRIC.
"The gold jewels of Jinnie, which are called by the Arabs El Herren, from the supposed charm they contain."—*Jackson.*

Note 333, p. 235.—*To keep him from the Siltim's harm.*
"A demon, supposed to haunt woods, etc., in a human shape."— *Richardson.*

Note 334, p. 235.—*Her Selim's smile to* NOURMAHAL.
The name of Jehan-Guire before his accession to the
throne.

Note 335, p. 236.—*Anemones and Seas of Gold.*
"Hemasagara, or the Sea or Gold, with flowers of
the brightest gold color."—*Sir W. Jones.*

Note 336, p. 236.—*Their buds on* CAMADEVA'S *quiver.*
"This tree (the Nagacesara) is one of the most
delightful on earth, and the delicious odor of its
blossoms justly gives them a place in the quiver of
Camadeva, or the God of Love. "—*Id.*

Note 337, p. 236.—*Is call'd the Mistress of the Night.*
"The Malayans style the tuberose (*Polianthes
tuberosa*) Sandal Malam, or the Mistress of the Night."
—*Pennant.*

Note 338, p. 236.—*That wander through* ZAMARA'S
shades.
The people of the Batta country in Sumatra (of
which Zamara is one of the ancient names), "when
not engaged in war, lead an idle, inactive life, passing
the day in playing on a kind of flute, crowned with
garlands of flowers, among which the globe-amaran-
thus, a native of the country, mostly prevails."—
Marsden.

Note 339, p. 236.—*From the divine Amrita tree.*
"The largest and richest sort (of the Jambu, or
rose-apple) is called Amrita, or immortal, and the
mythologists of Tibet apply the same word to a celestial tree, bearing ambrosial fruit."—*Sir W. Jones.*

Note 340, p. 236.—*Down to the basil tuft, that waves.*
Sweet basil, called Rayhan in Persia, and generally
found in churchyards.
"The women in Egypt go, at least two days in the
week, to pray and weep at the sepulchres of the dead :
and the custom then is to throw upon the tombs a sort
of herb, which the Arabs call *rihan,* and which is our
sweet basil."—*Maillet,* Lett. 10.

Note 341 p. 237.—*To scent the desert and the dead.*
"In the Great Desert are found many stalks of lavender and rosemary."—*Asiatic Researches.*

Note 342, p. 238.—*That blooms on a leafless bough.*
"The almond-tree, with white flowers, blossoms on the bare branches."—*Hasselquist.*

Note 343, p. 238.—*Inhabit the mountain-herb, that dyes.*

An herb on Mount Libanus, which is said to communicate a yellow golden hue to the teeth of the goats and other animals that graze upon it.

Niebuhr thinks this may be the herb which the Eastern alchymists look to as a means of making gold. "Most of those alchymical enthusiasts think themselves sure of success, if they could but find out the herb which gilds the teeth and gives a yellow color to the flesh of the sheep that eat it. Even the oil of this plant must be of a golden color. It is called *Haschischat ed dab.*"

Father Jerom Dandini, however, asserts that the teeth of the goats at Mount Libanus are of a *silver* color; and adds, "This confirms to me that which I observed in Candia: to wit, that the animals that live on Mount Ida eat a certain herb which renders their teeth of a golden color; which, according to my judgment, cannot otherwise proceed than from the mines which are under ground."—*Dandini's Voyage to Mount Libanus.*

Note 344, p. 239.—*Of Azab blew, was full of scents.*—The myrrh country.

Note 345, p. 239.—*Where Love himself, of old, lay sleeping.*
"This idea (of deities living in shells) was not unknown to the Greeks, who represent the young Nerites, one of the Cupids, as living in shells on the shores of the Red Sea."—*Wilford.*

Note 346, p. 239.—*From* CHINDARA'S *warbling fount*
I come.

" A fabulous fountain, where instruments are said
to be constantly playing."—*Richardson.*

Note 347, p. 240.—*The cinnamon-seed from grove to*
grove.

"The Pompadour pigeon is the species, which, by
carrying the fruit of the cinnamon to different places,
is a great disseminator of this valuable tree."—(See
Brown's Illustr. Tab. 19.)

Note 348, p. 240.—*The past, the present, and future*
of pleasure.

" Whenever our pleasure arises from a succession of
sounds, it is a perception of a complicated nature,
made up of a *sensation* of the present sound or note,
and an *idea* or remembrance of the foregoing, while
their mixture and concurrence produce such a
mysterious delight, as neither could have produced
alone. And it is often heightened by an anticipation
of the succeeding notes. Thus Sense, Memory, and
Imagination are conjunctively employed.—*Gerrard*
on Taste.

This is exactly the Epicurean theory of Pleasure, as
explained by Cicero :—" Quocirca corpus gaudere
tamdiu, dum præsentem sentiat voluptatem : animum
et præsentem percipere pariter cum corpore, et pros-
picere venientem, nec præteritam præterfluere
sinere."

Madame de Stael accounts upon the same principle
for the gratification we derive from *rhyme :*—" Elle
est l'image de l'espérance et du souvenir. Un son
nous fait désirer celui qui doit lui répondre, et quand
le second retentit il nous rappelle celui qui vient de
nous échapper.

Note 349, p. 241.—*Whose glimpses are again with-*
drawn.

"The Persians have two mornings, the Soobhi
Kazim and the Soobhi Sadig, the false and the real
daybreak. They account for this phenomenon in a

most whimsical manner. They say that as the sun rises from behind the Kohl Qaf (Mount Caucasus), it passes a hole perforated through that mountain, and that darting its rays through it, it is the cause of the Soobhi Kazim, or this temporary appearance of day-break. As it ascends, the earth is again veiled in darkness, until the sun rises above the mountain and brings with it the Soobhi Sadig, or real morning."— *Scott Waring.* He thinks Milton may allude to this, when he says :

> "Ere the blabbing Eastern scout,
> The nice morn, on the Indian steep
> From her cabin'd loop-hole peep."

Note 350, p. 242.—*In his magnificent Shalimar.*

"In the centre of the plain, as it approaches the Lake, one of the Delhi Emperors, I believe Shah Jehan, constructed a spacious garden called the Shalimar, which is abundantly stored with fruit-trees and flowering shrubs. Some of the rivulets which intersect the plain are led into a canal at the back of the garden, and flowing through its centre, or occasionally thrown into a variety of waterworks, compose the chief beauty of the Shalimar. To decorate this spot, the Mogul princes of India have displayed an equal magnificence and taste ; especially Jehan Gheer, who, with the enchanting Noor Mahl, made Kashmire his usual residence during the summer months. On arches thrown over the canal are erected, at equal distances, four or five suites of apartments, each consisting of a saloon, with four rooms at the angles, where the followers of the court attend, and the servants prepare sherbets, coffee and the hookah. The frame of the doors of the principal saloon is composed of pieces of a stone of a black color, streaked with yellow lines, and of a closer grain and higher polish than porphyry. They were taken, it is said, from a Hindoo temple, by one of the Mogul princes, and are esteemed of great value."—*Forster.*

21

Note 351, p. 242.—*Of beauty from its founts and streams.*

"The waters of Cachemir are the most renowned from its being supposed that the Cachemirians are indebted for their beauty to them."—*Ali Yezdi.*

Note 352, p. 242.—*Singing in gardens of the South.*

" From him I received the following little Gazzel, or Love Song, the notes of which he committed to paper from the voice of one of those singing girls of Cashmere, who wander from that delightful valley over the various parts of India."—*Persian Miscellanies.*

Note 353, p. 242.—*Delicate as the roses there.*

" The roses of the Jinan Nile, or the Garden of the Nile (attached to the Emperor of Marocco's palace), re unequalled, and mattresses are made of their aves for the men of rank to recline upon."—*Jackson.*

Note 354, p. 242.—*With Paphian crystals in their locks.*

" On the side of a mountain near Paphos there is a cavern which produces the most beautiful rock-crystal. On account of its brilliancy it has been called the Paphian diamond."—*Mariti.*

Note 355, p. 242.—*On the gold meads of Candahar.*

"There is a part of Candahar, called Peria, or Fairy Land."—*Thevenot.* In some of those countries to the north of India, vegetable gold is supposed to be produced.

Note 356, p. 242.—*Had been by magic all set flying.*

" These are the butterflies which are called in the Chinese language Flying Leaves. Some of them have such shining colors, and are so variegated, that they may be called flying flowers ; and indeed they are always produced in the finest flower-gardens."—*Dunn.*

Note 357, p. 243.—*The features of young Arab maids.*

" The Arabian women wear black masks with little

clasps prettily ordered." — *Carreri.* Niebuhr mentions their showing but one eye in conversation.

Note 358, p. 243.—*On* CASBIN'S *hills.*
"The golden grapes of Casbin."—*Description of Persia.*

Note 359, p. 243.—*And sunniest apples that* CAUBUL—
"The fruits exported from Caubul are apples, pears, pomegranates," etc.—*Elphinstone.*

Note 360, p. 243.—*In all its thousand gardens bears.*
"We sat down under a tree, listened to the birds, and talked with the son of our Mehmaundar about our country and Caubul, of which he gave an enchanting account : that city and its 100,000 gardens," etc.—*Id.*

Note 361, p. 243.—MALAYA'S *nectar'd mangusteen.*
"The mangusteen, the most delicate fruit in the world ; the of the Malay Islands."—*Ma*

Note 362, *ed of the Sun, from* IL
"A delicious kind of apricot, called by the Persians Tokm-ek-shems, signifying sun's seed."—*Description of Persia.*

Note 363, p. 244.—*With rich conserve of Visna cherries.*
"Sweetmeats, in a crystal cup, consisting of rose-leaves in conserve, with lemon of Visna cherry, orange-flowers," etc.—*Russel.*

Note 364, p. 244.—*Feed on in* ERAC'S *rocky dells.*
"Antelopes, cropping the fresh berries of Erac."—*The Moallakat,* Poem of Tarafa.

Note 365, p. 244.—*And urns of porcelain from that isle.*
Mauri-ga-Sima, an island near Formosa, supposed to have been sunk in the sea for the crimes of its inhabitants. The vessels which the fishermen and divers bring up from it are sold at an immense price in China and Japan. (See *Kaempfer.*)

Note 366, p. 244.—*Amber Rosolli.*—Persian Tales.

Note 367, p. 244.—*From vineyards of the Green Sea gushing.*

The white wine of Kishma.

Note 368, p. 244.—*Offered a city's wealth.*

"The King of Zeilan is said to have the very finest ruby that was ever seen. Kublai-Khan sent and offered the value of a city for it, but the King answered he would not give it for the treasure of the world."—*Marco Polo.*

Note 369, p. 245.—*Upon a rosy lotus wreath.*

The Indians feign that Cupid was first seen floating down the Ganges on the *Nymphæa Nelumbo.* (See *Pennant.*)

Note 370, p. 245. *When warm, they rise from* TEFLIS' *brooks.*

Teflis is celebrated for its natural warm baths. (See *Ebn Haukal.*)

Note 371, p. 245.—*Of a syrinda.*

"The Indian Syrinda, or guitar."—*Symes.*

Note 372, p. 246.—*It is this, it is this.*

"Around the exterior of the Dewan Khass (a building of Shah Allum's), in the cornice are the following lines in letters of gold upon a ground of white marble :—' If there be a paradise upon earth, it is this, it is this.' "—*Franklin.*

Note 375, p. 246.—*As the flower of the Amra just op'd by a bee.*

"Delightful are the flowers of the Amra trees on the mountain-tops, while the murmuring bees pursue their voluptuous toil."—*Song of Jayadeva.*

Note 374, p. 246.—*And precious their tears as the rain from the sky.*

"The Nisan or drops of spring rain, which they believe to produce pearls if they fall into shells."—*Richardson.*

Note 375, p. 246.—*Who for wine of this earth left the fountains above.*

For an account of the share which wine had in the fall of the angels, see Mariti.

Note 376, p. 246.—*Of* ISRAFIL, *the Angel, there.*
The Angel of Music. See note 293, p. 311.

Note 377, p. 249.—*When first 't is by the lapwing found.*
The Hudhud, or Lapwing, is supposed to have the power of discovering water under ground.

Note 378, p. 250.—*Of her dream.*—See p. 250.

Note 379, p. 251.—*Like that painted porcelain.*—
"The Chinese had formerly the art of painting on the side of porcelain vessels fish and other animals, which were only perceptible when the vessel was full of some liquor. They call this species Kia-tsin ; that is, *azure is put in press,* on account of the manner in which the azure is laid on."—"They are every now and then trying to recover the art of this magical painting, but to no purpose."—*Dunn.*

Note 380, p. 252.—*House of Azor.*—An eminent carver of idols, said in the Koran to be father to Abraham. " I have such a lovely idol as is not to be met with in the house of Azor."—*Hafiz.*

Note 381, p. 252.—*The Unequalled.*—Kachmire be Nazeer.—*Forster.*

Note 382, p. 253.—*Miraculous fountains.*—" The pardonable superstition of the sequestered inhabitants has multiplied the places of worship of Mahadeo, of Beshan, and of Brama. All Cashmere is holy land, and miraculous fountains abound."—*Major Rennel's Memoirs of a Map of Hindostan.*

Jehan-Guire mentions " a fountain in Cashmere called Tirnagh, which signifies a snake ; probably because some large snake had formerly been seen there."—" During the lifetime of my father, I went

twice to this fountain, which is about twenty coss
from the city of Cashmere.   The vestiges of places of
worship and sanctity are to be traced without number
amongst the ruins and the caves which are inter-
spersed in its neighborhood."—*Toozek Jehangeery.*
Vide *Asiat. Misc.* vol. ii.

There is another account of Cashmere by Abul-
Fazil, the author of the Ayin-Acbaree, "who," says
Major Rennel, "appears to have caught some of the
enthusiasm of the valley, by his description of the
holy places in it."

Note 383, p. 253.—*Roofed with flowers.*—"On a
standing roof of wood is laid a covering of fine earth,
which shelters the building from the great quantity
of snow that falls in the winter season. This fence
communicates an equal warmth in winter, as a refreshing coolness in the summer season, when the tops
of the houses, which are planted with a variety of
flowers, present at a distance the spacious view of a
beautifully chequered parterre." — *Forster.*

Note 384. p. 253.—*The triple-colored tortoise-shell of
Pegu.*—"Two hundred slaves there are who have no
other office than t Lunt the woods and marshes for
triple-colored tortoises for the King's Vivary. Of the
shells of these also lanterns are made."—*Vincent le
Blanc's Travels.*

Note 385, p. 254.—*Like the meteors of the north as
they are seen by those hunters.*—For a description of
the Aurora Borealis as it appears to these hunters,
vide *Encyclopædia.*

Note 386, p. 254.—*Odoriferous wind.*—This wind,
which is to blow from Syria Damascena, is, according
to the Mahometans, one of the signs of the Last Day's
approach.

Another of the signs is, "Great distress in the
world, so that a man when he passes by another's
grave shall say, 'Would to God I were in his place!'"
—*Sale's Preliminary Discourse.*

Note 387, p. 256.—*As precious as the Cerulean Throne of Coolburga.*—"On Mahommed Shaw's return to Koolburga (the capital of Dekkan), he made a great festival, and mounted this throne with much pomp and magnificence, calling it Firozeh or Cerulean. I have heard some old persons, who saw the throne Firozeh in the reign of Sultan Mamood Bhamenee, describe it. They say that it was in length nine feet, and three in breadth: made of ebony, covered with plates of pure gold, and set with precious stones of immense value. Every prince of the house of Bhamenee, who possessed this throne, made a point of adding to it some rich stones: so that when, in the reign of Sultan Mamood, it was taken to pieces, to remove some of the jewels to be set in vases and cups, the jewellers valued it at one corore of oons (nearly four millions sterling). I learned also that it was called Firozah from being partly enamelled of a sky-blue color, which was in time fully covered by the number of jewels. — *Ferishta.*